Converging Ways?
Conversion and Belongir
Buddhism and Christian.

edited by
John D'Arcy May

Converging Ways?

Conversion and Belonging in Buddhism and Christianity

edited by

John D'Arcy May

Bibliografische Information der Deutschen Bibliothek
Die Deutsche Bibliothek verzeichnet diese Publikation
in der Deutschen Nationalbibliografie; detaillierte bibliografische
Daten sind im Internet über http://dnb.ddb.de abrufbar

Biblographic information published by Die Deutsche Bibliothek
Die Deutsche Bibliothek lists this publication in the Deutsche
Nationalbibliografie; detailed bibliographic data is available
in the Internet at http://dnb.ddb.de

ISBN 978-3-8306-7251-7

Converging Ways?
Conversion and Belonging in
Buddhism and Christianity

John D'Arcy May
Introduction 7

I. Benedictine and Buddhist

Thomas Josef Götz OSB
Catholic Monk, Buddhist Monk: The Monastic Interreligious
Dialogue with Japanese Zen 11

Thomas Timpte OSB
Conversion and Identity: Moving Between Buddhism and
Christianity in Korea 25

II. Conflict and Conversion

Elizabeth J. Harris
Confrontation Over Conversions: A Case Study from Sri Lanka 37

Jørgen Skov Sørensen
Imperial or Emprical? On Boundaries of Religious Identity
in India and Europe 55

III. Conversion and Controversy

Perry Schmidt-Leukel
'Light and Darkness' or 'Looking Through a Dim Mirror'?
A Reply to Paul Williams from a Christian Perspective 67

José Ignacio Cabezón
A Buddhist Response to Paul Williams's *The Unexpected Way*   89

Paul Williams
Buddhism, God, Aquinas and Morality: An Only Partially
Repentant Reply to Perry Schmidt-Leukel and José Cabezón   117

IV. Belonging and Identity

Kajsa Ahlstrand
Boundaries of Religious Identity: Baptised Buddhists in Enköping 155

Ruben L.F. Habito
Being Buddhist, Being Christian: Being Both, Being Neither   165

Michael von Brück
A Theology of Multiple Religious Identity   181

Contributors   207

JOHN D'ARCY MAY

Unexpected Ways to Religious Identity

There is currently considerable discussion of the relationship between religious conversion – both in the sense of *Bekehrung*, changing one's religious allegiance, and *Umkehr*, deepening or rediscovering one's adherence to a particular religious tradition – and the possibility of multiple religious belonging. Raimon Panikkar famously claimed to be at one and the same time Hindu, Buddhist and Christian, but the question has been discussed from many different points of view.[1] One of the pioneers of 'religious bi-lingualism' was Hugo Enomiya-Lassalle, the Jesuit missionary to Japan who became a practitioner and teacher of Zen, but whether such a stance is really possible is still a matter of intensive discussion.[2]

This book, which arose out of the sixth conference of the European Network of Buddhist-Christian Studies in the Benedictine Archabbey of St Ottilien near Munich on 10-13 June, 2005, presents a variety of approaches to the problem which differ in both content and genre. There are autobiographical accounts based on intense personal experience (Goetz, Timpte, Habito), examples of historical research and its interpretation (Harris, Skov Sørensen), data from empirical studies (Ahlstrand) and an attempt at a comprehensive theory of multiple religious belonging (von Brück).

This variety is appropriate because at the centre of the conference was an example of a very personal and very public conversion which repudiated any suggestion of double belonging and which was defended with rational arguments. It was also a conversion quite against the trend of Western Christians 'going East' and claiming to discover in

---

[1] See Raimon Panikkar, *The Intra-Religious Dialogue*. New York: Paulist Press, 1999 (3rd rev. ed.); Catherine Cornille, ed., *Many Mansions? Multiple Religious Belonging and Christian Identity.* Maryknoll: Orbis Books, 2002.
[2] See Ursula Baatz, "Zen und christliche Spiritualität. Eine Zwischenbilanz", Karl Baier, ed., *Handbuch Spiritualität. Zugänge, Traditionen, interreligiöse Prozesse.* Darmstadt: Wissenschaftliche Buchgesellschaft, 2006: 304-328.

Asian traditions what their European Christianity allegedly lacks – spirituality, mysticism, meditation, generally as ciphers for an escape from oppressive dogmatism and intellectualism. Paul Williams, professor of Indian and Buddhist philosophy at the University of Bristol in England and a well-known convert to the Tibetan Buddhist tradition (the *Vajrayāna* or 'Diamond Vehicle' in conventional Buddhist terms, as distinct from the *Theravāda* or 'Way of the Elders' in South and Southeast Asia and the East Asian *Mahāyāna* or 'Great Vehicle'), announced to an astonished public that he had become a Roman Catholic, lock, stock and barrel, with no concessions or apologies. In response to the furore that ensued, he gave a personal account of his conversion which was also an intellectual defence in his moving and entertaining book, *The Unexpected Way*.[3] At the centre of his concern is the difficult – and not very fashionable – question of religious truth. For him, the attractive thing about Catholicism is that Catholics believe in the existence of a creator God who raised Jesus from the dead, claims that make no sense to Buddhists but are decisive for Williams. In order to defend his position he engages in philosophical argument about the possibility of metaphysics as a way of demonstrating the literal truth of such propositions.

Thanks to the persuasive powers of my colleague Perry Schmidt-Leukel, Williams was prevailed upon to attend the conference and debate his position with two other converts, Schmidt-Leukel himself (formerly Catholic, now Episcopal Church of Scotland) and José Cabezón (formerly Catholic, now Tibetan Buddhist in the Gelukpa tradition). The resulting texts, which form the centrepiece of this volume, are demanding because of their technical terminology and scholarly apparatus, but I can assure readers that the audience, which was largely German or otherwise non-English speaking, was fascinated by the debate and followed it with great intensity. Chairing the proceedings, I compared the participants – somewhat incongruously in the circumstances – to prizefighters in the ring, reeling under the blows of their opponents but still standing to deliver effective counterblows. It is comparatively rare in these days of liberal tolerance in the West to experience a full-blown, no-holds-barred religious argument at an extremely high intellectual level, such as was commonplace in the

---

[3] Paul Williams, *The Unexpected Way: On Converting from Buddhism to Catholicism.* London and New York: T. & T. Clark-Continuum, 2002.

medieval universities of both European Christians and Asian Buddhists.

It is my hope that readers will be able to thread their way through the widely diverse contributions, from the accounts of shared and contested monastic experience in Part I and the stories of historical controversy and misunderstanding in Part II to the debate about unequivocal conversion in Part III and the evidence for multiple belonging which crosses the boundaries of identity in Part IV. May both contest and convergence stimulate further discussion of these important issues in the irenic spirit demonstrated here.

I would like to thank my colleagues on the board of the European Network of Buddhist-Christian Studies for their cooperation in organising the St Ottilien conference and Martin Trischberger of EOS Verlag for producing the book so efficiently. Paul O'Grady of the philosophy department in Trinity College Dublin kindly shared with me his thoughts on Paul Williams's conversion. Finally, the conference speakers unfailingly sent me their manuscripts and their revisions in good time, the greatest favour any editor can ask of an author.

THOMAS JOSEF GÖTZ OSB

Catholic Monk, Buddhist Monk The Monastic Interreligious Dialogue with Japanese Zen

1. Introduction

For several years Catholic and Buddhist monks have met regularly and they are discovering many things in common in their ways of life. Both 'ways' have been developing independently for more than a thousand years. The meetings are part of the larger movement of inter-religious dialogue. This dialogue takes place on many levels: the so-cial-political level, the intellectual-scholarly level, the philosophical-theological level and the ascetic-spiritual level. Thus, as Pope John Paul II puts it in his encyclical Redemptoris Missio, the dialogue is open to a wide field and can take many forms of expression. It can consist in an exchange of thoughts among experts of the religious tra-ditions concerned or their official representatives. It can take the form of cooperation for the holistic development and preservation of reli-gious values, from information about spiritual experiences to the so-called 'dialogue of life', in which believers testify to their own human and religious values and help each other to live according to them, thus creating a more just and fraternal community.

The intermonastic meetings of the last two decades have taken place on different levels, but their main emphasis was on the encounter in the everyday life of the Benedictines and the exchange of spiritual experiences in monastic life. From a Christian perspective, one's view of Buddhism is limited because of inevitable short-sightedness and distortions with regard to Buddhism. Wrong ideas about Buddhism are widespread in Europe. On the other hand, the Christian perspective is free from the blind spots which prevent the Buddhist monk from see-ing things that could be criticised in his own context. The same holds true, of course, for the observations made by Buddhist monks in Benedictine communities. This is the opportunity offered by the inter-monastic encounter: it sharpens our perception of our own tradition, deepens it, and brings about a renewal of spiritual life in East and West. At a deeper level the interreligious dialogue can even become an 'intrareligious dialogue', leading to a more intensive engagement with one's own tradition.

The literature on the spiritual basis of Buddhist and Christian mona-sticism is fairly voluminous. Yet there are few accounts of monastic daily life, especially in Buddhism. Because the forms taken by daily life in Benedictine and Zen monasteries are the result of a thousand years of development, the way the monks live today can be under-stood against the background of the history and spirituality of the mo-nastic life.

2. Encounters before the Second Vatican Council

In the early Christian centuries Christian communities had already learned of the existence of Buddhist traditions. Clement of Alexandria writes around 200 CE: 'Among the Indians there are followers of the Buddha, whom they worship like a god because of his outstanding holiness' (*Stromata* I.XV.71.6). The geopolitical significance of Alex-andria as the axis of East and West made it possible that Buddhist ideas became known around the turn of the second to the third centu-ry. Clement of Alexandria called all non-Christians barbarians, a poli-te expression used by the Greeks to refer to non-Greeks. These barba-rians, whose philosophies were in Clement's view a 'light for the peoples', included Indian wisdom as well.

There was a Greek in the fourth century who seems to have been deeply rooted in non-Hellenistic spirituality: Evagrius of Pontus. In the opinion of Hans Urs von Balthasar, Evagrius was very close to the thought and spirituality of Mahāyāna Buddhism. Marco Polo was pro-bably the first to acquaint Europeans with the novelty that the life of Buddha, as it was related in Sri Lanka, resembled in all its details the life of Joasaph in the *Vitae Patrum* ('Lives of the Fathers'). Marco Polo visited Sri Lanka in 1293. The Bollandists have vouched for the fact that the 'St Joasaph' venerated as a saint in the medieval Church was none other than the Buddha himself. The legend of Josaphat and St Barlaam, which was very popular among Christians in the Middle

Ages, has its origins in corruptions of the terms *Bodhisattva* and *Bhagavan* (the Venerable One). From the vulgarised *Bodhisat* via the Arabic *Judasaf* we get *Joasaph* (Latin *Josaphat*), while *Bhagavan* (Arabic *Bilauhar*) became *Barlaam*. Their veneration by the people led to their canonisation. In 1370 St Joasaph appears in the *Catalogus Sanctorum* of Peter de Natalibus. St Joasaph has since been removed from the calendar of the saints.

In the encounter with European colonialism in the nineteenth century a new Buddhist self-confidence developed in many countries. In addition, Buddhist texts were received in Europe enthusiastically at times, for example by Schopenhauer, Hegel and Nietzsche. A kind of 'Protestant Buddhism' arose in small circles in Europe, understanding itself as a protest against the predominance of European Christianity and mistakenly stylising Buddhism as a religion of reason and meditation. Developments such as these hindered dialogue, in the end, by playing the religions off against one another rather than finding out what they had in common. One of the first Catholics to adopt a positive attitude to Buddhism was Romano Guardini. In his book *The Lord* he writes:

> Only one person ever seriously attempted to go farther: to lay hands on being – Buddha. He desired more than mere moral progress or peace outside the world. He attempted the inconceivable: himself part of existence, he tried to lift all existence by its 'bootstraps'. So far no Christian has succeeded in comprehending and evaluating Buddha's conception of Nirvana, that ultimate awakening, cessation of illusion and being. To do this one must have become entirely free in the love of God's Son, yet remain linked by a profound reverence to the great and mysterious man who lived six centuries before the Lord.[1]

Apart from Guardini, Henri de Lubac also spoke openly and positively of Buddhism. In this way both contributed to the opening of the Catholic Church at the Second Vatican Council.

---

[1] Romano Guardini, *The Lord,* tr. by Elinor Castendyk. London: Longmans Green, 1956: 305-306.

3. After the Second Vatican Council

The Council's Declaration on the Church's Relationship to Non-Christian Religions, *Nostra Aetate*, is a decisive step towards the dialogue of religions. The Declaration is a key document of the Council, because without it all other statements about the necessity of dialogue would have no basis. In the Declaration *Nostra Aetate* the Second Vatican Council spoke positively and in detail about the other religions as such:

> The Catholic Church rejects nothing which is true and holy in these religions. She looks with sincere respect upon those ways of conduct and of life, those rules and teachings which, though differing in many particulars from what she holds and sets forth, nevertheless often reflect a ray of that Truth which enlightens all men. (*NA* 2)

In the solemn vote on the document in November 1965 2,221 were in favour with 88 against.

This document became the basis of interreligious dialogue in the years after the Council. The Buddhist-Christian dialogue found its own particular expression in the 'Monastic Interreligious Dialogue'. At a conference of *Aide à l'Implantation Monastique* (AIM, an organisation of Benedictine monasteries which supports monastic communities in mission countries) in Bangkok, intermonastic dialogue was officially adopted in 1968. Pioneers of intermonastic dialogue were invited to this conference, among them Thomas Merton, who died during the conference as the result of an accident. Some weeks earlier he had concluded his speech at a meeting of religious superiors in Calcutta with the words:

> And the deepest level of communication is not communication, but communion. It is wordless. It is beyond words, and it is beyond speech, and it is beyond concept. Not that we discover a new unity. We discover an older unity.

Cardinal Pignedoli, the president of the Secretariat for Non-Christians, wrote in 1973 to the Abbot Primate of the Benedictines in Rome, Rembert Weakland:

> Even our limited experience in interreligious dialogue has already shown very clearly the great importance that monasticism has in this field, especially in Asia. The monk typifies historically and par excellence the *homo religiosus* of all times, and is a point of reference for Christians and non-Christians alike. The existence of monasticism at the very heart of the church is like a bridge to all religions.

After receiving Pignedoli's letter the Abbot Primate, after consultation with the Abbot General of the Trappists, asked the Secretariat of the AIM to make proposals on the organisation of intermonastic dialogue. In 1977 the two commissions *Dialogue Interreligieux Monastique* (DIM) for Europe and the North American Board for East-West Dialogue (NABEWD) for North America were founded. In the period after 1977 there were various meetings and undertakings, which were attentively observed by the AIM and the Secretariat for the Non-Christian Religions in Rome. Eventually the intermonastic dialogue was integrated institutionally into the work of the Pontifical Council for Interreligious Dialogue. The task of DIM is thus 'to promote dialogue among Christian and non-Christian monks, placing these different forms of monasticism in the general context of interreligious dialogue'.

4. Encounters between East and West

In 1979, for the first time, a group of Buddhist monks and nuns came to Europe to acquaint themselves with the practice of Christian life in Benedictine monasteries. In St Ottilien we too opened not only our doors but also our hearts. It was known as 'The First East-West Spiritual Exchange', in which 22 Buddhist monks, two nuns, two Shinto priests and 13 other guests from Japan took part. During their stay they shared in groups of five or six participants in the life of communities in monasteries of the Benedictine tradition in Germany, Holland, Belgium, France and Italy. The Japanese guests took part in the daily life of the Christian monks, so that the exchange, while also an exchange of thoughts, was predominantly a mutual experience of learning. During the exchange there were conferences and meetings in common, with cultural and academic lectures and performances of Zen arts. Finally, there was a trip to Rome and a symposium at which the Buddhist and Christian participants could exchange and discuss their experiences and impressions.

For the second 'East-West Spiritual Exchange' in 1983, 14 Catholic monks, two nuns and a secular priest from England, France, Italy, Germany, Belgium and the Netherlands travelled to Japan to experience for themselves the daily life of Zen monks. In order to familiarise the guests with this form of life, for the first few days they were introduced to Zen monastic customs in Sogenji, after which they broke up into small groups to spend their first week in different Zen monasteries of both the Sōtō and Rinzai traditions. After spending time in a monastery and sharing life in the Zendo the European participants visited the great centres of Japanese Buddhism, where they learned about the culture and art of Zen through visits and lectures. During a symposium in Kyoto each Benedictine visitor reported on his or her impressions. These were marked by their deeply fraternal reception in the Zen monasteries, the beauty of Zen culture and the profound effects of Zazen. In particular, all shared the experience that living with others is an encouragement but also a questioning of one's own monastic life.

The exchange was characterised from the beginning by genuine fraternity, and it was obvious to each participant that this open friendship would continue. There were thus further meetings in 1984, 1987 and 1991, alternately in Zen monasteries in Japan and monasteries of the Benedictine tradition in Europe. Since 1991 the exchange has concentrated more on visits by individual Japanese monks to European monasteries and experiences of individual Benedictines who travelled to Japan to spend time in Zen monasteries. During this period there were more and more conferences and meetings in both Europe and Japan on various aspects of the monastic interreligious dialogue. In this way friendly relations could be established between Buddhist centres and Benedictine communities in Europe in the spirit of dialogue.

In what follows I would like to present some aspects of the experiences and observations in a Zen monastery in Japan as a Benedictine from Europe encounters them. One's first experience is that 'Buddhism', such as one knows it from the European literature, has little to do with the everyday reality of a Zen monastery. One's own idea of Buddhism can be strongly influenced by Western ways of thinking. Concrete Buddhist practice does not always correspond to the view of one's own religion determined by ideology, Western philosophies, theology and dogma. Our way of thinking sets different emphases, so that we interpret the meaning of Buddhist concepts wrongly. One comes to know the religion of others mainly through the people who live and practise it and have been influenced by it all their lives. Only so can the visitor recognise the *Sitz im Leben* of the foreign religion and the real meaning of particular aspects internal to Buddhism. Using one's reason and through books one can only partially recognise what sustains and concerns the other. A sojourn in a Zen monastery opens up to the visitor a new, hitherto unknown horizon of religious practice and lived tradition within Zen Buddhism. One not only learns to know the other, one learns to respect and appreciate her, and to be in immense awe of a tradition which is thousands of years old.

A second observation was that in the end it is our rootedness in and knowledge of our own monastic tradition that made possible a better understanding of life in a Zen monastery. One rediscovers many of one's familiar spiritual aids and experiences in a Zen monastery. Indeed, one is overcome by a feeling of being at home, so many traditions did we recognise from our Benedictine daily routine: the significance of monastic silence, the place of the liturgy, the experience of living in community, the position of the Abbot and the Rōshi as spiritual leaders in a monastic community, and many more. Our years of experience in the Benedictine tradition were a decisive bridge to understanding Buddhism as we came to know it. A person living in a Christian tradition locates statements such as 'Nirvana is peace and tranquillity' or 'The Buddha-nature is immortal' in a spiritual context which transcends the purely historical or exegetical meaning of these statements. One 'knows' as a Christian phrases from the Western Christian tradition which in a certain sense are similar.

'Zen' in Japanese is the transliteration of the Chinese 'Ch'an-na', which again is the equivalent of the Sanskrit word *dhyāna* and means the mental absorption of contemplation, in which all dualistic distinctions such as I/Thou, subject/object, true/false are invalidated. Zen can be defined in two ways. It is a school of Mahāyāna Buddhism which developed out of the encounter of the Dhyāna Buddhism transmitted to China by Bodhidarma and Taoism in the sixth and seventh centuries. As such Zen is a religion whose teachings and practices are intended to lead to the disclosure of the True Self (*Kensho, Satori*) and finally to complete awakening or enlightenment. Yet at the same time Zen is not a religion at all, but the indefinable, incommunicable root experience, which each individual must experience for him or herself and from which all religions spring as ways of expressing this experience. This root is devoid of all names, descriptions and concepts. In this sense Zen is not linked to any religion, not even to Buddhist tradition. It is the primordial perfection of all that exists as experienced by great wise ones, saints and religious founders of all times and cultures. Zen is thus not a method, but the immediate expression and making present of the perfection which exists in every human being at every moment.

Zazen, often translated as 'sitting in contemplation', signifies the most intensive and direct meditative practice which leads to enlightenment. Zazen, however, is not meditation as we know it from our Western tradition. It does not involve concentrating on a text or an object of meditation. Zazen is supposed to liberate the mind from slavery to any kind of fixation, form of thought, thing or representation, no matter how noble and holy these might be. In its purest form Zazen means dwelling in a state of wide-awake attention devoid of thoughts, not directed towards any object and without content.

We experienced Zen and the practice of Zen meditation in all its variations as something very rich and deep. It was a new experience for us that meditation can involve coping with the pain in our knees. Sitting silently with the inevitable pain one is 'forced' in a positive sense not to flee from oneself and to face up to one's own reality. Zen meditation is objectless. One becomes quiet, calm, breathing more slowly and deeply, and abdominally. It is extremely important to adhere strictly to the sitting position. Thus one achieves a deep unity and harmony with nature and the whole environment. The separation between the human and nature is overcome, and the implicit dualism caused by this separation between me and the objects that surround me is gradually extinguished. Zazen means meditating in the lotus posture, in which one sits on a cushion and places the right foot on the left thigh and the left foot on the right thigh. During what were for us long periods of meditation the community aspect became evident. A lot of energy comes from the group in which each one is observing the numerous rites and rules of behaviour before and after meditation. We meditated together eight times a day for up to 45 minutes. Alone, without the support of the community, one could have managed at most a few sessions of 25 minutes. The realisation that Zen is not just meditation in the lotus posture was new to us. Zen is an entire programme for life, of which meditation in the lotus posture is only one expression, even though it is the most important. Zen is an expression of the way I walk, work, meet people and deal with nature. A person permeated by Zen is always on the move yet mentally present. The Zen masters (Rōshis) were shocked to learn that in Europe Zen is almost exclusively known as sitting in the lotus posture.

In Zen work is an important aspect of practice, though it takes second place to spiritual practice in the monastery. Work has its own spiritual value, and consists almost exclusively of gardening and cleaning. It is regrettable that this rich and ancient tradition is no longer widely known in Japanese public life. Zen would be an answer and an orientation for many uprooted people in Japan. Japanese society seemed to us to be at least as consumer-orientated as European society.

Zen and meditation in the lotus posture (Zazen) are immensely valuable and deep sources of religious experience. With great tact, discretion and love we were introduced to the practice of Zen. The Zen masters who guided us through Zen practice did so with the explicit intention of opening up for us a new source and thus – as they repeatedly said – to help us become better Christians. It must be mentioned here that Zen monks living in Europe were very surprised and impressed to find that Benedictine monasteries are equipped with the latest technical appliances and run schools, printing presses and workshops to the same standards as are found elsewhere in their countries. A Zen monastery can better be compared with an educational training centre for young monks. Life in a Zen monastery is stricter and more spartan. The young monks live there for about four years, after which they found a family and become temple priests in a parish. In other East Asian countries the Buddhist monastic community is a community for life.

In Christian monasteries object-related meditation is widespread. One meditates and ruminates on a text from Holy Scripture, for example, reading it not simply to obtain information but in such a way that the reading issues in prayer. The reading becomes prayer and ideally a 'vision of God', an experience beyond the text. Many Christian authors call this contemplation. By ruminating and meditating on the sayings of Holy Scripture one enters into the reality of Christ, praying and at the same time trying to make the text one's own, in order to realise it later in one's life. *Lectio, meditatio* and *oratio* have entered the history of spirituality as the Benedictine method of prayer. It would be too restrictive to see this only in connection with prayer. The real thrust of this method is to recognise God's call clearly in each situation.

Nothing is so characteristic of Benedictine life as liturgical worship and the divine office. Benedict appropriates from previous traditions at this point. He defines monastic life as one that takes concrete shape in prayer. Benedict regulates the communal prayer of the monks in his Rule, which becomes determinative for the West. One searches in vain in the Rule for a theological foundation for prayer; instead, the structure and conduct of the individual hours and the inner attitudes necessary for performing them in a dignified way are described at length. Prayer takes priority over every other activity, it determines the rhythm of the day, opening, accompanying and closing it. In this ritual and spiritual shaping there is a great similarity between Buddhist and Christian monastic communities. The whole life and work of a monk in a Benedictine monastery is surrounded and permeated by prayer. Only he who is aware of God in everything and lives in God's presence will not offend God. The image of God in Benedict's Rule and for the monks of his time is definitely accentuated in the present, not in the past or the future. To pray is to be aware of God and to enter into God's presence and be absorbed by it. A monk seeks and experiences God not so much in memory as in the here and now of existence. What happens in the present is determined by God. In prayer God and the present are held together in their interrelationship, becoming transparent in their connectedness and in their reliance on faith. In prayer life is regarded from the perspective of the ever-present God in celebration, gratitude and healing. The same form of life orientated to concrete practice is found in Zen monasteries as well. The here and now is what matters. For Benedict's Rule work is an important part of the way to God, but it takes second place to prayer. In this sense work has a definite theological place in the life of the monastic community. Benedict's instructions regarding a balanced distribution and a sensible alternation of prayer, reading and work are all directed towards God. Prayer, reading and work are not simply juxtaposed but form a living unity, in which one may not be overdone or neglected in favour of the others without endangering or falsifying the primary intention of seeking God. Work for Benedict has an explicitly spiritual value, just as work in a Zen monastery is subordinate above all to the Zen training in the fullest sense.

In the Zen monasteries we learned that ceremonies and modes of encounter are important bearers and mediators of a spiritual tradition. Haven't we in Europe very often lost sight of the importance of manners and ritual? The tea ceremony, for example, we found to be a deep form of wordless communication and communion. The monks' frequent bows before one another and their Zen master were not empty forms but signs of deep mutual respect.

5. Basic Spiritual Attitudes as Places of Encounter

The encounters of everyday life in the monastery correspond to encounters in spirituality. In the spiritual attitudes of both monastic traditions there is much in common which can be brought into relationship, though there are also significant differences which separate us. This is particularly true of the ways we understand the person and ultimate reality. This is an area fraught with difficulty in Buddhist-Christian dialogue, both an obstacle and an opportunity. It is too superficial to deny that Buddhism has any concept of the person or to force upon it a Christian conception of the person. It would be just as wrong to speak unreflectively of God in a Buddhist context or to classify Buddhism as 'godless'.

Benedict begins his Rule with the summons: 'Listen, child of God, to the guidance of your teacher'.[2] Benedict wishes to set up in the monastery a 'school for the Lord's service'. The true Master is Christ, as the Gospel of John testifies (Jn 13:13). Being a Christian means becoming more and more Christlike. Benedict concludes the Prologue with the words: 'Thus we never want to withdraw from his instruction, but to persevere in his teachings in the monastery until death. If we thus patiently share in the sufferings of Christ we may also inherit his kingdom with him'. Following instruction does not simply mean keeping traditional rules, but is a determined walking in the way of the Lord, which becomes most apparent when we share his suffering.

In Buddhism, too, the Teaching (*Dharma*) and the Way or 'Vehicle' (*Yāna*) are one; here, too, the monk strives to follow the way of the Buddha. The first step consists in taking upon oneself, like Buddha, a life of homelessness. In monastic life the monk tries to become closer to Buddha by honouring him, by making an effort, like him, to achieve enlightenment through meditation, and by instructing lay disciples in the teaching. In the Mahāyāna it is very definitely a matter of un-

---

[2] From the new translation by Patrick Barry OSB, in Patrick Henry, ed., *Benedict's Dharma: Buddhists Reflect on the Rule of Saint Benedict.* New York: Riverhead Books, 2001: 142.

folding and realising the Buddha-nature. The 'Dharma-body' is acknowledged as the highest reality in which all Buddhas share and are one. The Dharma-body is beyond emotions, it is at one and the same time law, rule and spiritual body of the Buddha. This perfect reality can only be grasped in enlightenment, in which this knowledge is bound up with the realisation of one's own Buddha-nature, in which one's deepest essence consists. The way of Zen is to lead to this enlightenment, for Zen, according to a short definition attributed to Bodhidharma, is 'a particular tradition outside the scriptures, independent of words and letters: an immediate disclosure of the human heart, by which one perceives one's own nature and becomes a Buddha'. Dōgen Zenghi, the founder of the Sōtō school of Zen in Japan, expresses the consequences of this for the follower of the Buddha-way thus: 'To learn the Buddha-way means to learn one's own self. To learn one's own self means to forget one's self'. Forgetting one's own self bears fruit in enlightenment, which however points beyond itself and must be lived as selflessness in everyday life.

In Christianity, too, Jesus summons us to deny ourselves by following the way of the cross: to know only Christ, no longer our self, to see only him, who goes before us, and not the way that is so difficult for us. In following Christ the monk must renounce self-will, as Benedict repeatedly demands in the chapter on humility. The way of the monk as an ascent to God is the descending way of self-emptying, for 'anyone who lays claim to a high position will be brought low and anyone who is modest in self-appraisal will be lifted up' (*Rule*, 7.1).

6. Kenosis as a Point of Contact between Buddhist and Christian Spirituality

Benedict regards humility as a way to maturity, which leads a person to his or her true self, to Christ and thus to God. It is a matter of having the mind of Christ. The way of Christ led ultimately to the cross, of which Abbot Hyperichius says: 'The tree of life touches heaven; but the humility of the monk can climb it nonetheless'. The cross is the expression of the utmost self-emptying (in Greek, *kenōsis*) of Christ and stands in the centre of Christian life. This kenosis distinguishes Christian faith from other religions, but as the way of letting go and becoming empty of self it can become a place of encounter in the dialogue with Buddhism. The Jesuit Aloysius Pieris, who lives in

Sri Lanka and is very committed to Buddhist-Christian dialogue, rightly says: 'The Buddhist will only enter into a genuine conversation with the Christian when he or she understands Christian dogmatics as a complicated but consistent advocacy of the freedom of an indescribable God, which is humanly unfathomable. The Christian, on his or her part, will only enter into a genuine conversation with the Buddhist when the existential achievement of his or her selflessness and self-emptying begins to speak, and with it the selflessness and self-emptying of Christ. The chance for both lies in letting go of self'. This is the decisive point of contact between Buddhist and Christian spirituality. Spiritual exchange makes possible the encounter in and with the very heart of the religions. In this way people rooted in their own tradition can exchange experiences as forms of expression and ways of searching for the Absolute. This kind of dialogue leads to mutual enrichment. We communicate to one another the reasons of our own faith, but this exchange does not stop in the face of sometimes fundamental contradictions; rather, one entrusts oneself humbly and confidently to God, 'who is greater than our heart' (1 Jn 3:20).

THOMAS TIMPTE OSB

Conversion and Identity Moving between Buddhism and Christianity in Korea

This is a talk of a Christian monk in relation with Buddhist monks. I have no competence as a scholar of religion. I accepted this challenge because in my experience very little is heard of about Korean Buddhism. But Koreans developed Buddhism which they received from China in a specific way. And Korean Buddhism had a decisive influence on Japan. Some Korean Buddhist teachers were even acknowledged in China where their scriptures would be studied. It is a pity that many studies about Buddhism do not mention Korea at all. During a sojourn in Japan 1983, I met Japanese monks who showed interest in Korean Buddhism, because they knew that Koreans retain many old traditions, especially Zen traditions in a more original form.

Background: Religions in Korea

Korea is a marvellous example of practical religious pluralism. It has a unique mixture of religions. There is no dominant religion. There are four main traditions, living in peaceful coexistence:

Shamanism is the original religion of the Korean people, which they brought with them when immigrating in different waves from Northeast Asia (Siberia).

Buddhism entered Korea from China since the 4th century CE, and soon became dominant. It remained the official religion during the unified Silla (668-918) and Koryo (918-1392) Dynasties. After 1392 (Choson Dynasty until 1910) Buddhism was suppressed by the new state ideology of Neo-Confucianism. The monasteries withdrew to the mountains, and the monks were considered backward and ignorant.

After 1945 Buddhism became completely free and especially since the 1990s we see a new flourishing of Buddhist monastic life.

Coming from China, Korean Buddhism is Mahāyāna Buddhism dominated by the Rinzai school of Zen since the latter part of the Koryo Dynasty. It has also incorporated a couple of popular beliefs like prayers to the mountain spirit and sacrifices for the deceased. Typical for Korea is the tolerance of different schools of thought within the same monastic order. Divisions result more from personality clashes. Since the time of the Japanese domination (1910-1945) a large order of married monks also came into being. The largest order, the Chogye Order, requires strict celibacy. It counts about 12,000 monks and nuns. The large number of nuns is also a special trait of Korean Buddhism. Their number is continuously increasing and must now be equal to that of the monks.

Confucianism started entering Korea from China in the first century BCE. Even in the Silla period it became the dominant thinking of the civil servants who used to be trained in China. Since about 1250 Neo-Confucianism extended its influence and since 1392 (Yi-Dynasty) became the official ideology in a very rigid form. One can say that Confucianism became the religion of Korean men until the present day.

Christianity came to Korea through books brought from China. A group of reform-minded Confucian scholars who studied Western science came upon books written by Jesuit missionaries in China and started living by Christian values and precepts. One of them was baptised in Beijing in 1784 and on his return to Korea baptised his companions. This date is considered as the beginning of the Catholic Church in Korea, which existed about 50 years without foreign missionaries and priests under continuous persecution. This is unique in the whole history of Christianity: the Christian faith coming to a country without missionaries. Faith, which is said to come by hearing, in this case came through reading. Protestants came to Korea after 1884, when the country was forced to open itself to the outside. For various reasons they soon overtook the Catholics in numbers.

Presently of the 48 million inhabitants of South Korea roughly one half profess to believe in a religion, and of these about half are Buddhist and half are Christian. According to a Gallup poll the religious population is increasing. This does not mean that almost every second Korean has no religion at all. The statistics only include those who belong to an organised religion. But what can be called 'diffuse religi-

ons' do not appear in this picture. In Korea nowadays nobody considers him or herself Shamanist, but tens of thousands of Shamans apparently can make a living because people believe in their powers to
relate to the spirits.

In the same way very few consider Confucianism as their religion.
Some question whether Confucianism is a religion at all and not just a
system of ethics and social cohesion. But there are also some people
who practise Confucianism explicitly as their religion. For others it
may be said to take the place of religion as it has done effectively for
Korean society over a period of several hundred years. The fact is that
there are many Buddhist or Christian Confucianists: people whose
moral and social values are influenced more by Confucianism than by
the religious community they belong to, mostly in good faith. Something similar is true for Shamanism, though hardly ever admitted, because Shamanism is considered as primitive and seen as more like a
superstition than a religion, though recently we find a kind of re-
evaluation.

To understand the relations and the movement between different religions in Korea it might be good to say something about homogeneity
and diversity in Korean society. Ethnically Korea is uniquely homo-
geneous. There are no ethnic minorities, unless you consider several
hundred thousand foreign workers, who moved to Korea from other
Asian countries during the last 10 years or so. Therefore religious
affiliation has nothing to do with belonging to an ethnic group. Nor
does it depend on social status. Actually there is a great social
mobility in Korea. This means that religious affiliation is very much
decided by personal choice. The only outside influence to be seriously
considered is that of the family. Pressure to remain in a certain
religion is stronger in the case of Christians. Among Christians, and
especially among Catholics, because of the rites of baptism and other
sacraments there is a strong sense of membership. The sense of
belonging to a certain religious group is strongest with Catholics from
families who have been Christians since the persecutions of the 19th
century. But as a general rule it is quite normal that members of the
same family belong to different religions. Of two sisters one may be a
Buddhist nun, the other one a Catholic sister. I know of a married
Buddhist monk, whose children were all Protestant or Catholic. One
of his sons became a Benedictine brother.

Conversion

The word 'conversion' may have two different meanings. One is changing one's religious affiliation, the other one is what the Bible calls *metanoia*, which means changing one's attitude to life. This comprises accepting new values or deciding to live according to the values hitherto only accepted in theory. There can be sudden experiences of conversion or there can be a gradual change of mind. One of the goals of interreligious dialogue is a conversion in this second sense which in certain cases may include a conversion in the first sense. In any case it should lead to a deeper commitment and understanding of one's own religion. Through dialogue we learn about other religions and at the same time learn to see our own faith with new eyes. This may lead to a new and enriched 'identity'.

Here I shall speak of conversion as embracing a religion or changing one's religion. In Korea this kind of conversion is a very frequent thing. Since most Christians are baptised as adults they are converts in this sense. In the case of Catholics only one fourth of believers were baptised as infants. According to a statistic of 1997, among the converts 17.4 per cent (1987: 21.3 per cent) claim to have been Buddhists, 16 per cent belonged to other Christian denominations, but 60 per cent did not belong to any religious group. There is a lot of movement from not believing in a religion to believing and vice-versa, and also from one religion to the other. Most converts to any religion in Korea come from those who have been without religious affiliation. And according to Gallup (1997) of the 22 million Koreans not believing in a religion almost half claimed to have belonged to a religion before. Of these 73 per cent had frequented a Protestant church for some time. This may be explained by the fact that Protestants have many activities for children and young people. Of the 22.6 million believers in a religion 16 per cent had belonged to another religion before. This shows that there is also a lot of movement between religious affiliations.

What brings about conversion to religion in general or to a specific religion? Many of course try religion because they were persuaded by a family member or friend or because they were contacted by a missionary. But more often than not there are quite personal reasons for the quest. For a few it is intellectual curiosity, looking for an answer to the mysteries of human existence. But most Koreans, when asked what they are looking for in religion, will answer: 'Peace of heart'. Concretely speaking often a sickness, a loss of a family member or some other calamity will bring about a conversion either from non-belief to belief or from one religion to another. Religion has to be of help in getting on with life. We find people shopping around in different religions to get healing or better counselling. I have known somebody who left Buddhism to become Protestant after he was healed from some mysterious sickness when he tried praying to Jesus, and a devout Catholic woman who became Buddhist after a monk healed her son.

In the case of Buddhists converting to Christianity, we have to consider that being Buddhist in Korea can mean two things. In the first case the belonging is quite vague and has more of a cultural meaning. In my experience, most of those who say that they were Buddhists before they came to a Church had little knowledge of Buddhist doctrine. It often just means that their grandmother or some other family members used to pray in a Buddhist temple.

The second case is different and difficult to find. It is very rare that a convinced Buddhist becomes a Christian. I actually never met a Christian believer who had been a Buddhist monk or nun before. When I was novice master at our monastery in the 1970s it happened twice that a Buddhist monk wanted to enter our Christian community. But both gave up after learning of the conditions to become a member of a Catholic religious order. They had not seen the fundamental differences in the approach of Christianity and Buddhism. On the contrary I know of many Catholics who converted to Buddhism, including members of Catholic religious congregations who became Buddhist nuns and at least one Buddhist monk who was a professed brother in a Catholic order.

This is explained by the deep penetration of Buddhism into Korean culture. For about 1,000 years Korea was a Buddhist country. So the whole culture and the mindset of Koreans are profoundly influenced by Buddhism. But because of the persecution by the Confucianist state, Buddhism had become mainly a religion of women of the lower classes. So when Christianity came to Korea it encountered a kind of religious vacuum created by Confucianism, which itself had become ossified and sterile. Until recently Christian faith was more attractive than Buddhism, because it was considered modern and promising social change. Buddhist monks who had been persecuted for centuries were considered backward and ignorant. Change came slowly after the end of the Japanese occupation in 1945 when Buddhist monastic life was reorganised according to the Korean traditions. For the last ten years or so conversions to Buddhism by non-believers or believers of other religions have become quite frequent. Buddhism is now the fastest growing religion.

Even deeply convinced Catholic believers tell me that the atmosphere of a Buddhist temple exercises a great attraction. There they feel often more at home than in a Catholic parish. Mind and will are strongly Christian, but the set-up of the Buddhist temple appeals more to their religious emotions. They might exclaim: 'This is ours!' Christians visit Buddhist temples all the time. But Buddhist nuns or monks rarely come to Catholic monasteries. One reason is of course that the temples are in the most beautiful places of Korea. But another reason is that the set-up of our places appears foreign to Buddhists. They look to them like Western, i.e. foreign places. According to a 1998 survey (Gallup), when asked what religion they would prefer if they wanted to join a religion, 41.8 per cent said they preferred Buddhism (Catholicism 36.7 per cent, Protestantism 21.4 per cent). Buddhist practitioners tend to see their doctrine as superior to Christian faith which in their eyes looks rather primitive. They cannot see the role of Christ other than as that of a religious teacher and exemplary practitioner.

Even more important is the emotional attraction (*Gemüt* in German). There is a book by Chung Hyun-kyung, a Protestant feminist theologian, of which the German title is *Christin im Kopf, Schamanin im Bauch* ('Buddhist in my Head, Shaman in my Belly'). For many Koreans I could add *Buddhistin im Herzen* ('Buddhist in my Heart'). Whatever the convictions, Buddhism retains a deep attractiveness for all Koreans. For Christians without a strong personal relation to Jesus Christ it will be easy to change allegiances. Change to Buddhism is also made easier because doctrines are not so important. Buddhism is above all a practical way to inner freedom. Christians who enter a Buddhist monastery are not asked expressly to renounce their Christian faith. Buddhism is a lot more tolerant about doctrines. And because of the cultural background, becoming a Buddhist can be experienced as a homecoming. Buddhism is received more naturally. A young lady who works for *Jungto-hoi,* a Buddhist social organisation, told us that she does not see herself as having had a conversion. For her it was progress in the same direction. She says: 'I never changed' and 'I respond better to Buddhism'. Her life as a socially engaged Christian was not fulfilled. In Buddhism she found the answer to her questions. In a similar way Hyongak, a Buddhist monk living in Hwagyesa (temple) in Seoul, tells me that he did not give up his Catholic faith.

He thinks that he is now a better follower of Christ than before. The question here is of course 'Who is Jesus Christ?'

Question of Identity

Until very recently in Europe religious identity was decided by a person's family background. Therefore multiple belonging or multiple identity was hardly a question. In Korea this was always quite different. Here people were always able to wander between different religions. Even if one stays nominally in one religion there can be an overlapping of different identities. In Korea multiple belonging is less a problem brought about by conversion from one religion to the other but is inherent in every believer because of the interpenetration of religions which has existed for many centuries.

Here I want to ask first what does it mean to 'have' a religion? For many Koreans it means to belong to a community, which gives them peace of heart (most frequently given as a motive for joining a religion) and a certain stability of mind. Doctrine is not so important. More important is the image the religion projects. From conversations I have often learned that people find it good to have a religion. Non-believing mostly means that somebody did not yet find the right place. People find it good to belong to a respected religion. To Koreans Christianity appears progressive and modern. It is perceived as championing justice and equality. During the eighties of the last century, when military dictatorship was at its worst, many were attracted to the Catholic Church because they had the impression that the Catholic clergy with the Cardinal Archbishop of Seoul at its head fought against dictatorship. They also had the impression that the Catholic Church was cleaner than other religious bodies, that it was relatively free from irregularities and greed. It seemed also less rigid and dogmatic than the Protestants, who in Korea almost exclusively belong to the tradition of Calvin and are mostly fundamentalist. Many of those new converts to Catholicism left later, when they found that the clergy was pretty authority-conscious and more rigid than they had presumed. The question is, whether they ever had a personal relation to Christ, which should be the decisive criterion for being a Christian believer. This question applies also for those who stay on. Converts are required to learn the catechism, but what they really believe is often quite vague. That makes it easier to change their allegiance if there is an emotional attraction.

Statistics and my own experience show in fact that Koreans pretty easily change their religious allegiance. This may have to do with their culture, as it developed in history. Here different religions have always penetrated each other. But easy change also has to do with the reasons why Koreans look for a religion at all. When asked what they are seeking in religion the most common answer is 'peace of heart'. If they have the impression that Buddhism is better equipped for providing this peace of mind or heart they may switch from Christianity to Buddhism. And it can also be the other way round.

For Buddhism this is much less a problem than for the Christian Churches. In Buddhism doctrinal belief is much less stressed than in the Christian tradition. Buddhism is a way of practice, a road to internal freedom. Buddhists may think that Christians, through their own practice, can advance on their way to freedom. As the Buddhists in Korea say, the important thing is the Heart. But most Buddhists would think that Christians would need to be born again as Buddhists to attain Nirvana. This is the kind of inclusivism most Buddhists seem to profess. Many Koreans also have a kind of Shamanistic approach to religion: religion has to 'work'. So a religion may be tried. But if after conversion life becomes more difficult instead of easier and more prosperous, one gives it up.

As to the question of identity consciousness in Korean Christians I find three different attitudes:

1. In new converts often there is an eagerness to become as Protestant or as Roman Catholic as possible. Frequently Korean Catholics adhere more strongly to traditions considered traditionally Catholic than European Catholics do (e.g. the rosary, statues of Our Lady, Novenas etc.). There is a fear of losing one's newfound identity. Therefore there is a reluctance to engage in dialogue with other religious groups. So contact with Buddhism is kept minimal. I know about cases where the teaching of Buddhist doctrine to students for the priesthood or young nuns was suspended because the students liked it too much. Their superiors feared that they could lose their Christian faith. In other words: Their Christian identity did not seem stable enough to those responsible for their formation. Indeed I found the same concern with Buddhist monks who did not want their students to be engaged in interreligious dialogue.

2. In other believers I find a syncretistic tendency. But this seems to be more a cultural than a religious phenomenon. It comes from the desire to be a true Korean. So we see Catholics make their prostrations before the Buddha exactly according to the Buddhist ritual. In the same way they may make an offering to a pig's head though they profess not to believe in Shamanism. For them it is a way to profess their allegiance to Korean culture.

3. Finally quite a number of Christians show a natural confidence in their Christian identity, without being self-conscious about it. In this case Buddhism is acknowledged and respected as a religion of deep human wisdom and part of the Korean cultural heritage. Such people sometimes give a Christian interpretation to Buddhist doctrines like universal interdependence or non-dualism. They may also feel enriched by originally Buddhist practices like Zen Mediation or use prostrations in their prayer.

It is not easy to analyse the components of the religious identity of Korean Christians, because in spite of the huge doctrinal differences between Buddhism and Christianity the religious and even more the moral values are very similar in both religions (think of charity-compassion, frugality, respect for nature, modesty etc). It is easier to spot Shamanist and Confucian attitudes and thinking in Christian believers because the differences are greater. Shamanism is decidedly this-worldly or even materialistic. Confucianism stresses hierarchy and ritualism. But because of the long standing of Confucian tradition, the highest moral value for a majority of Koreans of any belief is filial piety.

The Question of Multiple Belonging

In Korea belonging to different religions in some way or other is a pervasive phenomenon. In practice the different religions often fulfil different functions. Van Bragt, quoted by Valkenberg, says the same about Japan. This kind of syncretism or eclecticism is described by professor Yoon Younghae in this way:

> In general for the important events in human life like marriage, funeral, sacrifices for the ancestors and similar rites of their social life Koreans follow the values and prescriptions of Confucianism. Most Koreans practise the rites for

the ancestors which are totally Confucian in character. By and by even Christians with a strong faith identity tend to accept the sacrifices for the ancestors. On the other hand in their view of human life and moral values most Koreans are deeply influenced by Buddhism, feeling the impermanence of human life and believing in rebirth and the law of Karma. And whatever faith they may belong to, when Koreans are confronted with problems which cannot be rationally resolved or find themselves in a great crisis, they seek the help of a soothsayer or a shaman... As to the implementing of political and social justice, Koreans of all beliefs will happily follow the Christian community.

As to this last point, however, it is remarkable how little Korean politicians put Christian ethics into concrete political practice such as legislation concerning social issues and human rights. This may be attributable to the quite common Korean opinion that true religion is something other-worldly and concerned with only personal perfection, which in turn is the Korean understanding of Buddhist religion embodied in the monk as spiritual seeker living in his hermitage in the mountains.

Bernard Senécal, a Canadian Jesuit living in Korea, has an interesting theory about religious identity. The term he uses is *multiple appartenance religieuse*. He says: 'We call the phenomenon of multiple belonging the situation of a person or a group of persons whose religious practices and beliefs are determined by several religious traditions at the same time'. This, he says, is true for all Koreans and has been so for a long time because of the coexistence of Shamanism, Buddhism and Confucianism, even before the arrival of Christianity. Senécal considers Korea as a microcosm where all the great tendencies of the development of religious history come together. He thinks therefore that Korea is a privileged place to study possible forms of expressions Christianity could take in the future

According to Senécal there are two possibilities of this multiple belonging. In the first case there is a centre which unifies the different elements. In the other case there is no single centre which unifies different beliefs and practices. This lack of inner integration may lead to psychological problems. In the first case Senécal distinguishes *Coréanocentrisme, Bouddhocentrisme* and *Christocentrisme*. He does not speak of *Shamanocentrisme* or *Confuciocentrisme*. He says however that 'Shamanism...constitutes a kind of diffuse atmosphere in which the totality of Korean life is immersed' and seems to imply that the ethical ideal of *Coréanocentrisme* is the wise man of Confucius. Here we only look at *Bouddhocentrisme* and *Christocentrisme*.

Senécal calls Christocentric a person who may live in a situation of multiple belonging but for whom Jesus Christ, Son of God, constitutes the existential centre which unifies the other non-Christian religious elements. For the Buddhocentric person the Buddha, whether seen as a kind of divinity to be implored or as the true nature of all beings to be realised in illumination, is the existential centre in which all other religious elements are integrated.

To illustrate the case of Christocentrism Senécal introduces a Mrs Kim, who had lived and practised as a Buddhist before converting to the Catholic faith. She is a strong believer who goes to mass every day, has a gift of healing and visits people in prison. Still, when she sees that her elder daughter refuses to be baptised she attributes this to the influence of Buddha to whom she prayed when she wanted to have a daughter. This daughter she still considers a gift of the Buddha. In order to avoid the influence of Buddha she does not go to Buddhist temples and refuses to see statues and other representations of the Buddha. In this way she avoids causing tension in herself by competition between Buddhocentrism and Christocentrism, which would be heavy to bear. In similar ways for many Koreans, though sure and definite in their allegiance to Jesus Christ, the Buddhist universe retains a certain reality.

We also see Christians, whether converts or not, consciously incorporate certain Buddhist teachings into their world view. This may be done by giving Buddhist teachings a Christian interpretation. We can see this for instance with the doctrine of dependent origination (*pratītya-samutpāda*, Chinese-Korean: *yongi*), quite often considered as the centre of Buddhist teaching. The interdependence of all beings becomes the foundation of Buddhist ethics. Because this doctrine denies the ego and teaches that there is no difference between me and the other, for Christians it can provide a wonderful motivation for true altruistic love as taught by Jesus. Buddhism with its teaching about the unity of all beings can also help Christians to re-evaluate the anthropocentrism of traditional Christianity.

In the multireligious environment of Korea it is not surprising that some Christians tend to hold Buddhist views which cannot be logically reconciled with Christian beliefs, such as the doctrine of Karma, the possibility of a previous life etc. For Korean Christians it is sometimes difficult really to grasp the meaning of the resurrection.

The same may be said for the influence of Shamanistic beliefs. Many Christians believe in the existence of spirits, though they are confident that they have escaped their power by their faith in Christ. To Koreans it is often not clear whether some belief or ceremony is Shamanist or Buddhist, because Shamans use many Buddhist symbols and some Shamanist or Taoist representations are integrated into popular Buddhism. In an even stronger way the Confucian component of the Korean soul makes itself felt in the way Korean Christians look at the world and act in society. This appears in the respect for hierarchy and order, the relation between husband and wife, in the importance of filial piety and the observance of ancestor worship. Talking about this phenomenon Senécal states somewhat drastically: 'For Mrs Kim to live the Gospel means to live the Confucian ethics'.

ELIZABETH J. HARRIS

Confrontation over Conversions: A Case Study from Sri Lanka

I begin with three cameos. Each illustrates a strand in the ongoing confrontation in Sri Lanka over the question of conversion from Buddhism to Christianity.

1. On 29 December 2003, the Venerable Dr Omalpe Sobitha launched a fast-unto-death opposite the Ministry of Buddha Sasana (Ministry of Buddhist Affairs) in Colombo demanding that the President and the Prime Minister of Sri Lanka should bring in legislation to prevent Buddhists being converted to other religions. He was a member of the Executive Committee of the National Bhikkhu Assembly and would become a key member of the Jathika Hela Urumaya (JHU - National Heritage Party), a new political party that would field Buddhist monks to fight the national elections in April 2004.[1] He was joined by many other *bhikkhus* (Buddhist monks), one hundred according to one newspaper report.[2]

2. On 7 May 2005 an organisation called 'Solidarity for Religious Freedom' and the Roman Catholic Diocese of Chilaw, in the west of Sri Lanka, held a rally that, according to the National Christian Evangelical Alliance of Sri Lanka, attracted over 2,500 people from different Christian denominations. The Roman Catholic Archbishop of Chilaw spoke, as did the Anglican Bishop of Kurunegala and the Honourable Milroy Fernando, the Minister for Christian Affairs within

---

[1] Reports in the *Divaina* and *The Island* on 30.12.2003 as reported in *The Present Religious Conflict: Sparked Off by the Demise of Ven.Gangodawila Soma Thera*, Kelaniya: Globe Information and Publicity Services, 2003: 10.
[2] *Daily News*, 30 December 2003: 11, quoted in *The Present Religious Conflict*.

the government. All speakers, including the government minister,[3] spoke against the anti-conversion legislation that was, by that time, pending. The Bishop of Kurunegala drew a parallel with the passing of a draconian Prevention of Terrorism Act in 1979. As the Act had been used to oppress Sri Lanka's minorities, he declared, so would the anti-conversion legislation. The first had oppressed the Tamils, the second would oppress the minority Christian and Muslim communities.

3. An Assembly of God Church at Ambalangoda in the Galle District, in the predominantly Buddhist south of the country, was destroyed by the tsunami on 26 December 2004. On 4 June 2005 the church finalised the purchase of new land and a building for worship. On the night of the 5th, rocks, stones and bottles filled with sand were thrown at the building, damaging windows. The next day at 10 a.m. a crowd of about 100 people surrounded the church shouting threats. They carried iron rods, shovels and two swords. At 3 p.m. they invaded the church and attacked two parishioners and the Pastor, injuring one person seriously.[4] The attackers believed that the Christians of the church were involved in 'unethical conversions', a phrase frequently used by Buddhists and Hindus in Sri Lanka to describe evangelistic methods that encouraged people to convert to Christianity through 'bribing' them with material gifts.

Conversion and religious identity have been charged issues in Sri Lanka for well over a hundred years. Calls for legislation to protect the identity of Buddhists and Hindus against 'unethical conversions' to Christianity began towards the end of the twentieth century. Serious attempts to initiate legislation, however, began only in 2002 with calls from the Minister of Hindu Affairs for a Bill modelled on legislation in Tamil Nadu. In 2003, in response to an incorporation bill that sought registration for a Christian organization, the Supreme Court ruled that, although the Constitution gave everyone the right to practise their religion, it did not give freedom to Christians to propagate their religion since this would go against Article 9 of the Constitution,

---

[3] As early as March 2005, Milroy Fernando had made it known that he would vote against the Anti-Conversion Bill. See 'Christian Affairs Minister to vote against the Bill', *The Sunday Leader*, 20 March 2005: 4.
[4] Update on Church Attacks, National Christian Evangelical Alliance of Sri Lanka: 7 June 2005.

which gave Buddhism 'foremost place'. Some thought this ruling would take away the need for anti-conversion legislation. It did not. Two separate Bills were drawn up in 2004. The first was the work of the JHU and the second of Ratnasiri Wickramanayake, then Minister of Buddha Sasana.

The JHU Bill targeted fraudulent or forced conversions. It was gazetted by the fast-unto-death Parliamentarian, Venerable Omalpe Sobitha, as a private member's bill, on 28 May 2004 and tabled in Parliament on 21 July. Immediately an almost equal number of petitions for and against the bill – 21 or 22 against and between 21 and 25 for – were filed in the Supreme Court. Those against the bill, filed by human rights specialists and Christian groups, argued that the legislation would violate the Constitution on issues of freedom of expression and belief. The Supreme Court agreed. It ruled, in August 2004, that two clauses of the Bill violated Articles 10 (freedom of thought and religion) and 14 (freedom of expression) of the Constitution, with the implication that the Bill could only be passed if it was treated as a constitutional amendment, needing a two thirds majority in Parliament and a national referendum.

By 2005, however, the Bill was back and so was the one compiled by the Minister of Buddha Sasana. They contained these clauses:

> No person shall convert or attempt to convert, either directly or otherwise, any person from one religion to another by the use of force or by allurement or by any fraudulent means nor shall any person aid or abet such conversion. (JHU Bill)[5]

> No person shall convert or attempt to convert another person to another religion, and no person shall provide assistance or encouragement towards such conversion to another religion.
> (Bill drafted by Hon. Ratnasiri Wickramanayake)[6]

---

[5] 'Prohibition of Forcible Conversion of Religion: to provide for prohibition of conversion from one religion to another by use of force or allurement or by fraudulent means and for matters incidental therewith or incendental thereto'. From *The Gazette of the Democratic Socialist Republic of Sri Lanka*: Part II of May 2004, Supplement: p. One, lines 23-26.

[6] Bill drafted by Hon. Ratnasiri Wickramanayake, Minister of Buddha Sasana, June 2004, translated to English from the Official Version in Sinhala: Clause 0.2.

In the first, 'force' is defined as 'including a threat of harm or injury of any kind or threat of religious displeasure or condemnation of any religion or religious faith'.[7] In the second, the summary of the clause in the English version of the text is, 'That conversion to another religion is illegal'. It is towards Christian activities that both Bills are directed, although it would equally prevent Buddhists attempting to convert Christians, Muslims or Hindus.

In this paper I will explore how Sri Lanka has reached a situation in which issues connected with conversion and religious identity have produced violence, intimidation, threatened fasts-unto-death and anti-conversion legislation. I will do this through looking at the situation from the Buddhist side, in search for an answer to the question that emerges from the three cameos at the beginning of the chapter: 'Why do some Sri Lankan Buddhists see conversion, particularly conversions from Buddhism to Christianity, as a threat?'

The Politics of Conversion

In the West, conversion from one religion to another is usually defined in personal terms and recognised as a human right. It is seen as the fruit of personal choice, informed by reason or experience, sometimes after a long spiritual quest. Buddhism also has long endorsed an individual person's right to change their religious belonging. After all, the Buddha's main message was, 'The way you see the world is wrong. Change.' And his invitation was, 'Come and see – see if the path I teach works.'[8] Many at the time of the Buddha did change their religious allegiance and took the Buddha and his disciples as their teachers.

This individualistic model usually explains conversion through accenting the previous history and experience of the convert. However, I would like to argue that this is inadequate by itself. The individual person's place in history is equally important in understanding the phenomenon of conversion. Every conversion has a historical, social

---

[7] *The Gazette of the Democratic Socialist Republic of Sri Lanka*: Part II of May 2004, Supplement: 4, lines 1-4.

[8] Peter Harvey for instance describes Buddhism, Christianity and Islam as the 'three great missionary religions of the world' but distinguishes between the methods used by the three, writing, 'Indeed it (Buddhism) describes its teaching and path as "come-see-ish", and monks have traditionally not been allowed to teach to a new audience unless they have been invited to do so…' (Peter Harvey, *Buddhism*, London and New York: Continuum, 2001: 3).

and political side that cannot be edited out of the picture. I am drawn to Ananda Abeysekara's theoretical model. In his book on Buddhism in Sri Lanka, *Colors of the Robe*, he argues that the meanings of the categories we use in our conversations about religion are not always self-evident. How they are defined is dependent on contingent debates, embedded in local contexts. One example he uses is involvement in politics by members of Sri Lanka's monastic community. Whether such political involvement is seen as Buddhist or non-Buddhist, he argues, mutates and changes according to altering local contexts.[9]

In a similar way, I would like to argue that the way conversion is seen in Sri Lanka, and indeed in other parts of Asia, is dependent on contingent factors. Whether the ability to change religion is simply seen as a human right or whether, as in Sri Lanka, some see it as a threat to the 'nation' is dependent on a variety of contingent factors. In this chapter, I will touch on the four broad factors that condition the national discourse in Sri Lanka:

– The activities of fundamentalist Christian groups
– Historical memory
– The long-standing ethnic conflict in the country
– Conspiracy theories surrounding the death in 2003 of a notable Buddhist monk, Ven. Gangodawila Soma Thero.

The Activities of Fundamentalist Groups

Let me begin this section with an article that I believe to contain genuine material, written by someone with the name Christian Eckert, apparently a German who was in Sri Lanka in December 2004 at the time of the tsunami and who returned in 2005 with a Sri Lankan-born journalist to travel 3,480 kilometres visiting 18 projects. An account of his experience appeared on the website of *The Lanka Academic* and was much circulated in Sri Lanka. I received it from the Principal of the Theological College of Lanka. It concentrated almost entirely on the activities of fringe Christian groups. He wrote of one encounter:

---

[9] See Ananda Abeysekara, *Colors of the Robe: Religion, Identity and Difference*, Columbia: University of South Carolina Press, 2002, particularly pp. 67-108.

We later met a Mr D.S., a well-known businessman in the South, his reputation flawless. He has been helping his people, effective and fast. And he, too, told us about this temporary housing area, where the Baptist Church of Omaha is ruling a strange religion. He took us to a Tsunami Camp where we met a young woman who had lost her beloved sewing machine in the tsunami. For her it was the income source for her family. The young woman was approached by members of this obscure church. She was told to attend services and masses for one week and pray to the Lord to give her a sewing machine.

A week later, after she had attended the services, she got a brand new sewing machine, worth 25,000 rupees (US $ 250). She was told that other needy things, too, could appear in that way, if she would keep up attending the Christian masses and bible reading hours.[10]

My first factor is simply that unethical evangelistic practices are taking place in Sri Lanka and Buddhists are aware of it, rumour often adding to fact. The mainline Christian denominations have officially distanced themselves from these. In November 1993, for instance, a joint statement was signed by Buddhist and Christian leaders deploring 'all campaigns of conversion of one religionist to another by forceful means or by any other subtle method.'[11] And in 2003, the Catholic Bishops' Conference of Sri Lanka issued a press statement distancing themselves from 'fundamentalist Christian Sects' declaring, 'We do not support any of these measures such as material enticements or undue pressures that are alleged to be made by these groups in order to carry out so-called unethical conversions'.[12] In addition, after the tsunami, the practice of the mainline Christian denominations was exemplary. All insisted that the aid they received – and it was considerable – should be distributed to all, irrespective of religion or ethnicity. The Church of Ceylon within the Anglican Communion was

---

[10] Christian Eckert, *The Next Tsunami coming to Sri Lanka is a Religious One*, 22 May 2005, posted on http://www.theacademic.org/ (The website of *The Lanka Academic*).
[11] 'Buddhist and Christian leaders take common stand on forced or subtle conversion', *Daily News*, 15 November, quoted in Elizabeth Harris, *Theravāda Buddhism and the British Encounter: Religious, missionary and colonial experience in nineteenth century Sri Lanka*, London and New York: Routledge, 2006: 211.
[12] From, 'No links with fundamentalist sects, say Catholic Bishops': a report of the statement and the text, on-line version of the *Daily News*, 19 December 2003.

adamant: tsunami relief should not be used to build the power of the churches.

Some Buddhists hear these statements and are able to distinguish between the mainline denominations and independent Christian groups. For instance, Part II of a report written by a Commission set up to look into the grievances of the Sinhala people, published in 2001, declared:

> There have been a variety of Christianities in South Asia for some centuries, as for example Roman Catholicism, Methodists, St Thomas Christians in Kerala. But these older Christian Sects had, if not being indigenised, acquired a modus vivendi with Buddhism and Hinduism and largely avoided confrontation with the older religions, Buddhism and Hinduism.[13]

The Report went on to mention a 'large influx of new Christian denominations' in many Asian countries, a development it condemned as political rather than religious.[14]

The distinction between mainline denominations and independent churches, though, is not as clear-cut as the Sinhala Commission makes out in the above clause. All Protestant churches in Sri Lanka have evangelical wings keen to promote primary evangelism.

So the first contingent factor is the very real presence of fundamentalist Christian groups who will exert pressure on Buddhist villagers to become Christians. The stories that circulate as a result anger, hurt and sadden Buddhists. Unable to sympathize with or even understand what motivates Christian evangelism, they use their own categories and judge the activities of evangelists unethical, harming the evangelists themselves, the people they attempt to convert and society in general.[15] The actions that flow from this judgement have varied from the

---

[13] *Report of The Sinhala Commission Part II*, Colombo: the National Joint Committee, 2001: 97.
[14] *Report of The Sinhala Commission Part II*, Colombo: 97-98
[15] The traditional Theravāda Buddhism of the Pāli texts encourages people ask themselves before they act whether the act will harm themselves, harm others or harm both. The action should be avoided if it does. For such action, according to the *Ambaṭṭhika-Rāhulovāda Sutta* is 'unskilled, its yield is anguish, its result is anguish' (*Majjhima Nikāya* 61/ I: 44-45).

selling of talismans to protect against fundamentalism[16] to protest meetings called by leaders of the Buddhist monastic Sangha to gang violence against churches and Christians, sometimes led by Buddhist monks.

The year 2003 was a particularly bad year for attacks on Christians and churches. Taking calculations up to 12 January 2004, it was a year when the National Christian Evangelical Alliance of Sri Lanka had 107 incidents of violence, threat or intimidation against Christian communities or churches reported to it. Many of these were attacks on independent churches – Heavenly Harvest Church, Assemblies of God, Eternal Church, Calvary Church, Gethsemane Prayer Centre. Only occasionally was a Methodist, an Anglican or a Catholic Church attacked.

The 2003 spate of attacks on churches died down after a gang of twelve was remanded on 12 February 2004, including a Sri Lankan who had returned to the country from Australia. But the attacks did not end. A further spree came in December 2004. A Catholic Church was burnt to the ground in Homagama and an independent church in Kuliyapitiya attacked. Some congregations were unable to hold Christmas services.[17]

Communal Memory: The Nineteenth Century[18]

The reaction to activities deemed 'unethical' does not arise in a vacuum. It interlocks with communal memory of the colonial era, particularly the nineteenth century. The passing of time then collapses, and threats faced in the past become fused with perceived threats in the present. My second factor concerns the way in which memory of Christian-Buddhist relationships in the past can intensify tensions in the present.

Sri Lanka had three colonial rulers, Portuguese, Dutch and British, the British taking over from the Dutch in 1795-96. The British admi-

[16] Thimbirigama Bandara, 'The Conspiracy of Converting People to Other Religions', *Ravaya*, 4 January 2004, summarized in *The Present Religious Conflict:* 19.
[17] See for instance, 'Christians spend Christmas in fear', *The Sunday Leader*, 26 December 2004, p. 13.
[18] The data from this section is drawn from a much longer account of Christian-Buddhist relationships in the nineteenth century in Part V of my book, *Theravāda Buddhism and the British Encounter*.

nistrators inherited a sizeable Roman Catholic population and a large number of people nominally baptised into the Dutch Reformed Church for political reasons. Close on the heels of the British administrators came Christian missionaries, employees of the independent missionary societies that were formed at the end of the eighteenth century as part of the evangelical revival. The first came in 1805 from the London Missionary Society. Within twelve years, Baptists, Wesleyan Methodists and Anglicans from the Church Missionary Society (CMS) had also arrived.[19] Some went to the predominantly Hindu north and east. Some remained in the predominantly Buddhist south.

Those in the south soon discovered what they deemed a very strange attitude among Buddhists to the religious 'other' – strange at least when compared to the missionary worldview. They found that Sri Lankan lay Buddhists saw no incompatibility between endorsing Christian tenets and retaining their Buddhist identity. They would listen eagerly to Christian preachers, ask intelligent questions and appear to agree, but remain Buddhists. As for the monks, missionary records show that some raised academic objections to Christianity. But most were willing to offer hospitality, even to the extent of allowing the missionaries to talk about Christianity inside Buddhist temples. Samuel Lambrick, CMS missionary, records this of one conversation with a monk:

> I found that he was for an intercommunity of Religions – that he was, in fact, of the same opinion as some of our own worldly-wise people at home, who think that every man may be saved, if he is sincere in the Religion which he professes. He appears, comparatively, shy of my company, since I told him that our God allowed of no rival – that if our Sacred Book was right, his must be wrong, and his worship of the Budhu sinful and abominable – and that, on the contrary, if he or any of his Sacred Books was in any degree or measure right, ours were all false, and a fabrication from beginning to end.[20]

---

[19] Missionaries from the Baptist Missionary Society arrived in 1812. Wesleyan Methodists arrived in 1814 and missionaries from the Church Missionary Society in 1818.
[20] *Proceedings of the Church Missionary Society* 1819-1820 (London): 192-3. For more evidence of the kind of 'dialogue' that took place see: *Proceedings of the Church Missionary Society* 1821-1822: 326-7.

When Christian evangelical missionary and Sri Lankan Buddhist monk met, it was not only two religions that met but also two orientations towards the religious 'other'. The Christian missionary placed competing truth claims at the centre. If the message of Christianity was right, then all other religious systems must be false; if all other systems were false then they had to be destroyed or superseded. Buddhist monks on the other hand were more concerned about peaceful co-existence than about conflicting truth claims. They had a sophisticated sense of what was true and what was heretical. They had a tradition of rational doctrinal debate as the work of Kitsiri Malalgoda shows.[21] They no doubt had cognitive problems with Christianity. But on the ground, all the data I've discovered suggests that they believed that people of different religions should co-exist peacefully and work together where possible, debating with each other maybe, but not offending each other.[22] They were therefore not, at first, opposed to Buddhist lay people listening to Christians or even having a form of dual belonging by attending Christian worship, as long as their Buddhist identity was primary. The tragedy of Buddhist-Christian relationships in Sri Lanka is that, when these two orientations met and interacted, it was the missionary orientation that eventually became dominant, because it was backed by imperial power.

Several scholars who have written about this period have taken an incident from 1815, at Kelaniya Mahā Vihāraya (the great monastery and temple at Kelaniya), to illustrate the emerging dynamic.[23] Revd Benjamin Clough, Wesleyan missionary, preaches to a large crowd of Buddhists close to the temple on John 3:16 [24] and seizes the opportu-

[21] See Kitsiri Malaloda, *Buddhism in Sinhalese Society 1750-1900*, Berkeley: University of California Press, 1976.
[22] I have looked further at the Buddhist model for co-existence in: Elizabeth J. Harris, 'Co-existence, Confrontation and Co-responsibility: Looking at Buddhist Models of Inter-religious Relations' in *Swedish Missiological Themes,* 92/3, 2004: 349-70.
[23] See Richard F. Young and G.P.V. Somaratna, *Debates: The Buddhist-Christian Controversies of Nineteenth Century Ceylon*, Publications of the De Nobili Research Library, Vol. XXIII, Vienna: University of Vienna, 1996: 61; Barbara A. R. Coplans, 'Methodism and Sinhalese Buddhism: the Wesleyan Encounter with Buddhism in Ceylon 1814-1864, with special reference to the work of Robert Spence Hardy', unpublished thesis, University of Leeds, 1980: 100-14; Charles W. Karunaratna, *Buddhism and Christianity in Colonial Ceylon: The British Period, 1796-1948*, published by the author, ISBN: 1-899367-01-2, 1999: 12   (thesis, University of London, 1974); Elizabeth J. Harris, 'Co-existence, Confrontation and Co-responsibility': 349-350 and *Theravāda Buddhism and the British Encounter*: 197.
[24] 'For God so loved the world that he gave his only Son, so that everyone who believes in him may not perish but may have eternal life' (New Revised Standard Version).

nity to challenge what he perceives to be the Buddhist concept of transmigration. The lay people, true to form, seem to respond well and invite the preachers back. The resident monks at Kelaniya Mahā Vihā-raya, however, are disturbed by what they hear about the content of the preaching. The head monk, therefore, sends a message to Clough, saying that he would hold a public debate with him on his next visit. A date is arranged. But when Clough returns on the arranged date, the Buddhists retreat from confrontation. The head monk is nowhere to be seen and when Clough finds the other monks, they refuse to talk about it. So preaching continues. The next step of the Buddhist monks is to send a petition to the Governor arguing that they had been abused.[25]

This was not an isolated case. The sending of petitions was one of the main initial strategies of the monastic Sangha. As Kitsiri Malalgo-da has shown, these petitions not only protested that there had been abuse but pleaded for religious toleration, the withdrawal of offensive publications and an agreement 'that no religious group should issue publications which are likely or calculated to offend and injure the feelings of other religious groups'.[26] They came at a point when the Buddhist community still believed that a co-existence model of inter-religious relations was possible through reasoned appeals to the need for religious harmony.

The inter-religious model outlined in these petitions has a striking affinity to models that were advanced in the West in the twentieth century, for instance by the Inter Faith Network for the United Kingdom.[27] In the nineteenth century, however, the petitions were either scorned or ignored. The Buddhist monks soon discovered that, in spite of the hospitality they had offered to missionaries, harmonious co-existence was not on the missionary agenda. The missionaries would do everything in their power to show contempt to Buddhism by representing it as nihilistic and soteriologically impotent. Sadly, but perhaps inevitably, the attitude of Buddhists towards the 'other' that was Christianity changed. The Christian missionaries became not only

---

[25] Benjamin Clough, 'Extract of a letter from Clough, to Mr John Barber, dated Colom-bo, Aug. 30, 1815', *Methodist Magazine*, XXXIV, 1816:198 (the letter from which my account of the incident is largely drawn).

[26] Malalgoda, 1976: 214, drawing on records in the Sri Lanka National Archives and the Colonial Office in London.

[27] The Inter Faith Network for the United Kingdom was established in 1987, and net-works over a hundred member bodies, which include representative bodies of nine faiths, regional and local inter faith groups and educational institutions. Its members have endorsed a code of conduct that is rooted in respect and courtesy.

representatives of a different religion but betrayers of hospitality and a threat to the Buddha Dhamma in a way that the Dutch had never been. For at least the Dutch had turned a blind eye when baptised Sri Lankans had continued going to the Buddhist temple. Their *predikants* were not children of the evangelical revival with its no compromise message.

To cut a long story short, the eventual consequence of this clash of world-views was that some Buddhists, in defence of their own identity, adopted the Christian missionary model of inter-religious encounter. Preference for the co-existence model continued in some places but, especially amongst the growing middle classes and the monastic community, it was replaced by a confrontation that demonised Christianity in the same way as the Christian missionaries had demonised Buddhism.

In the 1860s and 1870s several Buddhist-Christian debates were held. The most important was the Panadura Debate in 1873 between the Venerable Mohoṭṭivattē Guṇānanda, revivalist Buddhist monk, and Rev. David de Silva, a Sri Lankan Methodist pupil of the missionaries. It is a good example of the slide towards confrontation and mutual demonisation.[28]

Venerable Mohoṭṭivattē Guṇānanda had done his research well, particularly into what western freethinkers such as Charles Bradlaugh were using to attack Christianity. Appealing meticulously to the letter of Hebrew scriptures, he accused Christians of worshipping a jealous, capricious, violent and demon-like god, linking Jehovah and Jesus to the world of the demonic.[29] How could Jesus be divine, he argued, if his birth was accompanied by so many deaths? How could words said by the murderer Moses be accounted good? Just as Christian missionaries had used literalism in approaching the Theravāda texts to 'prove' that Buddhism was atheistic and nihilistic, so Buddhists did the same with the Bible. After the Debate, Buddhist-Christian confrontation continued, taking new forms as help from western theosophists arrived.

---

[28] See Elizabeth J. Harris, *Theravāda Buddhism and the British Encounter*: 202-203.

[29] Reference can be made to the first speech of Guṇānanda in which Exodus 4:24 is cited as similar to the kind of offering given in Sri Lanka to appease the devil. See J.M. Peebles, *Buddhism and Christianity: Being an Oral Debate held at Panadura between the Rev. Migettuwatte Gunananda, a Buddhist Priest, and the Rev. David de Silva, Wesleyan Clergyman*, Colombo: All Ceylon Buddhist Congress, 1994 (an annotated reprint of Peebles' original): 67-68. The same theme is continued in further speeches, for example that both the devil and the Christian God love blood (Peebles 1994: 92, 122).

My point in this section is that this history is not dead. It feeds mistrust against Christians in the present, confrontational attitudes towards truth claims and a determination to defend Buddhism against threat. On 24 August 2003, for instance, a commemorative public rally was held in Sri Lanka to mark the one hundred and thirtieth anniversary of the Panadura Debate and a postage stamp was issued.[30] And an article published on 19 September 2004 could declare in the context of the anti-conversion debate:

> At the open debate between the Buddhist Bhikkhu and the Christian Father held at Panadura, it was convincingly argued and proved to the world, the doctrinal superiority of the Buddha Dhamma over Christianity.
> It is thus quite clear that converting a Buddhist to Christianity certainly cannot be to ensure his spiritual advancement but possibly for some other sinister and covert motive.[31]

The 'covert motive' that some Buddhists suspect Christians of is no less than a destruction of Buddhism in Sri Lanka, not only through conversions but through support for the separatism of Tamil militants.

The Ethnic Conflict

Sri Lanka's ethnic conflict is not a religious conflict, but religion is not innocent within it. Its principal cause is the failure of the centralised parliamentary structure, which the country agreed to at independence in 1948, to accommodate the need of the Tamil minority in the North and East of the country to have a say both in their own governance and in the governance of the country as a whole. This constitutional flaw and the failure of non-violent methods of negotiation led, in the middle of the twentieth century, to the emergence of several militant Tamil youth groups, which demanded a separate state in the North and East. By the time the Liberation Tigers of Tamil Eelam (LTTE) had

---

[30] The rally was organised by the Council for the Commemoration of the Great Debate of Panadura. See 'That controversial clash', D.C. Ranatunga, *The Sunday Times Plus*, August 24, 2003: 9.
[31] Asoka Devendra, 'Conversion: Sinister and covert motives', *The Sunday Times Plus*, 19 September 2004: 2.

gained dominance of these groups in the early 1980s, a violent ethnic conflict had begun.

There has been a ceasefire in the conflict since February 2002, but it is fragile and subject to numerous violations, increasingly so after the LTTE withdrew from peace talks in April 2003. Some progress towards the resumption of talks was made on 24 June 2005, when, in the face of much opposition in the South, a Memorandum of Understanding concerning a joint mechanism for tsunami relief (the Post-Tsunami Operational Management Structure – P-TOMS) was signed between the government and the LTTE. Even that is now under threat with the election of a new President, Mahinda Rajapakse, in November 2005.

The ethnic conflict feeds into the conversion debate, increasing the mistrust of some Buddhists towards Christianity, because the Tamil 'other' and the Christian 'other' are conflated in the words of some vocal Buddhists, the perceived threat from one feeding into the perceived threat from the other. There are two levels to this. First, probably at a subconscious level, there is a replay of emotions and reactions present in the nineteenth century. In the nineteenth century, Christian missionaries were eventually cast as betrayers of the trust, hospitality and tolerance of the Sinhala Buddhists of Sri Lanka. This fuelled a vigorous and sometimes venomous confrontation. In a surprisingly similar dynamic, the LTTE, in the twentieth century, has also been cast as betrayer of the goodwill of the Sinhala people as well as of their historical and demographic rights. I first drew attention to this parallel in 2001, when I wrote:

> Each action taken by the Tamil community to draw attention to their need for more control over their own affairs within a democratic framework has been taken by these groups (nationalist Buddhist groups) as a humiliating attack on the self-definition of the Sinhala people, amounting to betrayal.[32]

I did not then know of Part II of the Report of the Sinhala Commission, which illustrates the victimhood associated with this mindset. Dismissing Tamil claims that they are oppressed as a 'big lie' and at-

---

[32] E.J. Harris, 'Buddhism and War: a study of cause and effect from Sri Lanka' in *Culture and Religion*, 2/2, Autumn 2001: 214.

tributing the growth of LTTE terrorism to British colonialism, it accuses foreign funded NGOs of being LTTE propagandists, 'fifth columnists under a hidden agenda'.[33] Whereas in the nineteenth century it could be argued that Sinhala Buddhists were justified in seeing themselves as victims of an alien view of inter-religious relations, the transference of this mindset to the LTTE in the twentieth century has prevented some Buddhists from seeing the deep-seated grievances of the Tamil people, with disastrous consequences.

The second level relates to the fact that there is a Christian element in the LTTE. The majority of Tamils in Sri Lanka are Hindu, but there is also a sizeable Christian Tamil community, some prominent members of which have been active supporters of the LTTE. Sri Lankan Buddhists know this and also that diaspora Tamil communities have successfully lobbied bodies such as the World Council of Churches in favour of a separatist agenda. 'The so-called peace process is a conspiracy led by foreign powers with the assistance of the church', one Sinhala leader of a Buddhist nationalist party could therefore declare in January 2004. He went on to argue that the LTTE must be destroyed militarily, and even undermined another Sinhala nationalist party, the *Sihala Urumaya* (Sinhala Heritage Party), for having Catholics within it, who, he implied, must be supporters of the LTTE.[34] In more populist vein, anonymous Buddhists in Colombo could move from criticism of Christian 'converters' to this, written to the press in 2000:

> This is a wake-up call to the sleeping Buddhists, who are about to lose their country, race and religion. Any other race would have jerked itself awake, seeing how Norway (chosen to be facilitator in the peace process), the only country that objected to Vesak being declared a holiday by the UN, is being accepted here with open arms and a red carpet welcome, each time a representative pops in to ascertain how far, with the help of the you-know native, the devilish work of the disintegration of the motherland is progressing. Is it true that the Sinhala Buddhist himself is progressing from deep sleep to total paralysis?[35]

---

[33] National Joint Committee, *Report of the Sinhala Commission Part* II: ix-x, 92.

[34] Harischandra Wijetunge, 'Sihala Urumaya is a Cat's Paw of the Church', *Lanka,* 11 Jan 2004, quoted in *The Present Religious Conflict:* 23-24 .

[35] Buddhists Colombo 6 and 7, 'Rise from your slumber, Buddhists told', 31 December 2000, *The Sunday Leader:* p. 6.

'Threat to the dhamma' is again the motif, but it is not only through conversions. It is through the combined impact of Christian proselytisation and Christian support for the LTTE, locally and internationally. A grand conspiracy theory emerges of Christians and the LTTE, supported by foreign non-governmental organisations, united in their wish to destroy the unity and identity of Sri Lanka, imaged as the only Sinhala Buddhist country in the world. Even Christians who eschew separatism but support a negotiated solution to the ethnic conflict are implicated.

Conspiracy Theories surrounding the Death in 2003 of a Notable Buddhist Monk, Ven. Gangodawila Soma Thero

The last factor conditioning the present conflict over conversion in Sri Lanka is more focussed and illustrates how mistrust already present can be whipped up and channelled. In December 2003, the Venerable Gangodawila Soma Thero died, at 54 years of age. Soma Thero became a monk at the age of 25 – a comparatively late age in Sri Lanka. He did not have a position in the Buddhist hierarchy, but he had excellent communication skills and a sound knowledge of the Theravāda tradition. He used these in the media, particularly television, to put across a reformist message that attracted thousands. He attacked religious practices that could be seen as non-Buddhist imports from Hinduism. He appealed to a simple, rigorous morality and denounced alcoholism and drug abuse. But he could also show ethnic bias in his denunciation of Tamil and Muslim traders and his urging of Sinhala Buddhists to have as many children as possible to counter population growth in the Muslim community.[36] 'Unethical' conversions were also attacked.

Soma Thero died in Russia in December 2003. He had told friends that he was going to a Russian institute for about ten days to receive an Honorary Doctorate.[37] At his funeral Ven. Ellawala Medhananda Thero, who later became a JHU monk, said, in Sinhala, that Soma

---

[36] Material taken from Jayadeva Uyangoda, 'Soma Thero: Significance of his life and death', *Polity* (Colombo), I/5, January-February 2004: 17-18; See also: 'Defending the Faith', Editorial in *The Sunday Leader*, 28 December 2003: 8.
[37] See for example: D.C. Ranatunge, 'Soma Hamuduru had a mission to fulfil', *The Sunday Times Plus*, 21 December 2003: 10; D.C. Ranatunge, 'When *Nena Pahana* went dim', *The Sunday Times Plus*, 12 December 2004: 3.

Thero had not passed away but had been made to pass away. And a leaflet was passed around the funeral procession, which was almost the largest Colombo had ever witnessed, asking 'Was it a natural death or was Soma Thero killed?'

These insinuations had a target: Christians. It became known that the Institute awarding Soma Thero his degree was Christian and that Christians had been involved in his invitation.[38] Relations and friends of Soma Thero insisted that he was fit when he left and, as a diabetic, always controlled his blood sugar.[39] Those predisposed to link Christians with conspiracy theories saw one here. Soma Thero must have been killed by Christians. What other conclusion could there be? So the story spread that Christians had had Soma Thero injected with poison, because of his opposition to unethical conversions.

The funeral was held on 24 December 2003. Christians feared a massive backlash against churches and Christians. Chandrika Kumaratunge, the President, however, took firm measures to prevent this by threatening the police with transfers or demotion if there was violence. The conspiracy theory, however, did not go away, even though a team of medical experts pronounced his death natural – probably due to his diabetes. Tension erupted on the anniversary of his funeral in December 2004. In October 2005, a Commission appointed by the President did not reach a unanimous answer. There are still some Buddhists who are convinced that Christians murdered Venerable Soma Thero, pioneer of a purer Buddhism.

Concluding Remarks

A newspaper article written by a Sri Lankan Buddhist in 1994 quoted one of the edicts of King Asoka, ruler of much of India in the 3rd century BCE:

---

[38] For reflection on the conspiracy theory, see Risidra Mendis, 'Guiding Light no more', *The Sunday Leader*, 21 December 2003: 11.

[39] See Risidra Mendis, 'Guiding Light No More': 11 where the Thero's younger brother is quoted as saying, 'The Thero always controlled his blood sugar level. When the Thero's body was flown back to the country, we found a blood sugar monitoring machine in his bag. The machine indicated that for the past few days the Thero's sugar level was normal'.

As regards inter-religious relations, the great Buddhist Emperor Asoka's Edict is universally applicable. It says: 'He who does reverence to his own sect while disparaging the sects of others wholly from attachment to his own, with intent to enhance the splendour to his own sect, in reality, by such conduct inflicts the severest injury to his own'.[40]

This is the ethic that most Sri Lankan Buddhists would like to see practised – a co-existence model where religions respect each other. Running parallel to the narratives in this chapter are other stories that speak of co-operation, joint action, dialogue and friendship between Christians and Buddhists throughout the twentieth century. Confrontation over the question of conversions and Christian support for the LTTE has always been only one, albeit significant, element in Sri Lanka's inter-religious patchwork. Some Christians working or living in rural areas would want to say it is the minority strand. For where respect for Buddhism is present, the hospitality and generosity of Buddhists in Sri Lanka is second to none. Where respect for Buddhism is present, the right of an individual to convert from one religion to another can also be endorsed. Christian students training for ordination at the Theological College of Lanka are encouraged to create a relationship of trust with their local Buddhist monastery and always to speak with the monastery if a Buddhist devotee wishes to convert to Christianity. Where this has been done, conversions have not caused mistrust. It is when contempt of Buddhist belief and practice is perceived or demonstrated, that conflict arises. This was the key to the rancour in the nineteenth century Buddhist Revival.[41] This is the key today. Where contempt of the *dhamma* is perceived, traditionally liberal approaches towards conversion and identity are overturned. Defence of the *dhamma* against threat takes its place and with it, a dangerous tendency towards violence and patterns of thought that simplify a complex situation.

---

[40] Gunaseela Vitanage, 'Buddhist-Christian relations: A Buddhist Response to the "Joint statement from the Christian Consultation of Sri Lanka",' *The Island*, 20 August 1994: 9.
[41] See E.J. Harris, *Theravāda Buddhism and the British Encounter*: Part V.

JØRGEN SKOV SØRENSEN

Imperial or Empirical?
On Boundaries of Religious Identity
in India and Europe

The declaration of a postmodern condition signifies a momentous change of mind. It entails in effect the rejection of intellectual modernity, how the modern world has been theorised and rationalised, towards something else. (Tim McGuigan)[1]

Introduction

For many years, one of my favourite text samples brought into play to stir up heated discussions among my students has been the Indian theologian Stanley Samartha's semi-classic account 'A Hindu Christian Funeral'.[2] The title alone is a semantic eyesore to most traditional-thinking European theologians. Many of us have grown used to thinking in pretty well established and fairly restricted entities when it comes to religious identity. How can anything – or indeed anyone – be *both* Hindu *and* Christian at the same time? Samartha's recollection of a bi-religious funeral of a friend, allegedly both a Christian and a Hindu at the very same time, somewhat disturbs the conventional picture of religious identity that we find prevalent in a European theological setting.

Let us take yet another example that highlights questions regarding 'boundaries of religious identity'. As I mentioned above, Samartha's

---

[1] Tim McGuigan, *Modernity and Postmodern Culture*, Issues in Cultural and Media Studies Series. Buckingham and Philadelphia: Open University Press, 1999: 31.
[2] S. J. Samartha, 'A Hindu Christian Funeral', in R. S. Sugirtharajah and Cecil Hargreaves (eds.), *Readings in Indian Christian Theology*, Vol. 1, ISPCK Study Guide 29, Delhi, ISPCK, 1994: 158-62.

text does indeed yield a good response when used pedagogically. However, in case one needs a 'quicker stir' among the students, if one is teaching, say, a somewhat droopy class just after lunch, I have seen very good results by applying – believe it or not – some statistics. How about the fact that according to national census material, each and every Japanese citizen on average adheres to 1.85 religions?[3] To many this is mind-blowing information – particularly in a hitherto fairly mono-religious Nordic European context (mine, currently!) where Christian exclusivist identity is still very much alive and kiccing.

Adding to this I have done my own, admittedly unscientific, however – I would say – still significant, observations during regular informal visits to Hindu places of worship in Britain where I was teaching some years back. Almost every Wednesday evening *puja* in one *mandir* in Birmingham would gather a good number of Sikhs from the local community to join in the celebrations. In another Hindu place of worship where I used to bring my students, Birmingham's small Jain community had set up their religious paraphernalia in a corner, coexisting and worshipping, it appeared, happily with the larger Hindu population of the area.[4] It seems that in this case the shared cultural background played a bigger role than the differences in religious expressions and in all three examples we experience what we may term 'soft boundaries' between religious identities.

Imperial or Empirical?

My illustrations and examples above are current ones. It would, however, be wrong to conclude that such observations are recent phe-

---

[3] This number is calculated on the basis of Ian Reader, *Religion in Contemporary Japan*. London: Macmillan, 1991: 6. Ian reader points to the fact that some of the numbers kept in the statistics may be inflated due to optimistic estimations by the various religious associations. However, he concludes that there is surely a substantial element of 'multiple affiliation' involved. Jan Van Bragt makes a comparable observation, pointing to the fact that whereas Japan's citizens total approximately 126 million, still, it is estimated that 100 million adhere to the Shinto faith and at the same time 95 million consider themselves as Buddhists. On top of this come other classic and new religions. Jan Van Bragt, 'Multiple Religious Belonging of the Japanese People', in Catherine Cornille (ed.), *Many Mansions: Multiple Religious Belonging and Christian Identity*. New York: Orbis Books, 2002: 8.
[4] Coincidentally all this took place in an old Christian Church building now converted into a *mandir* hosting the Hindus – and Jains – of the neighbourhood.

nomena only. This is far from being the case. On the contrary, I owe a substantial debt to observers who went before me. During modern times among the first to open up the question of such 'soft boundaries' between religious traditions was the legendary Jesuit missionary to China, Matteo Ricci (1552-1610). Ricci in his mission practices borrowed extensively from Chinese culture, so much so that he eventually fell out with the Vatican. The conflict later turned into the so-called 'rites controversy', a theological struggle precisely about the compatibility and continuity, and indeed the lack of the same, between Christian faith and Chinese cultural and religious rites and observances. Undeniably, Ricci is a classic example of the questions raised about the nature of 'boundaries of religious identity' and only one on a long list of people who, in line with the escalating globalisation of world affairs – including, as one would expect, religious matters – have experienced the emergence of comparable questions relating to the nature of religious boundaries.[5]

A less well-known example, however of analogous scope and relevance, is given by Harjot Oberoi in his monograph on culture, identity and diversity in the Sikh tradition.[6] Oberoi's recollection is strikingly illustrative of a lived experience of religion that counteracts traditional western perceptions and understandings of the nature of 'religions' and the exclusiveness of the same. Briefly put, Oberoi claims that European thought systems and concepts have fashioned to a great extent the ways in which scholars from that very part of the world have perceived and understood 'other religions'. In fact, Oberoi goes as far as suggesting that 'religions' – understood as well-defined entities of religious identity like Hindu*ism* and Buddh*ism* – exist only as imaginations in the minds of the very same scholars. In consequence, there is no such thing as what the western world of modernity and academia would consider independent, self-contained 'religious systems'.[7]

---

[5] The controversy eventually came to a close with Pope Clement XI favouring a more conservative view of discontinuity between the traditions in question.

[6] Harjot Oberoi, *The Construction of Religious Boundaries. Culture, Identity, and Diversity in the Sikh Tradition*. Chicago and Oxford, The University of Chicago Press 1994:8ff. I am grateful to Professor John Hull, Birmingham University, for this reference.

[7] Bringing in Oberoi's critical remarks urges me for the rest of this article to use the term 'religion' and its derived notions only in inverted commas as an indication that my suggestions question this terminology.

Oberoi vividly illustrates his suggestion with empirical evidence from the 'Report on the Census of the Panjab, 1881'.[8] He quotes from the wording of an obviously frustrated civil servant, D. C. J. Ibbetson, reporting that:

> [...] the various observances and beliefs which distinguish the followers of the [...] faiths in their purity are so strangely blended and intermingled, that it is often impossible to say that one prevails rather than another, or to decide in what category the people shall be classed.[9]

Whereas it is obvious that Ibbetson feels uneasy about his empirical observations, his report on the other hand appears to show little – if any – systematic concern for the potential conclusion that his embedded and deep-rooted European (i.e. imperial) categories of religious adherence are wrong and therefore do not and cannot reflect the reality Ibbetson encounters in this imperial Indian setting.[10]

Revelation or Revolution?

As with Ricci above, this sort of colonially inherited knowledge of the complexity and at times unanticipated nature of the world continued in the nineteenth century as part of the development into today's overwhelming globalisation. At least potential changes began with the uneasiness or even the astonishment of the 'colonial masters', and the same potential changes were carried along with the, at times, startling reports sent back to audiences in Europe by missionaries and imperial civil servants, who encountered astonishing religious sentiments and attitudes among the Asian and African peoples.

These, to the European, new experiences of 'the other' eventually revealed a hugely more multifaceted image of the nature of the human mind and its derived cultural and 'religious' expressions. To a vast

---

[8] D. C. J. Ibbetson, *Report on the Census of the Panjab, 1881, Vol. I,* Calcutta, 1883.
[9] Ibbetson (1883: 101). Reference from Oberoi (1994: 9).
[10] For a recently published, well researched and well written account of the issues of colonial constructions of 'Hinduism' see Sharada Sugirtharajah, *Imagining Hinduism: A Postcolonial Perspective.* London and New York: Routledge, 2003. For a fine collection of primary text material on the issue of Hinduism as a colonial construction, see P. J. Marshall (ed.), *The British Discovery of Hinduism in the Eighteenth Century.* Cambridge: Cambridge University Press, 1970.

number of people today, increased mobility along with migration on a hitherto unseen scale has contributed to potential transformations in the way we view 'religion'. Where we have been used to see 'religion' as a discernible and objective entity (that is indeed what Ibbetson was looking for) this may well be changing into views on 'religion' as phenomena comprising different – even conflicting – faith experiences of various individuals within the very same, established, tradition. In other words, the boundaries of religious identity appear to be more soft than western modernity thinkers anticipated.

In the early 1960s, Wilfred Cantwell Smith's neo-classic work *The Meaning and End of Religion* epitomised provisionally this development with regard to the understanding of 'religion' in a truly 'revolutionary' way, as the subtitle of the book self-confidently puts it.[11] Cantwell Smith develops his ideas around the thesis that due to the fact of experience telling us that the term 'religion' is 'notoriously difficult to define'[12] we must reconsider the western category, notion, idea or typology of 'religion'. According to Cantwell Smith we have to question the traditional way of looking at 'religions' defined as counterposed socio-theological entities that – owing to their essentially similar 'religious' nature – are in innate competition with one another.

Cantwell Smith's comprehensive analysis of the history of 'religion' as a term and an entity brings him to his fundamental conclusion. Modern European Enlightenment thinking with its love for an 'intellectualist and impersonal schematisation of things'[13] could be traced as the impetus for what he saw as the still widespread understanding of 'religion' as belief systems with clear-cut structures, impenetrable boundaries and exclusive doctrinal compositions.[14] And it is true that Ibbetson's choice of words above is very illustrative of the Enligh-

---

[11] Wilfred Cantwell Smith, *The Meaning and End of Religion: A Revolutionary Approach to the Great Religious Traditions*. London: SPCK, 1978. References below will be made to this SPCK edition (the book was initially published in the USA by Macmillan in 1963).

[12] Cantwell Smith (1978:17). I.e. experiences as we have seen them illustrated in the British census reports above.

[13] Cantwell Smith (1978:40).

[14] Although Smith is writing this back in 1963, i.e. before the great intellectual upheavals of the 1970s, one should remember that my illustrations with Western students feeling 'uneasy' about uninhibited religious intermingling are recent ones taken from within the last few years. Traditional, modern, understandings – both popular and academic – are still 'widespread' and in this way Cantwell Smith's call for 'reconsideration' and questioning of traditional ways is indeed still relevant today.

tenment, or modern, mind-set as Cantwell Smith defines it, viz. an 'impersonal schematisation of things'.

Making use of terminology such as 'purity' in his description of the 'religions' of the Subcontinent, Ibbetson reveals modernity's un-critical presuppositions of a number of distinguishable and 'pure' reli-gious systems; systems that can be traced and described in minute detail. Looking deeper into his terminology, this thoroughly modern attitude is further stressed by the way he underscores the term 'catego-ries' according to which the subjects of the 1881 census 'shall be clas-sed'.

Taking Ibbetson's 'fuzzy'[15] empirical material at face value and combining it with my own and borrowed examples presented during the introduction above, may it not at this stage be appropriate to ask ourselves whether the apparent lack of razor-sharp religious bounda-ries is more suitably seen as a *revelation* rather than a *revolution*? Or in other words, could we imagine religious boundaries as something a modern mind-set has imposed on a *fundamentally fuzzy world*? In that case Cantwell Smith's analysis is certainly more like a revelation than it is a revolution. However, that by no means disqualifies his observa-tions. On the contrary, as we shall see below.

The West and the Rest?

Working through the examples given above, one may easily be inspi-red by Cantwell Smith's thesis – be it revolutionary or 'just' revela-tionary. The claim and discursive voice of this article into a discussion on the nature of 'Boundaries of Religious Identity' is that the ex-amples above are indeed all illustrations in one way or the other that a modern Enlightenment preconception of the typology 'religion' – i.e. 'religion' as a universally applicable entity that can be intellectually systematised and thereafter confined into boxes of doctrinal under-standing – has over the years successfully become normative. Diffe-rently put, the western intellectually and politically determined mani-festations of non-western 'religions' are revealed as creations made in our own modern image.

In spite of the apparent shortcoming – i.e. according to the empirical 1881 census results – of both the thought of predetermined 'catego-

---

[15] I.e. 'fuzzy' in the eyes of the modern beholder.

ries' and the conception of a 'pure faith' which would lend itself to be treated as an objective entity, Ibbetson's imperial approach of unwavering classification is not severely shaken. If anything, it is at the most momentarily stirred a little by the observations that seem to question his modern systematisation. Ibbetson embodies the hard core colonial attitude, characteristic for his time and his modern Enlightenment mind-set. However, where Cantwell Smith largely represents an analytical intellectual attitude to this mind-set, other contemporaries demonstrate a more direct critique of the colonial approach.

The refreshingly critical missiologist Werner Ustorf at the University of Birmingham has elsewhere intriguingly described this modern approach in the context of what has been commonly known as 'the modern mission movement'. In spite of important differences in this movement's agenda compared with the agenda of the administrative colonial masters, the modern mission movement fundamentally had arisen out of the same progressive ideology as the imperial project, viz. the understanding of Europe as the executor of (divine) history. Ustorf writes:

> Protestant missions [...] had repackaged the knowledge of God, putting it within the safe confines of a modern interpretation of Christianity as an absolute religion, and came to see themselves as the executors of divine history. This divine mandate included the conversion of anybody who might think differently [...]. At the centre stood a desire to tame any independent or local designs for life and religion, and with this to take control of their social forms. The intention was to master the ambiguity and fuzziness of the world by applying a universal religious rationality.[16]

This article is not focussing on the strictly missiological aspects brought to the table by Ustorf's claims, even though these aspects are both interesting in their own right and, most certainly, part of an Enlightenment-driven colonial discourse, too. What is interesting in our context is, however, mainly the exposed attitude of modernity pinpointed by Ustorf. For whereas Ibbetson from his own modern and

---

[16] Werner Ustorf, 'Protestantism and Missions', in Alister E. McGrath and Darren C. Marks (eds.), *The Blackwell Companion to Protestantism*. Oxford: Blackwell, 2004: 397-98.

imperial starting point can uncritically speak of 'pure faith', 'categories' and 'classification' as matters of course, Ustorf takes an openly critical standpoint to that very attitude. Modern confines and interpretations are – according to Ustorf – really ideological means to 'tame any independent or local designs for life and religion' and not least to 'master the ambiguity and fuzziness of the world'.

To Ustorf the importance lies in revealing the modern mindset as basically one of applying an alleged universal rationality – in this particular case 'a universal *religious* rationality' – to everything and anybody, a move made in the wake of the Enlightenment and increasingly during modern times by 'the West' and on 'the Rest', as the sociologist Stuart Hall has so brilliantly expressed it.[17] It may be argued that this analytic and critical view of modernity as the lens through which the West views the Rest has become everyman's speak nowadays. However, if the statistical information of 1.85 religions adhered to by each and every individual Japanese citizen can still rouse heated discussions even in 2005, maybe we still have a mission to call for further attention to the problem encountered here.[18]

Modern or Postmodern?

I shall set out in these final stages of the current article to touch upon matters that are both more theological and more theoretical than has been the case above. Cantwell Smith and others with him have made their point clear, but it also appears that not everyone has listened, understood, or maybe even wanted to understand.[19] It is a fact that

[17] Stuart Hall, 'The West and the Rest: Discourse and Power', in Stuart Hall and Bram Gieben (eds.), *Formations of Modernity*, Understanding Modern Societies Series. Cambridge: Polity Press, 1992: 318.

[18] A noteworthy publication in this debate, however from a point of view embedded in a strictly religious studies context is Russell T. McCutcheon, *Manufacturing Religion: The Discourse on Sui Generis Religion and the Politics of Nostalgia.* Oxford and New York, Oxford University Press 1997. In this book McCutcheon offers a political reading of 'religion' in academia, claiming a strong interrelationship between the traditional way of understanding 'religious studies' and society's larger system of political domination and cultural imperialism. Further to this debate, a couple of recent publications offer a variety of approaches, cf. Timothy Fitzgerald, *The Ideology of Religious Studies.* New York and Oxford, Oxford University Press 2000, and Gavin Flood, *Beyond Phenomenology: Rethinking the Study of Religion.* London and New York, Cassell 1999.

[19] Here, we cannot but conclude that Cantwell Smith was too bold when, back in the early 1960s – as we have seen him questioning normative terminology such as 'Christianity', 'Buddhism' and even the term 'religion' as such – he declared that 'I am

many (however, by no means all) scholars of 'religion' seem to have had their eyes opened to the empirical fact of fuzzy religious boundaries – Wilfred Cantwell Smith is one such prominent example.[20] It seems to me, however, that generally speaking, most Christian theologians appear to suffer rather than rejoice when they encounter the empirical evidence which revelations of the fuzzy nature of religious boundaries have brought about in the wake of globalisation.

A systematic theological questioning of the term 'religions' defined as belief systems with clear-cut structures, impenetrable boundaries and exclusive doctrinal compositions would, however, bring about much needed relief from some of the stubborn theological questions of our time. This applies particularly in the way such questions have been phrased within recent 'theologies of religion' in more or less appealing shapes and forms. Common for most of these attempts, however, is the fact that they fall to the floor in real life, because they reflect a modern *universalising* foundation speaking into what is now increasingly recognised as a postmodern *localising* context. And here, perhaps, lies the core of the problem, viz. the fundamental incompatibility between post-modern questions and modern answers. Tim McGuigan touches this nerve in the opening quotation above:

> The declaration of a postmodern condition signifies a momentous change of mind. It entails in effect the rejection of intellectual modernity, how the modern world has been theorized and rationalized, towards something else.[21]

---

anity', 'Buddhism' and even the term 'religion' as such – he declared that 'I am bold enough to speculate whether these terms will not in fact have disappeared from serious writing and careful speech within twenty-five years' (1963: 195). This can easily be dismissed with our knowledge gained since then as a naïve self-absorbed prediction. It may, however, also be interpreted as a sign of a genuine sense of new ideas emerging on the religious, theological and societal scenes in the early 1960s.

[20] Instead of dismissing the traditional terminology of 'religion', 'religious' and 'religiosity', as suggested by Cantwell Smith, it seems, however, that some have found a 'middle way', where the terminology is kept, but where definitions vary according to context. Walter H. Capps points in that direction when he writes that religion is 'a subject that possesses a variety of referents and can be employed within numerous frames of discourse, and thus can be defined in a multiplicity of ways. One cannot make sense of the word until one knows the context, frame of reference, or world of discourse the word is intended to register', Walter H. Capps, *Religious Studies: The Making of a Discipline*. Minneapolis, Augsburg: Fortress Press, 1995: xx.

[21] Tim McGuigan (1999: 31).

What is this 'something else' then? Well, again according to recent large scale surveys,[22] it seems that growing sections of our western societies turn towards 'something else'. 'Something else' which – in our case – turns out differently from traditional, modern, definitions of 'religions'; something different from 'religions' as socio-theological entities which – owing to their, purportedly, essentially similar 'religious' nature – are in innate competition with one another. Interestingly, this sort of 'turn' was exactly what Cantwell Smith called for in the 1960s.

This development, combined with the question of 'boundaries of religious identity' as well as with the notion of 'The West and the Rest', may well point to the significance of our pooled observations. The western Enlightenment understanding of what 'religion' *essentially* is, viz. clear-cut and well ordered structures of belief, is about to fall. It is conquered by overwhelming empiric evidence brought about by globalisation, and by the subsequent revelations of the world as a much more complex site than the Enlightenment's rigid systems would ever allow for. 'Religion' – it now appears – is not only questionable as a universally applicable term. 'Religion' seems more fuzzy at the edges than we previously believed, too. With the terminology of the sociologist Zygmunt Bauman, Western intellectuals can no longer consider themselves to be universal *legislators* using universal, one-size-fit-for-all definitions.[23] The postmodern intellectual has instead become the *interpreter* of local pieces of complex empirical evidence, characterising the postmodern era.[24]

---

[22] E.g. The Kendal Project conducted by researchers from Lancaster University, UK, and documented in Paul Heelas and Linda Woodhead, *The Spiritual Revolution: Why religion is giving way to spirituality*. Oxford, Blackwell Publishing 2005. A similar project is currently conducted in Enköping, Sweden, under the guidance of Kajsa Ahlstrand.

[23] This is what Cantwell Smith called modernity's 'intellectualist and impersonal schematization of things' (see note 13) and Ustorf critiqued as 'a desire to tame any independent or local designs for life and religion' (see note 16).

[24] Zygmunt Bauman, *Legislators and Interpreters: On Modernity, Postmodernity and Intellectuals*. Cambridge: Polity Press, 1987. Chapters that particularly deal with this transformation are *The fall of the Legislator*, basically a review and analysis of the modern crisis during the last part of the twentieth century, i.e. the fall of the intellectual as legislator, and in this way also the basis for postmodernity to establish itself, and *The Rise of the Interpreter*, i.e. the rise of the intellectual as interpreter. Bauman builds his understanding and definitions of modernity and postmodernity on the distinction between the role of the intellectual within the two paradigms. Thus he writes in his introduction to *Legislators and Interpreters* that '[...] the concepts of modernity and postmodernity stand for two sharply different contexts in which the 'intellectual role' is

A couple of interesting questions linger in the wake of Bauman's analysis. Is the development from *legislator* to *interpreter* the fundamental reason why Christian theologians hesitate to embrace the postmodern condition? Is the prospect of the weakened role as an *interpreter* unacceptable? Is the acknowledgement of fuzzy religious identity too much for Christian Church theology which is basically shaped by a modern *legislator* mind-set? William E. Paden in his classic anthology *Religious Worlds* may have found the centre of gravity inherent in this question as he applies the following descriptive and interpretative words to the fact of globalisation:

> Other worlds and other gods do co-exist with our own world and our own gods, and they are threatening precisely because they have a different set of premises from ours and thus explicitly or implicitly call into question the absoluteness of our own assumptions and commitments.[25]

However, as we know, the questioning of the absoluteness of Christian assumptions and commitments has never been particularly popular within the Church.

Conclusions or Diffusions?[26]

A complex, postmodern world somehow prohibits conclusions of a strong nature. Thus, I shall follow the underlying ethos of this article and refrain from such. Alternatively, in my section heading above I have suggested 'diffusions' as a potentially more suitable signal to use in this context. In this way I have wished to indicate the interrelati-

---

performed', and he adds a little later to that 'The opposition between modernity and postmodernity has been employed here in the service of theorising the last three centuries of West European history (or West European dominated history) from the perspective of intellectual practice. It is this praxis that can be modern or postmodern; the dominance of one or other of the two modes (not necessarily without exceptions) distinguishes modernity and postmodernity as periods in intellectual history' (Bauman, 1987: 3).

[25] William E. Paden, *Religious Worlds: The Comparative Study of Religion.* Boston, Beacon Press 1994:16.

[26] 'Cultural diffusion: in anthropology, the process by which a cultural trait, material object, idea, or behavior pattern is spread from one society to another'. Cf. *Webster's New Millennium Dictionary of English, Preview Edition 2003-2005 Lexico Publishing Group, LLC.* This definition can with advantage be kept in mind here.

onship and 'fuzzy logic' between coexisting world views in most societies today.

Werner Ustorf speaks in comparable terms. Based on studies of various expressions of world Christianity interacting with a variety of secular and religious worldviews, Ustorf incisively characterises our time as an era of 'theological untidiness'. His main point is that current theological discourses should not be seen as processes moving towards 'a "safe haven" of unwavering knowledge' but that the process itself is an expression of contemporary theology.[27] I take his words as a fruitful and constructive attempt to describe our contemporary situation as well as a suitable arrival point for the current article summing up our findings and suggestions with the following words.

Contemporary Christian theologians work in a time characterised by 'theological untidiness'. Established truisms regarding religious identity are questioned. The understanding of 'religion' based on a Western Enlightenment preconception and 'one-size-fit-for-all' definition is under attack from self-confident, post-colonial voices in Asia and Africa, but also from empirical surveys within Europe. In this way, dialogue between believers of various sorts is bound to question the absoluteness of our assumptions and commitments. Again, with Tim McGuigan 'the declaration of a postmodern condition signifies a momentous change of mind'.[28]

Are Christians ready to embrace this untidiness? Are Buddhists?

---

[27] Werner Ustorf, 'The Philanthropy of God and Western Culture', Aasulv Lande and Werner Ustorf (eds.), *Mission in a Pluralist World*, Studies in the Intercultural History of Christianity Series Vol. 97. Frankfurt am Main: Peter Lang Verlag, 1996: 123, 125. For the very same reason a number of Christian theologians have in recent years suggested the terminology 'constructive theology' in preference to the more traditional 'systematic theology'. For a particularly comprehensive account, see Peter C. Hodgson, *Winds of the Spirit. A Constructive Christian Theology*. London: SCM, 1994.
[28] See note 21.

PERRY SCHMIDT-LEUKEL

'Light and Darkness' or 'Looking Through a Dim Mirror'? A Reply to Paul Williams from a Christian Perspective

When asked about his prior object of meditation, Paul Williams once responded that this is for most of the time 'paper'.[1] This is definitely something that we have in common. Further, we both share a deep and long fascination with Buddhism. That is, if we don't gaze at empty paper, the form which emptiness takes has usually something to do with Buddhism. Thirdly, we are both Christians. However, theologically we seem to be moving in exactly opposite directions. I don't mean the more trivial fact that Paul started as an Anglican and converted to Roman Catholicism, while I started as a Roman Catholic and became an Anglican. I mean something far more important: It is in our understanding of Buddhism that we diverge, or more precisely, in our understanding of Buddhism in relation to Christianity, which has huge theological implications for the understanding of Christianity in relation to other religions in general – and, finally, for understanding our religious identity. Hence Paul has turned away from Buddhism, while my Christian faith has become deeply penetrated by Buddhism.

In his book *The Unexpected Way: On Converting from Buddhism to Catholicism* Paul makes two statements which I find hard to reconcile. On the one hand, he assures his 'Buddhist friends' that his reflections in that book are of a very personal nature and are 'not intended' 'as an attack on Buddhism'.[2] On the other hand, Paul tells his 'Christian friends' that we should seek to discriminate between truth and falsity in religion by strictly rational arguments and emphasises that his conver-

---

[1] See Paul Williams, *The Unexpected Way. On Converting from Buddhism to Catholicism*. Edinburgh: T.&T. Clark, 2002: xiii.
[2] Ibid.: xiv.

sion from Buddhism to Catholicism was primarily triggered by his belief in the objective truth of Christianity.[3] For Paul the truth of Christianity entails the falsity of Buddhism and – as he says elsewhere – the denial of the possibility that 'Buddhists too (*qua* Buddhists) attain true peace.'[4] I cannot see how this could not be taken as an 'attack on Buddhism'. I am aware that Paul subscribes frequently to an epistemological fallibilism admitting that either the Buddhists or the Christians or both may be wrong (by the way – how does this fit in with his consent to the Roman doctrine of infallibility?[5]). But what Paul affirms within his fallibilist framework is nothing less than the cognitive and soteriological falsity of Buddhism. The difference between Buddhism and Christianity seems for Paul to be one of darkness and light. That is, he asserts – as his subjective opinion, which admittedly may be false – that Buddhism is an objectively false religion and not only that Buddhism is subjectively 'false', i.e. unsuitable for Paul.

Now this is precisely what I am interested in. I am not interested in analysing or debating any of Paul's more personal motives in his conversion process. I would find that rather inappropriate. And I am not questioning his individual spiritual development which led him finally into the Roman Catholic Church. Hence, I am not going to deal with psychology but primarily with philosophy and to some extent history (here again, I suppose, Paul and I are on common ground). I am only interested in the cognitive aspect of Paul's conversion story[6] and I will argue that his attack on Buddhism is in several respects wrong or at least highly debatable. However, I share Paul's fallibilism. So he could nevertheless be right. But I will further argue that if he were right, that is if Buddhism were indeed a false religion and soteriologi-

---

[3] See ibid.: xv-xvii.

[4] Paul Williams, 'Aquinas Meets the Buddhists: Prolegomenon to an Authentically Thomas-ist Basis for Dialogue'. *Modern Theology* 20 (2004): 91-121, 112.

[5] If it cannot be conclusively proven that God exists, the assertion that God exists must be seen – in technical terminology – as a hypothesis. Consequently, any further assertion which logically depends on this basic assumption must also be treated as hypothetical. So if the magisterium of the Roman Catholic Church declares as an infallible doctrine any idea that logically presupposes the existence of God, the 'infallible' doctrine would have to be treated as a fallible hypothesis. This would amount to the assumption that *if* some statement (of belief or something else) is true, it is infallibly true. However, this is a rather trivial assertion and most certainly not what Vatican I had in mind when it declared infallibility.

[6] For this reason I base my critique not only on Paul's conversion record in *The Unexpected Way* but also draw on several others of his writings where he makes the same, or related, points.

cally unwholesome, this would also undermine the credibility of Christianity. I think that the truth of Buddhism and the truth of Christianity are tied together and that, therefore, the existential and the theological issue is, in the end, not a question of conversion but – on both sides – the challenge of how to integrate the truth of the other.

1. Buddhist Atheism?

Paul's understanding of Buddhism as a false religion is primarily based on his reading of Buddhism as a form of Atheism.

> Buddhists do not believe in the existence of God. There need be no debating about this.[7]

While I'm not denying Paul's outstanding competence in matters of Buddhism, I nevertheless want to debate precisely this. Paul himself adds several interesting qualifications. Of course, says Paul, Buddhism, traditionally, believes in the existence of 'gods' (*devas*), but the *devas* are saṃsāric beings. They are not transcendent but are still part of *this* world in the sense of *saṃsāra*. Hence they are still in need of salvation and are unable to function as that kind of reality which *provides ultimate salvation/liberation or fulfilment*.[8] However, says Paul, these are crucial features of what Christians mean when they speak of 'God', and, therefore, Buddhism indeed denies – at least implicitly – the existence of that reality which Christians call 'God'. In this sense Buddhism is Atheism:

> … a God that is not necessary to spiritual fulfilment is not God as taught by Christianity. Thus if Buddhism does not need *that* sort of God, it must hold that such a God does not exist. … then the God referred to by Christians is indeed being denied. From a Christian point of view Buddhism is clearly a form of atheism.[9]

---

[7] Williams, *The Unexpected Way*: 25.
[8] See ibid.: 25f.
[9] Ibid.: 26.

Paul adds another important qualifier. What Buddhists deny, says Paul, is a God who is the *creator of everything*. This again, from a Christian perspective, makes Buddhism a form of Atheism.[10]

> If Buddhist texts refute the existence of a creator of everything then they deny the existence of God as understood by Christianity.[11]

However, for Paul the main emphasis lies with the first aspect of the supposed atheism, that is, the purported irrelevance of God as a precondition of our salvation. So Paul adds that from a Buddhist perspective:

> ... even if there were to be a creator God, He would not be – as He is for Thomas [Aquinas; PSL] – the teleological goal as well as the origin of creation, in whom lies our final spiritual perfection.[12]

Finally, Paul alleges that Buddhism denies 'completely' the existence of a 'creator deity, who can be thought of in some sense as a person'.[13] Or, briefer and more focused:

> ... Buddhism denies altogether the existence of a *loving* creator God ...[14]

To summarise, for Paul, Buddhism is indisputably a form of Atheism because it denies God in the triple sense of a transcendent reality which is
1) immediately *relevant to our salvation*; which is
2) the *creator* of everything; and which is
3) in some sense a *loving person*.

---

[10] Williams, 'Aquinas Meets the Buddhists': 93.
[11] Ibid.: 94.
[12] Ibid.: 95.
[13] Paul Williams (with Anthony Tribe), *Buddhist Thought: A Complete Introduction to the Indian Tradition*. London-New York: Routledge, 2000: 4.
[14] Paul Williams, *Songs of Love, Poems of Sadness: The Erotic Verses of the Sixth Dalai Lama*. I.B. Tauris: New York, 2004: 2, my emphasis.

2. Buddhism and transcendence

First of all, one must not forget that early and classical Buddhism did not explicitly deny *the*, or *a*, Christian concept of God, for such a thing was simply unknown to them. The very few critical remarks that we find in the Pāli Canon and the more elaborate polemics present in some classical doctrinal and philosophical Buddhist treatises were directed against various Hindu concepts of the Divine or certain features of them. Therefore an important question is whether (and, if so, to what extent) what Buddhists criticised is identical with what Christians affirm.[15] (And, apart from that, how far it really matches with the targeted Hindu ideas.) In modern times as well as in the contemporary situation we do of course find Buddhists criticising explicitly Christian concepts of God. This was primarily the case during the various Buddhist encounters with Christian mission and colonialist interests in several Asian countries, and, somewhat later, as part and parcel of the formation of a Western Buddhism in the late nineteenth and twentieth centuries. But once again, it needs to be seen whether Asian Buddhists made themselves really familiar with the Christian ideas they were criticising or whether they more or less applied the traditional arguments of anti-Hindu Buddhist polemical writings to the Christian God. Further, it needs to be checked how far Western Buddhists have identified traditional Buddhist arguments against some forms of Hinduism too quickly with those Western atheist traditions by which many Western Buddhists were, and to some extent still are, shaped and which were indeed developed directly against Christianity.

These sorts of hermeneutical considerations are as important as they are difficult to deal with. This can certainly not be done satisfactorily in a brief essay like this. But let me at least indicate the sort of strategy which I find most promising, that is, to disentangle the various elements which make up (or can make up) the God-idea and look at them separately. In doing so I follow the three respects in which – according to the preceding analysis of Paul Williams's attack – Buddhism denies implicitly the Christian God.

---

[15] Needless to say, Paul Williams is of course fully aware of this hermeneutical issue. It is, however, a different question whether he has sufficiently considered all of its implications.

2.1 The transcendent as ground and goal of our salvation

The earliest atheists of whose existence we have good evidence lived in India and were contemporaries of the Buddha, the Cārvākas. But the Buddha was not one of them, nor was he particularly sympathetic with them. Quite the contrary, the Cārvākas' teachings were seen by the Buddhists as seriously unwholesome, among other things for the reason that they denied reincarnation and any other reality apart from this world, which is why their system is also called *lokāyata*. But Buddhists believed in transcendence, quite literally in something 'beyond this world' (*lokottara*). And 'this world' means for the Buddhists the whole of the five or six saṃsāric realms. But there must be something 'beyond' *saṃsāra*, otherwise any release from *saṃsāra* would be impossible. This is most clearly expressed in the following famous passage from the *Udāna* and *Itivuttaka*:

> There is, monks, a not-born (ajātaṃ), a not-brought-to-being (abhūtaṃ), a not-made (akataṃ), a not-conditioned (asaṅkhataṃ). If, monks, there were no not-born, not-brought-to-being, not-made, not-conditioned, no escape would be discerned from what is born, brought-to-being, made, conditioned. But since there is a not-born, a not-brought-to-being, a not-made, a not-conditioned, therefore an escape is discerned from what is born, brought-to-being, made, conditioned.[16]

This passage does not only emphasise that 'there is' a transcendent reality. It also underlines its genuine transcendence in the most explicit way by distinguishing it ontologically from the major features of the saṃsāric world. It is transcendent in the sense that it is not-born, not-brought-to-being, not-made, not-conditioned, while everything that makes up saṃsāric existence is born, brought-to-being, made and conditioned. Without the existence of such a truly transcendent reality, any salvation/liberation from *saṃsāra* would be inconceivable, i.e. impossible. We would be totally encapsulated by the transitory world of conditioned existence. The transcendent reality which our passage speaks of is *nirvāṇa*. It is the truly 'deathless' (*amṛta, amata*) and the-

---

[16] *Udāna* 8:3; and *Itivuttaka* 43. See John Ireland (transl.), *The Udāna and Itivuttaka*. Kandy: Buddhist Publication Society, 1997: 103, 180.

refore it must be unconditioned. For everything that underlies the mechanism of conditioned origination is, according to Buddhist principles, liable to decay. In order to be free from decay, something has to be free from conditioned origination, i.e. it must be unconditioned (*asaṃskṛta, asaṅkhata*) and this is what *nirvāṇa* truly is. This argument is explicitly presented in important classical treatises, such as the *Milindapañha*[17] and Buddhaghosa's *Visuddhimagga*.[18]

Moreover, as is stated in both texts, the characterisation of *nirvāṇa* as an 'unconditioned' reality entails that *nirvāṇa* cannot be regarded as being just a state, that is the state of the fully enlightened one. If it were merely a state, *nirvāṇa* would be conditioned: it would come into existence as a result of the successful completion of the Noble Eightfold Path. But then it would be no longer the un-become and unconditioned reality which alone can be free from death and decay. Therefore *nirvāṇa* needs to be understood as a reality which exists independently. Enlightenment is the state of arriving at this reality, or as a classical formula of the Pāli Canon has it: Enlightenment is the 'plunging into *nirvāṇa*'.[19] But *nirvāṇa* itself exists whether someone plunges into it or not. It is not conditioned by someone's attainment of Enlightenment. It is just the other way round. The unconditioned existence of *nirvāṇa* is the condition that makes Enlightenment possible.

Hence we find in another major treatise of classical Buddhism, i.e. in the influential *Abhidharmakośabhāṣyam*, an interesting debate: Does the fact that *nirvāṇa*, while being itself unconditioned, conditions our salvation, entail that it is in some sense 'active'? Being 'outside of time' *nirvāṇa* can 'neither project nor produce a result' in time.[20] However, it is not entirely without any form of causal effectiveness. Firstly, it can be the object of human experience, that is it can be a kind of causal condition for cognition.[21] Secondly, as an object of cognition it 'causes an obstacle to the vices' – 'as the stars are not visible when the sun shines'.[22] That is, the cognition of *nirvāṇa* puts a lasting end to all the defilements and is thus the cause of their final cessation.

---

[17] *Milindapañha* 269f.
[18] *Visuddhimagga* 507ff.
[19] E.g. *Aṅguttara-Nikāya* V 107.
[20] See Leo Pruden (transl.), *Abhidharmakośabhāṣyam* (by Louis de La Vallée Poussin), Volume I. Berkeley: Asian Humanities Press, 1991: 279.
[21] See ibid.: 256f, 279, 302.
[22] Ibid.: 255.

However, it is a 'cause' in the sense of the 'unmoved mover', who brings the effects about simply by its attractive presence.

So Paul is seriously wrong in his first allegation. That is, Buddhism does affirm the existence of a transcendent reality and it does so precisely in the sense that this reality is the ultimate condition of our salvation. This reality is of utter relevance to the attainment of fulfilment, for without this reality, such a fulfilment would be impossible. As Christians, we need to ask ourselves whether this is not a clear Buddhist testimony to that reality which we call – for various historical reasons – 'God'.[23]

This is where Paul's two further qualifiers could become relevant. That is, even if one admits that Buddhism acknowledges the existence of a transcendent reality as the decisive condition of our salvation, one could hold that this sort of transcendent reality would still be quite different from what Christians mean by God, because the Buddhist transcendence does not fulfil the two essential conditions of being the 'creator of everything' and 'somehow' a loving person. Therefore, one could argue, it seems to be rather inappropriate to regard the type of transcendent reality of which Buddhism speaks as an analogue or functional equivalent to the Christian concept of 'God'.[24]

Again, there is not enough space to discuss these two issues as fully as they deserve to be discussed.[25] But I would like to make a few brief remarks which indicate the route to what – as I believe – would be a constructive discussion.

---

[23] Paul admits that there are passages in the Pāli Canon where nirvāṇa is obviously spoken of 'as an Absolute Reality, … like … the ineffable "Godhead" of some religious teachings' (Williams, *Buddhist Thought*: 50). He addresses this fact as a 'complication' and calls this 'unfortunately', quite understandably given the rather modernist and reductionist, i.e. atheist, interpretation of *nirvāṇa* which he favours (see ibid.: 49). Paul claims that an absolutist interpretation of *nirvāṇa* is based on the attribute 'realm' (*dhātu*). But I think the crucial point is the attribute 'unconditioned' (*asaṃskṛta*) which excludes (in the eyes of rather mainline classical Buddhist texts) Paul's interpretation of *nirvāṇa* as 'an occurrence, an event' (ibid.: 48). Strong evidence in support of an 'absolutist' interpretation of *nirvāṇa* can be found in S. Collins, *Nirvana and Other Buddhist Felicities*. Cambridge: Cambridge University Press, 1998: 161-185.

[24] This is basically the argument of Christopher Gowans in his excellent study *Philosophy of the Buddha*. London-New York: Routledge, 2003: 151.

[25] All this is dealt with far more extensively in my 'The Unbridgeable Gulf? Towards a Buddhist-Christian Theology of Creation'. P. Schmidt-Leukel (ed.), *Buddhism, Christianity and the Question of Creation: Karmic or Divine?* Aldershot: Ashgate, 2006: 109-178.

2.2 Transcendent Reality as 'creative'

I think that two sets of questions are of particular importance:
First, what do we, as Christians, mean when we call God the creator of the world? And how does this relate to the Buddhist objections against the idea of divine creation?
Second, why did Buddhists criticise the idea of divine creation? And how does this relate to the Christian affirmation of it?

In response to the first set of questions, I pick out one example from the Christian tradition which is still rather influential and is seen as crucial by Paul Williams himself, that is, Thomas Aquinas. If we follow Aquinas, creation does not mean an act in time. It is – says Thomas – not an act of 'making' (*facere*).[26] Hence, the created world could also be everlasting, that is, without beginning or end, and nevertheless still be a created world – as, for example, was assumed by Aristotle. If the world had no beginning in time, it would nevertheless exist as an eternally created world, that is it would totally depend on God. But this dependence is, according to Aquinas, not the sort of dependence that we find *within* the chain of chronological events which are linked through efficient causal connection. God is not the cause of the world in the sense in which innerworldly efficient causes (in Aquinas's terminology: the *causae secundae*) function. Otherwise, the idea of creation would necessarily require a beginning in time.[27] But quite the contrary, Thomas affirms that God's existence could be shown even better under the presupposition of the world's eternity.[28] Hence, God is not the 'first cause' (*causa prima*) in any chronological sense of 'first'.[29] 'First' is rather a matter of logical or metaphysical priority. God is that which gives beings their particular form of existence including their own genuine causality.[30] And this is true independent of whether the chain of innerworldly efficient causes reaches back into the past indefinitely or whether there is something like a first moment. But in this case too, as Thomas holds with a strong line of

---

[26] See J. Schneider, 'The Eternity of the World: Thomas Aquinas and Boethius of Dacia', in: *Archives D'Histoire Doctrinale et Littéraire du Moyen Age* 66 (1999): 121-141, 133f, n. 46.
[27] See *Summa Theologiae* I 46:2.
[28] See *Summa contra Gentiles* 13.
[29] See for example *Summa Theologiae* I 46:2 ad 7.
[30] See *Summa Theologiae* I 8:1.

patristic Christian thinking, God does not create *in time* but creates time, or better, the world as a chronologically ordered universe.

So in what sense of causality can God then be called a 'cause'? First of all, if Aquinas calls God a 'cause' this is as much a form of analogical predication as any other term that is taken from the created realm and applied to the creator. It is not literally true in the sense of applying univocally. When we apply these terms to God, they acquire a meaning which we do not really understand.[31] I come back to this later. Apart from this principal proviso, Aquinas makes it clear that we cannot understand God as an efficient cause in the same sense as any other efficient causes, precisely because of the fundamental difference between the way the *causae secundae* function and the way the *causa prima* does. This distinction is thoroughly retained at crucial stages in Thomas's argumentation throughout his exposition of the 'five ways' (*quinque viae*) to show – or better: identify[32] – God's existence. In the second way, Thomas does indeed call God *causa efficiens*, but in the sense of the *causa prima* (*causam efficientem primam*). In his discussion of the second objection (*Summa Theologiae* I 2:3 ad 2) Thomas makes it clear that the *causa prima* functions primarily as the ultimate *teleological cause*. The objection holds that everything in the world can be explained by other innerworldly causes, i.e. natural events by (the laws of) nature, historical events by human reason and will. Against this Thomas argues that nature and the human mind (*ratio et voluntas*) need some further explanation because they are determined *towards some final goal* and insofar God should be seen as their 'first cause' or, more precisely, as the 'first immovable principle' (*primum principium immobile*). Elsewhere Thomas explains that the teleological cause (*causa finalis*) is the basis of all other causes, the primary cause of all causes.[33]

All of this is in line with the basic Aristotelian structure of Thomas's philosophical theology. God is the first cause of the world in the sense of the 'unmoved mover'. Hence Thomas says in the 'first way', the argument from movement, that everything moved is moved *to-*

---

[31] This is rightly emphasised by R. Heinzmann, *Thomas von Aquin.* Stuttgart: Kohlhammer, 1994: 63.

[32] I don't think they succeed as proofs in any strict sense. However, it seems that Thomas himself is more interested in pointing out what he basically means by 'God' (*hoc dicimus deum*) through showing five different ways of introducing the God-idea.

[33] See *Summa Theologiae* I-II 1:2.

wards something (*ad illud ad quod movetur*[34]). In the end, everything is moved by the attractive force of the ultimate good of all things, which is God – as Thomas explains at length in *Summa Contra Gentiles* 13 and 37.[35] Everything exists – even if it would exist without beginning in time – because it is ordered towards God.[36] To call God creator' is in a way subservient to calling God the final goal and highest good of the world. God is the *alpha* of the world precisely as its *omega*. The question 'why is there something rather than nothing' should – from a Thomist perspective – be read as asking for the ultimate *telos* of everything: 'why' in the sense of 'for what'?

The Buddhist criticism of the idea of a divine creator is – insofar as it entails ontological argumentation – usually directed against the idea of God as a kind of innerworldly *causa efficiens* and hence connected with the idea of creation in time. Therefore an understanding of creation *à la* Thomas is not really affected by this critique. But does the ultimate transcendent reality which Buddhism affirms posses a comparable teleological function? I think it does. It is a kind of Buddhist axiom that all beings are 'yearning for happiness and recoiling from pain'.[37] It is on the basis of this assumption that the Buddha proclaims the Four Noble Truths about suffering and its final cessation. Ultimate happiness, peace and lasting satisfaction can only come from *nirvāṇa*: the 'supreme bliss' (*nibbānaṁ paramaṁ sukhaṁ, Dhammapada* 204) and the 'deathless' (*amata*).[38] We suffer under the (potentially everlasting) transitory saṁsāric existence precisely because we are inclined towards the 'deathless'. The 'noble', non-deluded search is therefore the one aiming at *nirvāṇa* rather than the perishable goods of the world.[39] In *Aṅguttara-Nikāya* 10:58 *nirvāṇa* is indeed presented as a kind of universal *telos*: 'all things have release for their essence, plunge into the deathless, with *nibbāna* for their conclusion'. Should we not understand the idea of the original purity or 'luminosity' of the

---

[34] *Summa Theologiae* I 2:3.
[35] See also *Summa Theologiae* I 44:4.
[36] In *Summa Contra Gentiles* 37 Thomas explains explicitly God as the 'unmoved mover' as that which moves by being striven for: '*Quod movet sicut desideratum. Deus igitur, cum sit primum movens immobile, est primum desideratum*'.
[37] *Majjhima-Nikāya* 94 (II 160).
[38] There is an abundance of similar positive statements about *nirvāṇa* in the Pāli Canon. See Chinda Chandrkaew, *Nibbāna: The Ultimate Truth of Buddhism*. Mahachula University, 1982: 32-36.
[39] See *Majjhima-Nikāya* 26.

mind[40] – which already appears in the Pāli Canon and later developed into the influential idea of the common Buddha-nature of all beings – as precisely that sort of natural inclination towards *nirvāṇa*?

So the place of the ultimate and highest good is held by *nirvāṇa* or by that ultimate reality to which Mahāyāna Buddhism refers with terms like *dharmakāya*[41], *dharmatā*, *Ādi-Buddha*, etc. It too functions as a kind of 'unmoved mover' in so far as it attracts all beings towards itself. In some later Tantric developments we even encounter the idea that the ultimate is indeed the 'Sovereign All-Creating Mind'.[42] At times, however, particularly in a Madhyamaka context, the idea of divine creation is criticised as part of the overall criticism of any causal relation whatsoever. But this includes Buddhist ideas of causality as well. Radical negation negates affirmation and negation alike. Nāgārjuna – just to mention the root-thinker of the school – rejects not only the Hindu notion of *ātman* but also the Buddhist notion of *anātman*.[43] And surely his famous negation of any difference between *saṃsāra* and *nirvāṇa* must be understood as equally rejecting any possible (monistic or otherwise) identification of *saṃsāra* and *nirvāṇa*. I think radical Madhyamaka criticism is best seen as an expression of the mystical conviction that in the end, reality is inconceivable,[44] while our concepts at best have instrumental, pragmatic value and are, in that sense, relatively true (*saṃvṛti satya*).

---

[40] See Peter Harvey, *The Selfless Mind: Personality, Consciousness and Nirvana in Early Buddhism*. London-New York: Curzon, repr. 2004: 166-179.

[41] Paul Williams (*Buddhist Thought*: 172ff) refers to Paul Harrison's view that – at least in pre-, early- and middle-Mahāyāna – the term '*dharmakāya*' should not be misunderstood as referring to 'a kind of Buddhist absolute' (P. Harrison, 'Is the Dharma-kāya the Real "Phantom Body" of the Buddha?'. *Journal of the International Association of Buddhist Studies* 15 (1992): 44-94, 44). According to Harrison the *dharmakāya* refers either to the Buddha's identification with the Dharma as his teaching or to those 'dharmas' which constitute the particular attributes of a Buddha. However, I think that in his argumentation Harrison presupposes a rather modern understanding of the Buddha's 'teaching' and attributes. According to a classical Buddhist understanding the 'teaching' reflects the Dharma as an eternal law that was not invented but rediscovered by the Buddha, and the attributes of a Buddha manifest precisely his nirvāṇised nature, that is, his existence as 'visible dharma'.

[42] See Eva Neumaier-Dargyay (transl.), *The Sovereign All-Creating Mind. The Motherly Buddha: A Translation of the Kun byed rgyal po'I mdo*. Albany: State University of New York Press, 1992.

[43] See *Mūlamadhyamakakārikā* 18:6.

[44] Again, the point of Nāgārjuna's argument is that the reality which constitutes *saṃsāra* is as incomprehensible as is (traditionally) affirmed of *nirvāṇa* (see *Mūlamadhyamakakārikā* 18:7-9). Hence, one could rather say that *saṃsāra* is elevated to the status of the transcendent than *nirvāṇa* being reduced to the mundane realm.

Now if the Buddhist criticism of divine creation is not motivated by this radical mysticism,[45] it is based on Buddhism's own doctrine of creation, which is – as most of the classical scholastic treatises tell us – the periodical creation of successive universes by the collective karma of the sentient beings. If the individual karma is responsible for the kind of realm into which that individual will be reborn, the fact that there are several individuals with the same karmic tendency is responsible for the emergence of these realms as part of a new saṃsāric universe following the inevitable decay of the preceding one. If we carefully investigate the Buddhist critique of Hindu concepts of divine creation, as put forward by Vasubandhu, Bhāvaviveka, Śāntarakṣita, Kamalaśīla, etc., we find ample evidence that there is one crucial argument: If the post-mortem fate of the individual is directed by its own karma, for which the individual bears full responsibility, the world is basically a just world since everybody – at least ultimately – earns what he or she deserves. But if the beings and their cosmic environments are not created by their own karma but by some divine *īśvara* a serious problem arises: If the *īśvara* is just, then he will act in accordance with the law of karma in everything he does. But this would make him redundant. If – on the other hand – he goes against the law of karma in his creative acts, he is gravely unjust and not worthy of veneration. The problem of evil, as seen by classical Buddhist thinkers, is produced by the idea of a divine creator acting against the principle of human responsibility and the law of just karmic retribution, for as Bhāvaviveka argues: Either 'God' is just another name for karma, or he is a terribly unjust and immoral being.[46] Against the idea of the unjust and arbitrary rule of some divine creator or cosmic tyrant Buddhists wanted to defend the ideas of free-will and of human responsibility for one's own personal and spiritual development.[47] I think that this is a concern which many Christians can share.

But Buddhism is also aware that the idea of a complete and comprehensive retribution of every singe deed would lead to cosmic determi-

---

[45] Mādhyamikas could and did of course also at times criticise the idea of a divine creator on this level of 'conventional truth'.

[46] See Christian Lindtner, 'Madhyamaka Causality'. *Hōrin. Vergleichende Studien zur japanischen Kultur* 6 (1999): 37-77, especially the translations from Bhāvaviveka's *Madhyamakahṛdaya*, ibid.: 64-74.

[47] This is already the case in the famous passage from *Aṅguttara-Nikāya* I 173ff.

nism thereby making salvation impossible.[48] Hence the Buddhist karma teaching seeks to avoid determinism by understanding the impact of karma on the individual as being primarily a mental disposition and further, by holding that the forces of good are stronger than the opposite, so that good karma or spiritual progress can swallow up any bad karma before it ripens. There is a sense of grace in Buddhism, particularly if we remind ourselves that every good achievement is ultimately enabled and inspired through the radiating presence of the transcendent.

But should we not expect that a loving God would entirely refrain from creating a world if it will contain so much evil as a result of the conditions and consequences of a karmically structured environment and of the evil choices made by free beings? Would not a truly benevolent God create only such a world which is entirely free from any sort of evil? We find this argument, for example, in Kamalaśīla's famous commentary on Śāntarakṣita.[49] It coheres with an interesting Mahāyāna development of the Buddhist idea of creation through karma, namely the doctrine that the Buddhas, out of their immense karmic merit, create pure Buddha Lands, paradisiacal worlds free from any suffering whatsoever, where one can easily attain Enlightenment. Is such a 'Pure Land' not the kind of world that one should expect from a good and compassionate creator?

However, at times Buddhists have shown an awareness that a world in which there is evil is an inevitable implication of the realisation of particular goods and values, which would be impossible in a paradisiacal world. Let me mention two examples.

In the *Mahāyānasaṃgraha* Asaṅga mentions the widespread Mahāyāna belief that highly developed Bodhisattvas are capable of benefiting others in every manner – 'mundane and transcendent'. But "[i]f there really are such bodhisattvas ... then why do we still see sentient beings encountering severe penury and suffering in the world?"[50] In response to this objection Asaṅga argues that simply bestowing riches

[48] See *Aṅguttara-Nikāya* I 249.
[49] 'If it were through compassion that he did it [i.e., creating the world – P.S-L], for the purpose of helping others, then he would not make it full of such dire miseries as those of Hell, etc. – he would make it entirely happy.' Kamalaśīla on *Tattvasaṃgraha* 6:156f. Ganganatha Jha (transl.), *The Tattvasaṅgraha of Shāntarakṣita. With the Commentary of Kamalashīla,* Vol. I. Delhi: Motilal Banarsidass, 1986: 133.
[50] *Mahāyānasaṃgraha* VIII. John Keenan (transl.), *The Summary of the Great Vehicle by Bodhisattva Asaṅga* (BDK English Tripiṭaka 46-III). Berkeley: Numata Center for Buddhist Translation and Research, 1992: 99.

on the people might result in creating spiritual obstacles and 'this would hinder the good that they (otherwise) might engender'.[51] In an even more fundamental statement the famous *Vimalakīrti-Nirdeśa* (chapter 10) explains that only in a world like ours, that is 'in a buddha-field of such intense hardships', can the ten bodhisattva-*pāramitās* be developed. In order to realise *dāna*, generosity, there must be poverty, in order to realise *śīla*, morality, there must be the possibility of immorality, in order to develop *kṣānti*, forbearance, there must be real hatred, etc.[52] This sort of thinking is very much in line with what is known as the 'free-will-defence' or 'person-making-theodicy' within the debate on theodicy. The occurrence of certain forms of evil may be the inevitable implication of the realisation of particular goods. To develop a morally good character presupposes free will and a sort of natural environment with genuine challenges. But if both of these conditions are fulfilled then there will also be moral and natural evil. However, if the values which are thereby enabled will in the end lead to some sort of ultimate good – potentially available to all –, then the existence of such evils seems to be compatible with the assumption of a good creator God. Hence it is not surprising that the *Vimalakīrti Nirdeśa* suggests that our world is in fact a pure Buddha Land, but that due to karmic blindness the beings usually don't see that.[53] That is, our world – with its specific evils and with its particular potential and promises – is a Buddha Land because it does in fact provide the ideal environment for genuine spiritual progress.

What sort of conclusion can we draw from all this? Firstly, within Buddhism transcendent reality is primarily perceived as the ultimate goal of salvation/liberation and as such it is at the same time the precondition of salvation. It is usually not seen as being also the creative ground of everything. But on the other hand there are some important

---

[51] Ibid.: 100.

[52] See Robert Thurman (transl.), *The Holy Teaching of Vimalakīrti: A Mahāyāna Scripture*. Delhi: Motilal Banarsidass, 1991: 82f.

[53] See *Vimalakīrti-Nirdeśa* 10 : 'Noble sons, a buddha-field is a field of pure space, but the Lord Buddhas, in order to develop living beings, do not reveal all at once the pure realm of the Buddha'. Thurman, *The Holy Teaching of* Vimalakīrti: 80. Or *Vimalakīrti-Nirdeśa* 11: 'Lord, when we first arrived in this buddha-field, we conceived a negative idea, but we now abandon this wrong idea. Why? Lord, the realms of the Buddhas and their skill in liberative technique are inconceivable. In order to develop living beings, they manifest such and such a field to suit the desire of such and such a living being.' Ibid.: 87. See also J. Cabezón, 'Three Buddhist Views of the Doctrines of Creation and Creator', P. Schmidt-Leukel (ed.), *Buddhism, Christianity and the Question of Creation*. Aldershot: Ashgate, 2006: 33-45.

strands within Buddhism which come very close to ascribing in some sense creative power also to the transcendent – and that precisely in a teleological manner. All worlds are not only a product of collective karma. In a deeper sense they are 'pure lands' created by Buddhas as a result of their immense karmic merits. But Buddhas became Buddhas only through the force of their Bodhisattva vows, which in turn are ultimately triggered by the radiating presence of the all-pervasive Buddha-Nature. Only because we all have some sort of natural inclination towards the highest good and peace of the 'deathless' can we feel the deep unsatisfactoriness of saṃsāric existence and strive for salvation. And only because the nature of the ultimate reveals itself in our lives as the fullness of wisdom and compassion is our search for salvation gradually transformed into the altruistic search for the salvation of all, so that we might become Bodhisattvas and Buddhas and finally share in the creative 'activity' (remember: the 'activity' of an unmoved, non-acting reality) of the transcendent. If creation is part and parcel of the saving 'activity' of God, Buddhism must not necessarily reject such a view, but indeed entertains its own version of it.

2.3 Transcendent Reality as a 'loving person'

But is it not the case that Buddhism at least denies a loving God because it denies that ultimate transcendent reality has any sort of personal features, and hence – by implication – cannot be seen as 'loving'? Again, what seems to be a rather straightforward contradiction – the personal God of Christianity versus the impersonal absolute of Buddhism – turns out to be far less clear if we look at this more carefully. For the Thomist tradition in Christian theology – which Paul Williams mostly refers to – it is axiomatic that if God is truly transcendent then God must be beyond everything that we could properly grasp by our concepts or accurately describe with our words. As do all the great Church fathers, Thomas subscribes to the central axiom of the so-called 'negative theology' according to which God's transcendence entails necessarily God's ineffability – expressed in a masterly way by Anselm of Canterbury in his argument that God can only be that than which nothing greater can be conceived, if God is greater than anything that can be conceived (*Proslogion* 15). Similarly Thomas holds that 'the utmost of human knowledge of God is to know that we cannot know God.'[54]

Traditionally 'negative theology' drew from this the conclusion that in the end all positive statements about God need to be negated, that is, ultimately we can only say what God is not but not what God is. Thomas too asserts that 'because we cannot know what God is, but rather what God is not, we have no means for considering how God is, but rather what God is not'.[55] However, Thomas insisted that we are nevertheless entitled also to make positive statements about God, provided that we keep in mind that they are only analogically true when referring to God. That is, the attributes which we apply to God do not have the very same literal or – in Thomas's terms – 'univocal' meaning that they have when we use them within their proper realm of reference, the created world.[56] But what does Thomas understand by analogical meaning? It is not a sort of mathematical proportional analogy, but rather a kind of disproportional one. The main reason why – according to Thomas – we are permitted to assume some kind of analogy is that all created things receive their being from God who alone is pure being and every limited perfection of the nature of created things can be regarded as a remote reflection of the inconceivable perfection of God. But because the difference between God and creation is not a gradual but an essential one, the terms deduced from the created realm do not convey any knowledge when applied to God. In relation to God any term 'leaves the thing signified as uncomprehended and as exceeding the signification of the name'.[57] God's essence, says Thomas, 'is above all that we understand and signify in words'.[58]

Even divine revelation does not change this – as Paul Williams seems to assume.[59] It is true that for Aquinas by way of revelation we receive more propositional information about God. But all these propositions are still in human terms and hence fall short of what God is in Godself. Revelation unites us with God, but, says Aquinas, we 'are united to Him as to an unknown'.[60]

---

[54] 'Illud est ultimum cognitionis humanae de deo quod sciat se deum nescire'. *De potentia*, q. 7, a. 5.
[55] *Summa Theologiae* I 3, opening section. See also *Summa Contra Gentiles* 14.
[56] See *Summa Theologiae* I 13:5.
[57] *Summa Theologiae* I 13:5.
[58] *Summa Theologiae* I 13,1 ad 1.
[59] See Williams, 'Aquinas Meets the Buddhists': 99.
[60] *Summa Theologiae* I 12,13 ad 1.

But what then is the point of Thomas's doctrine of analogy? Why does he insist that we are justified in making positive statements about God if he admits that these statements thereby acquire a meaning which we don't understand and do not convey any knowledge of God's nature? What is the use of insisting that God can be called 'a person', i.e. 'father', who is 'wise' and 'good' or 'loving', if we do not know or understand what these terms mean when applied to God? Thomas's doctrine of analogy could easily be regarded as an empty gesture. But I suggest that there is a good justification for using such positive statements. They are useful analogies in so far as they bring us into the right existential disposition when we approach the divine mystery. They mirror how God is mirrored in and by his creatures. But they are not literally true descriptions conveying a correct knowledge of God.

In Buddhism we find the similar conviction that ultimate reality is inconceivable and ineffable. Nevertheless, the ultimate is manifested in every enlightened being, particularly in those who have attained Buddhahood and thus realised the highest perfection of wisdom and compassion. Already in the Pāli Canon it is said that *nirvāṇa* is visible through the perfected lives of the enlightened ones.[61] Later on, in the context of the *trikāya*-doctrine, Mahāyāna Buddhism developed the idea that the Buddhas of *nirmāṇakāya* and *saṃbhogakāya*, that is the earthly Buddhas and the heavenly, supranatural Buddhas whose incarnations the earthly Buddhas are, are form-ly manifestations of the form-less *dharmakāya*, that is the ultimate Buddha-Nature in its inconceivability. Let me quote Paul Williams on this who says – and I think rightly so – that the Buddhas of *nirmāṇakāya* and *saṃbhogakāya* are 'ultimately ... the spontaneous compassionate "overflow" of the *dharmakāya*'.[62] Hence for Buddhism too the last and highest symbolic representation of ultimate, ineffable reality is the image of a person full of wisdom and compassion.

I hope my scattered remarks have at least indicated that the issues of creation *versus* non-creation, or better, of divine creation *versus* karmic creation, and the contrast between a personal God and an impersonal Absolute are not as unbridgeable as they might seem to be *prima facie* and that there are plenty of points which invite a fruitful constructive dialogue in joint search for truth rather than a confrontational

---

[61] See *Aṅguttara-Nikāya* I 157-159.
[62] Williams, *Buddhist Thought*: 176.

exchange of mutual attempts to prove irreconcilability[63] and thus the falsity of the other. In constructive dialogue both partners will discover significant truths on the side of the other.

From here let me proceed to some concluding remarks on the theological implications of my dispute with Paul.

3. Christianity and the truth of Buddhism

First of all, I strongly hold that it is misleading to call Buddhism a form of Atheism. Buddhism is certainly non-theistic but to call it 'atheistic' would easily associate it with either the Eastern materialism or naturalism of the Cārvākas or with the materialism and naturalism of Western Atheists as we find it since about the eighteenth century. And perhaps one should also be somewhat hesitant in simply calling Christianity a form of Theism. For if 'theism' would entail that God is a person – just straightforwardly so without any qualification – and that this divine person created the world in a sort of innerworldly causal act, then major sections of mainstream Christianity could not be properly called 'theistic'.

Now Paul Williams is of course by no means the first to call Buddhism 'Atheism'. Rather, he is part of a relatively long tradition in the Western interpretation of Buddhism. But this has nevertheless always been just one strand, rivalled by an equally long tradition which sees Buddhism as a form of mysticism.[64] This may have its own problems, but I think it is definitely less misleading.

But what are the roots of the Western understanding of Buddhism as a form of Atheism? On the one hand, this certainly has to do with the traditional Hindu-Buddhist controversies over the īśvara issue. But I suggest that atheist conclusions have been drawn too hastily from this. We need to look afresh and far more carefully at these controversies and identify what these debates were really all about. It would be highly desirable to draw Hindus into this field of enquiry, and to support,

---

[63] See Williams, 'Aquinas Meets the Buddhists': 113.
[64] See on this G.R. Welbon, *The Buddhist Nirvāna and Its Western Interpreters*. Chicago: The University of Chicago Press, 1968; P. Schmidt-Leukel, *'Den Löwen brüllen hören'. Zur Hermeneutik eines christlichen Verständnisses der buddhistischen Heilsbotschaft*. Paderborn: Schöningh, 1992: 36-141.

wherever possible, an open-minded Hindu-Buddhist dialogue which is for numerous reasons urgently needed.[65]

However, a far more important root of the Western understanding of Buddhism as Atheism lies in the struggles internal to the West of the nineteenth century.[66] Western Atheists thought that Buddhism was a welcome ally in their criticism of Christianity, particularly because they erroneously assumed that Buddhism was by far the largest among the world religions. Conversely, the attempts of Christian apologetics to defend Christianity against those critics and the Christian counter-attacks were then also directed against Buddhism as the suspected ally.[67] Further, the dominant theological mood of the time was exclusivistic. It was shaped by the dream that Christian mission would succeed in the near future and Christianise the whole world thereby overcoming all other religions. Thus, every interpretation of other religions which painted them in the darkest colours, was favoured and adopted. This again caused among the modernist defenders of Buddhism a kind of obstinate self-definition along the lines of the Western polemical image of Buddhism – even in certain Asian countries, particularly when the Buddhist modernists had learned their Buddhism from English textbooks rather than from their own ancient traditions. To some extent this may also explain why Paul has been able to change sides without changing his understanding of Buddhism: i.e., he always understood Buddhism as Atheism, initially in opposition to Christianity and now in Christian opposition to Buddhism.

I think that the Christian exclusivistic scenario, according to which all other religions are false and soteriologically harmful, has disastrous implications for Christianity itself: If God can be portrayed, in the

---

[65] Something like a first attempt has been undertaken by K. Singh and D. Ikeda, *Humanity at the Crossroads: An Inter-cultural Dialogue*. Delhi: Oxford University Press, 1988. In our context it is worth noting that in his dialogue with the Hindu Karan Singh the Buddhist Daisaku Ikeda does not hesitate to present the 'eternal Buddha' of the *Lotus Sutra* as 'the fundamental source of all things in the universe', ibid.: 115.

[66] See the accurate assessment of the situation by Klaus-Josef Notz, *Der Buddhismus in Deutschland in seinen Selbstdarstellungen*. Frankfurt am Main: Peter Lang, 1984: 22: 'Alle diese Elemente abendländischen religionskritischen Denkens bauen sich zum Hintergrundszenarium dieser Fundamentalkrise des Christentums auf, in der sich der Buddhismus als Alternative für die "abgedankte" christliche Religion vorstellt'.

[67] See, for example, Barthélemy Saint-Hilaire's statement: 'I believe that the study of Buddhism … will show how a religion which has at the present day more adherents than any other on the surface of the globe, has contributed so little to the happiness of mankind …'. Jules Barthélemy Saint-Hilaire, *Le Bouddha et sa religion*, 3rd ed. Paris: Didier, 1866: xxix f., as quoted in Welbon, *Buddhist Nirvāna*: 69.

mode of metaphorical and analogical language, as a loving father whose love encompasses everyone, who – as Jesus says – 'causes His sun to rise on the evil and the good, and sends rain on the righteous and the unrighteous' (Mt 5:45), then we should expect to find numerous reflections of the saving presence of the divine around the world, in all cultures and religions and at any given time. The central Christian criterion for identifying these reflections is mentioned in 1 John 4:7: 'everyone who loves is born of God and knows God'. I think it is abundantly evident that – on this criterion – many Buddhists are born of God and know God and that Buddhism through its teachings and practices has served as a sacrament to bring this sort of birth and knowledge about. I am aware that Paul has in some places tried to argue for the opposite, that is, to show that Buddhist teachings undermine the flourishing of true love.[68] I don't have the time to go into any further discussion of this,[69] but I think this is again, at least in part, based on his misperception of Buddhism as Atheism.[70]

But what do we then make of the differences between the basically theistic and the primarily non-theistic expressions of ultimate reality in Christianity and Buddhism? Well, if the ultimate is truly transcendent, we should not expect to find exactly the same sort of reflections of His/Her/Its presence everywhere. Being truly transcendent, the ultimate necessarily exceeds human concepts and this is something that is indeed universally affirmed. We are only looking through a dim mirror, as St Paul says (1 Cor 13:12). The divine light shines through it, but the mirror also reflects our own image. Human experiences of the divine are as diverse as humanity itself. Hence, I am not suggesting that the concepts of Nirvāṇa and God are identical. I suggest that from a religious point of view they can be interpreted as expressing and mediating *different salvific experiences with the same ultimate reality* which shines through both of them. Or to use one of the beautiful parables of the *Saddharmapuṇḍarīka Sūtra*, it is the water originating from the one great cloud of the transcendent Buddha that nourishes in its own particular way the vast variety of different plants, and that is taken up by each of them according to their own form. So Buddhists too have a good reason to watch and see if they find evidence of

---

[68] See Paul Williams, *Altruism and Reality: Studies in the Philosophy of the Bodhicaryāvatāra*. Richmond: Curzon, 1998: 164-174; id., 'Aquinas Meets the Buddhists': 110f.

[69] Hence I am happy that José Cabezón has devoted large parts of his paper to this issue.

[70] This is particularly evident in Williams, 'Aquinas Meets the Buddhists': 110f.

this in other religions. Both, Christianity and Buddhism, need to integrate the truth that they discover in the faith of the other. If they are serious about this, it will certainly lead to significant transformations of identity in both traditions. Conversion may always be an individual option or even become a spiritual necessity on one's personal way. But I cannot see any rational arguments that would *coerce* Christians and Buddhists into the alternative either to convert to the other's faith or to reject it as false.

My hope for Paul is that his rediscovery of Christianity might also lead him to a rediscovery of Buddhism, that is, that he may overcome the inadequacies of the Western misunderstanding of Buddhism as Atheism seeing that God has not left himself without witness (Acts 14:17) among the Buddhists.[71]

---

[71] This is a revised version of the paper that was read at the Sixth Conference of the European Network of Buddhist-Christian Studies in St. Ottilien, June 2005. I am grateful to Paul Williams, José Cabezón and the conference participants for their critical remarks which forced me and helped me to clarify my position. I felt that this debate was a delight and intellectually highly stimulating. I am also grateful to Rose Drew for her helpful comments on various drafts of this chapter.

José Ignacio Cabezón

A Response to Paul Williams's
The Unexpected Way

Introduction

Let me begin with a word of appreciation for this book. If the goal of good writing is to make us think – if it is to provoke – then Paul Williams's *The Unexpected Way* is certainly a success, at least in the mind of this reader. The Indian Buddhist Pramāṇikas, or logicians, claimed that all conceptual knowledge arises through a process of negation; knowledge comes about apophatically, if you will. Only by contrasting a thing with what it is not can one come to understand what that thing actually is. If this is true, it applies as much to religious traditions as it does to the other more mundane affairs of the world. Hence, understanding Buddhism requires understanding what Buddhism *is not*. By forcing us to think long and hard about how Buddhism is not Christianity, and, vice versa, how Christianity is not Buddhism, Paul's 'meditation' has contributed much to our understanding of both religions, of what each of them *is*. As a Buddhist, I personally am grateful for such an opportunity.

Moreover, in the present intellectual climate, where honest and bold polemical exchange is all but a thing of the past, I find the tenor of Paul's work energising. Having been intellectually formed in large part on the debate grounds of one of Tibet's great monastic universities, I am a strange beast, I realise. But for better or worse, this background has nurtured in me a real appreciation – indeed, even a yearning – for good arguments. *Du choc des opinions, jaillit la verité* ('Truth emerges from the clash of opinions'), as the saying goes. *The Unexpected Way* has provided this reader with many an interesting argument for contemplation.

Finally, in fields like Religious Studies and Buddhist Studies, where confession – the declaration of the scholar's own religious subjectivity – is all but taboo, I find it refreshing to see a leading figure in the field writing candidly and unapologetically about his own religious identity and views, grappling with doctrinal issues as though they mattered (they do!), and transgressing the bounds of fixed genres by self-consciously mixing autobiography, theology, philosophy and even prayer. Those in our field who insist that there is but one form of serious intellectual exchange, who wince at the intrusion of religious subjectivity and piety into scholarly writing, who believe that there is a fixed and clearly demarcated line between buddhology and theology, will summarily dismiss this book, but they do so to their own detriment.

In what follows I will focus almost exclusively *on differences* – on the points over which Paul and I disagree. That is to be expected, I think. Scholars with philosophical inclinations aren't very good at celebrating similarities. So perhaps it is worth signalling at the outset that *there are* many points on which Paul and I are in essential agreement. We agree, for example, that 'it is simply not true that all religions are saying the same thing'. (67)[1] We agree as regards the fact that doctrine matters, and that accepting classical Buddhist doctrinal positions is often incompatible with accepting classical Christian ones (and vice versa). We agree that many contemporary religious movements have reduced truth to good vibes (my words, not his). (74) We agree that Buddhism and Christianity as institutions have 'always been subject to corruption'. (100) We agree that both Buddhism and Christianity make astonishing claims (122), and that attempts to denude religion of the supernatural make religion both less interesting and less compelling. (147, 165-66, 180) Put another way, Paul and I are both attracted to the 'magic and mystery' in religion. So there is plenty on which Paul and I agree, but, as I have said, dwelling on similarities is not nearly as interesting as contemplating differences, and so my focus will be on the latter.

What, in light of this book, do I think *of Paul*? Are we, Paul Williams's Buddhist friends, obliged *as Buddhists* to think any less of him because of his conversion or because he has written this book? Paul tells us that his rejection of Buddhism in favour of Catholicism means that 'my Buddhist friends have to face the fact that I am heading for

---

[1] References to the page numbers in Paul's book throughout this essay are to Paul Williams, *The Unexpected Way: On Converting from Buddhism to Catholicism.* London: T. & T. Clark, 2002.

hell'. (p. 98) (He contrasts this with the Christian perspective that 'leaves the issue of hell to the mercy and justice of God'.) But it is not at all clear to this Buddhist, who considers Paul Williams his friend, that he is destined for hell. It is not at all inconsistent with the teachings of Buddhism to see a Buddhist's conversion to Christianity as a positive thing in its own right. It all depends on what kind of a Buddhist one was, and what kind of a Christian one becomes. In the end what is most important is not the label – 'Buddhist' or 'Christian' – that an individual adopts, but the life that unfolds under the rubric of that label, or indeed under the rubric of no label at all. Paul's conversion appears to have resulted in many positive things for him and for those around him. True, Buddhism is exclusivistic. (On this point Paul and I agree.) No one, including Paul, reaches perfect and complete enlightenment without cultivating many factors: extraordinary compassion, a direct and intuitive understanding of the nature of reality (precisely as this is taught in specific Buddhist texts), and much else besides. But even exclusivistic Buddhists like me can and do acknowledge the intrinsic value of a committed Christian life. It is just not true, as Paul implies (85), that, because Buddhists have a long view of history and because they believe that everyone will eventually be led to embrace the truth of Buddhism, Buddhists therefore practise a passive tolerance of Christianity, waiting it out, as it were, until time brings them to the true path. I for one do not consider Christianity to be a mere 'holding pattern'. I *proactively* value Christianity as a religion. I acknowledge the contributions it has made to the spiritual development of individuals and of our world, and I rejoice in the virtues of a passionate and committed Christian life. There is no reason, therefore, for Paul to think that his Buddhist friends must consider his conversion to be a step backward, much less the first step on the road to perdition!

I have often thought that committing to a religious tradition is like getting married. There is a period of courtship and infatuation, and then one takes the plunge. In so doing one accepts one's partner (or one's religious tradition) 'for better or for worse'. Of course, marriages don't always work. Sometimes the fit is not good, in which case both parties may be better off separating. If belonging to a religious tradition is like marriage, then conversion is perhaps like divorce and remarriage. When this happens, a good friend will be supportive of one through this transition. But this can sometimes be difficult and awkward for that friend, especially if he or she is also well acquainted with one's former spouse.

Reading through Paul's book, I have often found myself in the position of that good friend. I can rejoice in Paul's finding fulfilment in the new 'object of his affection', and I realise that the 'divorce' requires that he distance himself emotionally and intellectually from his old 'partner' (Buddhism). But I also know this 'ex' rather intimately. So I shall put myself here in the position of 'defending the former spouse'. I shall act as her advocate. And perhaps that is the best way for the reader to view the remarks that follow – as the remarks of a friend who knows both parties rather intimately, and who wants to bring some sense of accountability to this parting of the ways.

Paul's book is an extended argument for Catholicism – a philosophical play in three acts. In the first act he argues for the plausibility of theism (mostly against Buddhism). In the second he makes a case for the plausibility of Christianity, and in the third he argues for the preeminence that should be accorded Catholicism among the various Christian options. It is in the first act that Paul really engages Buddhism, and so most of my remarks are based on what he says in this first (and by far the longest) chapter of his book. The presumed audiences for Chapters Two and Three are not principally Buddhists, but rather other (non-Catholic) theists – Jews, Protestants, and Eastern Orthodox Christians. Paul's argument for Christianity (Chapter Two) is largely a discussion of the evidence for the resurrection. As a Tibetan Buddhist, and therefore as a lover of magic and mystery, I have no problem accepting that Jesus came back from the dead. Miracles like this are plentiful throughout the world's religions, and if the validity of a religion were to be judged on the basis of the occurrence of extraordinary or supernatural incidents, then it seems to me that Tibetan Buddhism might well win hands down (at least if the outlandishness and sheer quantity of such events is the criterion).[2] But neither Paul (133-

---

[2] Paul states that 'it does not seem to me that any other religion or spiritual teaching has anything so dramatic or convincing as the resurrection from the dead... to support its claims. Buddhists (and others) sometimes talk about the wonders their spiritual heroes and heroines have done and can do. But nowhere is there a case so clearly and plausibly demonstrated as the resurrection'. (134) But this seems to me either false or at the very least unsupportable. How does one compare the Buddha's miracle of levitating into space and emitting fire and water from different parts of his body with an event like the resurrection? Can one such miracle be said to be more dramatic or convincing than the other? Can one really say that when a Tibetan monk turns his body into a rainbow and exits the world in this way that this is *less* dramatic than the ascension of the Virgin

(133-34) nor I believe that the teachings of Buddhism and Christianity can be validated on the basis of miracles. I, for one, would be happy to leave it at that, but Paul wants to go further:

> If the resurrection happened to Jesus, and He was a religious teacher – a teacher of meaning – then the chances are that the meaning of the resurrection is something like the one that He himself gave it. And is it really likely that Jesus could come back from the dead, explain what it all meant, and yet the Christian tradition that follows him proceeded to get it all hideously wrong? (134)

Let us leave aside the question of whether or not we know what Jesus said – a thorny issue that has preoccupied Biblical scholars from the nineteenth century up to the Jesus Seminar – and let us simply assume that what we have in the New Testament is an accurate account of what Jesus actually said. And let us also assume that the Christian tradition has preserved Jesus' interpretation intact, and that there is consensus among Christians about what this interpretation is. *For a Buddhist*, the answer to Paul's rhetorical question – 'Could Jesus and the subsequent Christian tradition have gotten it wrong?' – is a simple *yes*. Indeed, for a Buddhist (at least of my ilk) there is no choice but to claim that they *must have* gotten it wrong.[3] There are many instances in which religious people (including Buddhists) have misinterpreted the meaning of extraordinary religious experiences and events. So where Paul exits from the discussion – with this rhetorical question – is precisely where, I think, it becomes most problematic (and therefore also most philosophically interesting). But this is a complex issue, and so I too am content to leave it for the time being at that – with my simple rhetorical answer to Paul's rhetorical question. Let me say, however, that even if I believe that the Christian tradition has gotten it wrong, the misinterpretation of the resurrection does not for this Buddhist invalidate the Christian tradition *as a whole*. The issues are com-

---

Mary? What criteria do we use to determine that one is more 'dramatic or convincing' than the other? It is precisely because of these types of problems that miracles are *not* a criterion on the basis of which to judge the relative validity of religious systems, or so it seems to me.

[3] I have outlined what those problems are from a Buddhist perspective in 'Jesus through a Buddhist's Eyes', *Buddhist-Christian Studies* 19 (1999): 51-61; subsequently republished in Rita M. Gross and Terry C. Muck, eds., *Buddhists Talk about Jesus, Christians Talk about Buddha*. New York: Continuum, 2000: 17-31.

plex enough that they are not reducible to rhetorical questions and answers.

The Unexpected Way as a Polemic

This book, Paul tells us, is 'an intensely personal document... an *apologia* and a confession. As an *apologia* I am defending myself. But to whom? To myself, to friends, and to others (in that order). As a confession it is a confession of confusion, and a confession of faith'. (xiii) But the work is also, he says, 'a defence for my apostasy from Buddhism'. (ibid.) While he claims that his book is *not* an attack on Buddhism, no intelligent reader – Buddhist or Christian – can be blind to the fact that as 'Māra's advocate' Paul offers his readers some incisive criticisms of Buddhism. Despite his attempts to couch this work as a personal meditation on his conversion – 'Please believe me when I say I am really trying to go over and clarify my own problems with Buddhism and the attractions of Christianity' – the fact is that these private meditations have been published, and as such they have become a public document.[4] Given its tone and content, there is no escaping the fact that *The Unexpected Way* will be read in large part as an argument for Christianity vis-à-vis Buddhism, as a polemic against Buddhism, and as a defence of Christianity against the charges made by Buddhism. But in my view this is a virtue of the work. No apologies necessary!

As a polemic, Paul's book attempts to create a clear divide between Buddhism and Christianity. It highlights the differences between the two religions. That is what polemical literature does. It shows us what and who we *are* by showing us what and who we *are not*. To accomplish this, it is of course necessary to resort to rhetorical strategies that construct *us* and *them* in such a way that differences are highlighted.

Take the issue of God and Buddha, for example. The tendency in Paul's work is to deny that there is anything in Buddhism that even

---

[4] It is not until the very end of *The Unexpected Way* (202) that Paul more forthrightly acknowledges that his book is, at least in part, a critique of Buddhism: 'Part of my concern here and elsewhere has been to provoke scholars working in Buddhist Studies to a far greater critical sensitivity. Christian philosophers have spent many years defending their positions against philosophical criticism. In the last twenty years this has borne fruit in some immensely sophisticated defences and sometimes modifications of traditional Christian positions. I can see only gain in engaging in the same constructive criticisms and defence of Buddhist philosophy'. I agree.

approaches a Christian notion of God. And, of course, there *are* differences between Buddha and God. God is one; buddhas are many (indeed infinite in number). God is omnipotent; buddhas are as powerful as any being could be, but no being can be omnipotent according to Buddhism. Christians believe that God is the creator of the universe, but according to Buddhism the universe has always existed, making a single first creation (or an ongoing 'ground of being') unnecessary.[5] Buddhists believe that the classical Christian notion of God is philosophically untenable, just as Christians believe that human beings are incapable of a form of perfection (buddhahood) as this is described in the Buddhist texts. So differences there are aplenty, but it is both possible and intellectually profitable to consider Buddha and God in parallel.[6] Both the Buddha and God are, for their respective traditions, 'maximally great' beings. In classical Indo-Tibetan Mahāyāna Buddhism the Buddha is conceived of as omniscient, omni-compassionate, and (in at least one of the Buddha's aspects) omnipresent, just as God is in classical Christianity. But when the agenda is polemical, as it is in Paul's work – that is, when it is to show not only the basic incompatibility of Buddhism and Christianity but, indeed, the utter uniqueness and superiority of Christianity and its God – such comparisons become *de facto* impossible. Engaging in such a comparison (even as an intellectual exercise) is precluded by the agenda. God is *in*comparable. This is not *per se* a critique of Paul's work. An apologist has the right to choose not only his adversaries but also the mode through which s/he engages them (polemically, for example, as opposed to comparatively[7]). It *is* to say that this is not the whole story – that in choosing a certain mode of engagement one foregoes others, others that paint a more complex (and arguably more complete) picture of the two religions, that encourage dialogue rather than debate. But in an age when real debate is all but a lost art, perhaps it is not inappropriate to sacrifice a bit of complexity in the hopes of some new and different insights.

---

[5] See the papers in Perry Schmidt Leukel, ed., *Buddhism, Christianity and the Question of Creation: Karmic or Divine?* Aldershot: Ashgate, 2006.
[6] Paul Griffiths does so, for example, in 'Buddha and God: A Contrastive Study in Maximal Greatness'. *Journal of Religion* 69 (October 1989): 502-529.
[7] By 'comparatively' here I mean it as a mode of discourse that is committed to an exploration of both similarities and differences. Clearly polemics is also comparative in another, broader sense.

Now there *is* a certain ambivalence in Paul's book regarding its own agenda. On the one hand, Paul tells us that his goal is *not* to disprove Buddhism: 'I am very concerned lest my Buddhist friends should read some of the things I say here as an attack on Buddhism'. (xiv) But his rhetoric, it seems to me, belies this disclaimer. True, Paul often qualifies his arguments as 'argument[s] to myself' (17), as truths that are true 'for me'. (27) He tells us that his goal is not to demonstrate that God exists or that Catholicism is true, but rather that a belief in God and a commitment to Catholicism is *no more or less rational* than a belief in no-God and a commitment to Buddhism. But despite this disclaimer – despite the subjective qualifiers – the intelligent reader cannot help but ask herself why all of this should not be true *for me too*. Paul tells us that Buddhism suffers from an "explanatory gap" – a gap that 'can only be filled with a necessary being', God. Sometimes he implies that this is true in general. (19) Sometimes he qualifies this by stating that it is something that is true 'for me'. (33) But can an intelligent reader avoid asking why this should not be true *for everyone*? Even the language – 'a gap that needs filling' – would seem to cry out for something that fills it. Is it a real choice not to fill a gap that needs filling? Is there a real choice here, or only a rhetorical one? What is more, this strategy of subjectively qualifying his arguments would seem to run counter to one of Paul's great concerns, the loss of a sense of objectivity resulting from an emphasis on private experiences. (18)

There is perhaps a more clear way in which to see that the agenda of this book is polemical. Central to the work are certain fundamental structural dichotomies that I think unveil the implicit polemical agenda of this work. They go something like this:

Christianity	Buddhism	Page numbers
Hope	Hopeless	15, 20
Individuals significant	Individuals *in*significant	15, 19, 81-83
Optimistic	Pessimistic	19, 20, 49
Communalistic/ family-orientation	Individualistic/ isolation from the world	8, 72, 85, 87
Dependence on An/other(s)	Independence from others	51, 85
Other-directed	Self-reflexive (narcissistic)	76-77
A religion of public behaviour/ Objective	A religion of private Experiences/ Solipsistic	18, 22, 65, 72-77
Goal is something positive	Goal is an absence	51
The religion of the doughnut	The religion of the hole	51
True love	Auto-eroticism	77

These are not simple contrasts that present us with two equally rational and viable options – 'two options that are equally balanced'. (19) They are value-laden distinctions that cry out for the choice of Christianity over Buddhism. Who would choose a religion of hopelessness, insignificance and pessimism over one of hope, significance and optimism? Who would opt for the hole when you can have the doughnut? Why then not simply acknowledge that the arguments offered to us in this book are not meant merely as personal and subjective meditations, but as arguments that apply to everyone (Buddhists, Christians and everyone else) – that is, that they are arguments that, like Paul's chosen religion, are *catholic*. And why not admit that these arguments are meant to prove the relative superiority of Christianity over Buddhism? Such an admission, it seems to me, is preferable to the occlusion of a polemical agenda behind a screen of subjective qualifications.

On God

Paul begins his discussion of God with Aquinas's version of the cosmological argument. The problems with this argument – as with other versions like Leibniz's and Duns Scotus's up to contemporary versions, like that found in Taylor and Swinburne – have been discussed by a variety of figures in the philosophy of religion.[8] I will not repeat these here. Instead, since Paul formulates the argument in conversation with a Buddhist interlocutor in mind, let me focus on what I see to be a specifically Buddhist response, replacing his unspecified Buddhist interlocutor with a real one (me). As it is formulated by Paul (27f), the cosmological argument goes like this:

1. Why is there anything rather than nothing at all?
2. The totality of all things, as something that is contingent – that is, as something that need not have existed – requires some sort of explanation, even if this totality can be traced infinitely back in time, as Buddhists maintain.
3. Appeal to any Buddhist notion like the *dharmatā* ('the reality of things') or 'Mind' does not work as an explanation, since these too are contingent – that is, since they themselves require explanation. ('Why are there minds in the first place rather than no minds at all?').
4. In the end the only thing that can adequately explain the totality of things is something that is *not* contingent. That is, only something that is necessary, self-sufficient, requiring no further explanation, is a final answer to the question.
5. That necessary, self-sufficient being – the ground of existence – is God.

Now Paul, as a good philosopher, anticipates what possible Buddhist replies might be. For example, the Buddhist could claim, he says, that the *dharmatā* is fundamental as a 'bedrock position' beyond which one 'could simply refuse to go.' (31) In this case, he implies, the Buddhist has stopped the inquiry at some fixed (Buddhist) point by fiat, making the position 'no more rational' (32) than the theist position: *a chacun son dogma*. Hence, we are left with two incommensurable and equally viable alternatives. The cosmological argument in this context 'is not intended as a proof of the existence of God' (33), but rather is meant to show that theism is no less rational than Buddhism.

---

[8] For a good (though brief) overview, see Bruce Reichenbach's entry, 'Cosmological Argument', in the *Stanford Encyclopedia of Philosophy*, found online at: http://plato.stanford.edu/entries/cosmological-argument/index.html#note-1. The piece has links to other, more extensive discussions.

If this is all that the cosmological argument is meant to prove – that the two religions are no more or less rational – then perhaps we might have been spared having to work through the intricacies of the argument in the first place. But of course that is not the traditional function of the cosmological argument. That argument is meant to prove the existence of God as the necessary ground of existence, and therefore the irrationality of atheism (understood as the claim that no such God exists). What if the cosmological argument were taken at face value – taken 'full throttle', as it were – not just for the sake of presenting theism as an equally viable alternative to Buddhism, but as a full blown challenge to Buddhism: as a reason for abandoning Buddhism and accepting theism. As far as I can tell there is nothing that (apart from Paul's disclaimer that he does not mean it in this way – and what, after all, do author's intentions matter in this postmodern day?! –) should stop us from considering it as such. How would a Buddhist respond? This is what I imagine such a response would look like.

There is something rather than nothing because there are sentient beings. The universe exists because sentient beings (beings with minds) create karma ('actions'), and karma brings the universe into existence as the place where the results of that karma are experienced. This, by the way, is the reason why there is also order in the universe. Not because a single being (God) created that order, but because the collective karma of sentient beings requires it. Karmic seeds 'collected' in an orderly universe 'ripen' as another orderly universe in the future. (If it is not already evident, this is the Buddhist response to the so-called 'argument from design'.) But why are there sentient beings rather than no sentient beings? Tautologically, there are sentient beings because there are beings with minds. But that just begs the question. Why are there minds rather than no minds? Isn't a universe without minds logically possible? Here, I think, the Buddhist answer is somewhat interesting, and perhaps unanticipated. The answer is no. A universe – existence – without minds is not logically possible. Why? Existence is, by definition, 'that which is cognised/imputed[9] by

---

[9] This distinction reflects two different Buddhists schools' versions of what it means to exist. The Pramāṇikas claim that existent things are those things 'cognised by minds' (*blo yul du 'char ba*). The Madhyamakas claim that existence is something imputed by the mind (*blos btags pa*). Such a notion of what it means 'to exist' is admittedly counterintuitive. For a Buddhist, this counterintuitiveness is due to the fact that we operate through the filter of 'ignorance' (*ma rig pa*) – that is, through habitual patterns that make it seem as though the world is independent of the mind. Given its counterintuitiveness, the theist might well argue that this version of what it means 'to exist' is a

minds'. This is not a trivial claim. To assert that what is not cognised or imputed by a mind cannot exist is to assert something about the fabric of existence.[10] Isn't it possible, though, to conceive of a universe without any minds in it – a universe of just dead matter? Although it may seem as though it is logically possible to conceive of such a universe, in fact it is not. Where would one be standing when one was conceiving of such a universe? Outside the universe? That is impossible. Since the universe is the totality of all things, it is impossible to stand outside it. Well then what if one were standing inside such a universe, peering at all the dead matter, as it were? Then, of course, there would be at least one mind in such a universe – the mind of the observer.

Even without rejecting the Principle of Sufficient Reason – a common way of countering the cosmological argument – it is possible for the Buddhist interlocutor to explain the existence of the universe without appeal to a necessary ground. Notice that the truth or falsity of the individual pieces of this counter-argument – the truth of karma, of rebirth, etc. – are irrelevant in this context. All that is required is an explanation of why there is something rather than nothing without appealing to a necessary ground. If this is possible – and the Buddhist would claim that her explanation is just that – then the 'full-throttle' version of the cosmological argument fails. God has not been proven.

God as 'a ground of being' is, in any case, impossible for other reasons. A necessary, unchanging ground that is self-sufficient simply could not function. Of course the theist will claim that the Buddhist has misunderstood the nature of the ground that is God, and of the grounding that God does. The ground, claims the theist, serves as the ontological basis or support – not as the causal underpinning – of the

---

faulty one. And it is true that at some point it behoves the Buddhist to provide good reasons for the truth of this notion of 'existence'. But for our purposes here – for the purpose of responding to the cosmological argument in 'round one' – it suffices simply to offer an explanation of existence that is an alternative to the theist's explanation: enough to offer an explanation of existence that does not require (as the theist claims) the positing of an independent ground of being. The Buddhist will claim that mind is such an explanation.

[10] While it may be true, as Paul says, that individual 'mental acts [seeing a book, tasting a strawberry, etc.] could have not existed' (30), a Buddhist would deny that there could *exist* a possible world in which there are no mental acts whatsoever. Existence *logically* requires the existence of minds. Why? Because this is the way existence *is defined*. Does such a definition of existence need to be defended? Clearly so. That, however, is a separate matter, and one that is beyond the scope of this paper. See also the previous note.

universe.[11] But what precisely does this mean? I understand how a definition might be said to ground the thing that it defines (the definiendum). For example, mind can be said to 'ground' existence because of its essential (definitional) relationship to existence. I can also understand how the earth might be called 'the ground' of the sprout. Without the earth as a cause, the sprout could not come about. But what does it mean to say that there exists some 'ground' for the sprout separate from the things that define it and separate from its causes – some ethereal principle that explains why the sprout should exist at all? It is not surprising that a Buddhist would claim at this point that this is simply a figment of the philosopher's imagination, an example of 'reification' *(sgro btags)*.

Let us pause to consider one of God's attributes: that of being 'personal'. Now I know what it means for someone to be a person, and I know what it means to relate to someone else as a person. Buddhas are (at least in one of their aspects) personal. They were once ordinary persons, and they have mental continua (*rgyud*) just as ordinary persons do. I therefore have some sense of how to relate to buddhas. One relates to them the way that one relates to extraordinary people who have the ability to help one. One tries to emulate them, one treats them with deference, one asks for their help. But how does one relate to a 'ground of being', to a being who 'does not change', who is 'outside time'? (37) That is less clear to me.

Likewise, I know what it means to be good, and to do good. But what does it mean to say that something (God) is 'the necessary ground of goodness', or 'Goodness itself'? (46) What does it mean to be the ground from which 'all good things flow' while simultaneously claiming that that ground of goodness, though personal, has 'no moral

---

[11] *The Unexpected Way* (39): 'The [Buddhist argument against God] urges that an unchanging thing could not act as a cause... But is this right? The argument seems to work with a very restricted idea of what it means to be a cause, and also what it is to be God. Causation and the creative function of God are here being specified in terms of *doing* something, rather than simply being. Paradoxically, the paradigmatic formula for causation adhered to by Buddhists is "This being, that occurs"... This means that for the Buddhist too it is quite possible for causal function to be exerted simply by being'. But of course, Paul, by focusing on the first part of the formula ('this being') is ignoring the second ('that occurs'). What is spoken of in this formula is nothing other than causality: when the causes are complete and present, the effect occurs. In no way would a Buddhist see this formula as claiming anything like non-causal, ontological dependence, much less that 'the formula is perfectly fulfilled by the existence of God'.

obligations'?[12] I know what it means to relate to a person who is good, but I have no idea of how to relate personally to abstract goodness or to the ground of goodness.

I also know what it means to love.[13] Love is an emotion, a mental state. It is (at least in part) the wish to bring happiness to another. But what does it mean to say that God is love? Does it mean that God is a mental state? Does it mean that God is the sum of all the mental states we call 'love' – a kind of psycho-pantheism? I can imagine many ways in which one might relate to love as an emotion. I know what it means to have love, and to want love. But how does one relate to love itself as a personal being? How does one relate personally to an emotion?

As a young boy I was a theist. I loved what I thought was God. But after reading The Unexpected Way I realize that what I loved was not God at all, for the object of my youthful devotions was not an unchanging, atemporal ground of being. 'He' (at least that was the pronoun in use back then) was good, but not goodness. He was loving but was not Himself love. Rather, what I loved, I realize now, was something like an extraordinary person. Maybe I was never really a Christian. Maybe I was a Buddhist – a lover of persons – all along.

---

[12] These claims are made as part of Paul's discussion of theodicy. (43-48) The gist of the argument is this: God is good and is, indeed, Goodness itself, but this does not entail that God need have created a better (less evil) world, for (in the case of God at least) being good does not entail having any moral obligations or duties. Why then did God create this particular world and not some other? This is 'at the moment a mystery'. God may at some point provide us with more information about why he chose this (not very nice) world to create, but he may not. Is this convincing? Until God is a little more forthcoming – until God makes the reason for such a cruel world a little less 'mysterious' – I reckon many of us will probably opt out of theism. In the meantime I ask myself this: Given that the problem of evil is *the* stumbling block for so many people, why didn't God provide just a little more information on the matter? It probably would have swelled the ranks of the theists. God is (we are told) good, and God wishes the good. God *could have* provided more information (at least there appears to be no logical stumbling block to having done so). Moreover, to have done so would have created more theists, and I take it that from a Christian vantage point this is a good. And yet God chose not to do so. This, I take it, is a problem.

[13] Paul suggests that 'love is a way of being with an other, with others, in community. It is a way of dwelling together, each in the light of the other, a way of caring. That is where we find God. That *is* God'. (76) I have some problems (see below) with conceiving of love as *just* 'a way of being', of 'dwelling together', since it seems to reduce love to certain forms of social interaction. But that issue aside, if this is what God *is*, if God *qua* love is simply being with others, caring for them, then Buddhists would be theists. But I doubt that this is what Paul (or most other theists) actually have in mind when they say they believe in God.

On Karma, Reincarnation and the Moral Order

According to Buddhism, certain actions (karma) bring happiness, certain actions bring suffering, and certain actions bring experiences that are neither. Those actions that bring happiness are called 'virtuous' or 'good'. Those that bring suffering are called 'evil' or 'bad'. Those that bring neither are called 'neutral actions'. This is simply the way 'good', 'bad' and 'neutral' are defined. Therefore, the statement 'good deeds bring about happiness' is a necessary – not a contingent – truth. It is something that is true by definition. In the face of this, any attempt to argue from the contingency of the moral order to a necessary cause (God), as Paul does (40-43), fails. Why? Because the moral order – the fact that good deeds bring happiness – is not contingent. It requires no explanation or ground. It is something that follows from the very definition of the word 'good'.[14]

In Buddhism the grounding for morality comes from the very structure of the universe – from the fact that certain actions lead to happiness and others to suffering. In classical Christianity morality is grounded in God and in God's will. 'There is no possible circumstance under which doing God's will would be the wrong thing to do'. (61) And this is true, Paul tells us, regardless 'of what follows for oneself, or indeed for others'. (61) The consequences of an action – whether it leads to happiness or to suffering for oneself or for another – are 'irrelevant'. Contrapuntally, for Buddhists the Buddha's will is, I believe,

---

[14] So much for the ontological status of goodness. But what of the epistemological question? How do we *know* that a certain action is good? How do we know that giving to the monastic community will bring about happiness? Without getting into the complexities of the issue, the later Indian Buddhist philosophical tradition claims that such facts are 'extremely hidden' (*atyantaparokṣa, shin tu lkog gyur*). As such, they are beyond the ken of ordinary individuals (individuals who do not have access to knowledge of past or future lives). That does not mean, however, that it is impossible to know such truths. They are knowable, the Pramāṇikas tell us, in reliance on trustworthy testimony (*śabda, lung*) – on the Buddha's word. Since the Buddha is omniscient, the Buddha knows first hand that actions like 'giving to the monastic community' always result in happiness, and are therefore good. We, in turn, know this second hand, not by seeing that this is an inviolable aspect of the way things are, but by relying on the testimony of someone who does. On this point, see José Ignacio Cabezón, *Buddhism and Language: A Study of Indo-Tibetan Scholasticism.* Albany: State University of New York Press, 1994: 99-111. Is this reliance on the Buddha a simple act of faith? It can be, of course, but the Pramāṇikas claim that it need not be, that we can come to an inferential understanding of the fact that the Buddha is a trustworthy person. On this question, see Roger R. Jackson, *Is Enlightenment Possible? Dharmakīrti and rGyal tshab on Knowledge, Rebirth, No-Self and Liberation.* Ithaca: Snow Lion, 1993.

irrelevant to the question of what is good. Buddhas know what is good, do what is good, and they wish what is good for others. But that is just to say that they know what actions lead to happiness, and that they wish that sentient beings would engage in the causes of their own happiness. Actions are not 'made' good – they do not receive their 'grounding' as good actions – by virtue of the fact that buddhas (or any one else, for that matter) consider them to be good. It is the other way around. The goodness of actions is 'grounded' *a priori* in the causal functioning of the universe. An action is good because it brings happiness for oneself and for others, and that is why buddhas will it. Hence, 'what follows for oneself or for another' from doing a certain action is what is *most* relevant to Buddhist moral considerations.

As Paul reminds us (61-62), the *motivations* for doing good deeds are also quite different in Buddhism and Christianity. Buddhists engage in virtuous actions for the sake of bringing about the welfare of self and other – for the sake of human flourishing. Trusting in the guidance provided by the scriptures, they expect certain positive effects to result from engaging in virtue. Christians engage in good actions, we are told, not because they believe that this will bring about happiness for themselves or for others – that, Paul tells us, is 'incidental and as such irrelevant' (61) to the doing of good – but because it is the will of God. While Christianity 'favours virtue and condemns vice' (71), the transformation of the mind that this entails 'is initiated by God in grace. The recipient does not at all bring it about'. (71) If this is true, the Buddhist (or indeed anyone committed to improving one's lot in life) cannot help but wonder what reason anyone should have to engage in virtue. Since any felicity (including, one assumes, emancipation) is not something wrought by human action – since it is 'an unpredictable and thereby totally unmerited act of God's grace' (61-62) – why be a moral person? Why exert oneself in virtue? To do so brings one no closer to the happiness of self and other. *Not* to do so does not necessarily doom one to suffering, for that, as we have seen, is also unpredictable, something that in the end is in the hands of God. (98)

Clearly the Buddhist and Christian visions of morality are incompatible, and the truth is that we probably have little to go on to choose one over the other. But let me ask a question that Paul asks repeatedly in this work: Which do I *hope* is true? I hope that there is something that I can do from my own side to bring about the happiness of myself and others. I hope that the universe is structured in such a way that what I do matters to others – not just in the here and now, but in the long run, in the broader scheme of things. Is it hubris to think that we can make a difference in the world? Maybe it is, or maybe it is just to be hopeful in a particularly Buddhist way.

On Buddhas and Dependence

Paul tells us that enlightenment in Buddhism 'does not require any help from divine intervention'. (25) This may be true for modernist, 'demythologised', de-metaphysicalised forms of Buddhism. But historically Buddhists have traditionally believed that it is not only possible but indeed necessary to achieve enlightenment in dependence upon the intervention of enlightened beings. This is the essence of what it means 'to go for refuge'. Buddhas therefore function for Buddhists – not just Pure Land Buddhists like Shinran, but for all Buddhists – in much the same way that God functions for Christians. We praise buddhas, ask for their blessings, and (in the refuge formula, for example) affirm our faith in their ability to protect us from suffering. While we acknowledge that buddhas cannot simply bestow on us emancipation through an act of their will – that they 'do not wash our sins away with water' *(sdig pa chu yis mi bkru pa)*, as the Buddhist saying goes – we believe that they can do everything that any being could do to help us. It is simply not true, therefore, that in Buddhism 'dependence on others is to be avoided'. (51)

Is Buddhism 'atheistic'? (26) If *theos* is equated with the classical Christian notion of God (or, indeed, with any one of a number of classical Indian notions of God), then, trivially, Buddhism is atheistic. But such a claim obscures the more complex relationship of God and Buddha. Even when a religion rejects the Christian notion of God (as Buddhism does), it is possible to have a real and sophisticated notion of 'divinity' and of dependence, one that affirms the existence of transcendental beings and that acknowledges that such beings can and do spiritually intervene on behalf of the world.

Paul tells us that 'for all its advocacy of compassion... the state of one who is enlightened, the state of a Buddha, from his or her own side is one of complete and utter self-sufficiency', that 'the goal is one of absence', 'an absence of dependence on others'. (51) While this is not an unfair portrayal of some minoritarian movements within Indian Buddhism (some Buddhists did indeed claim that Buddhas 'go poof' at the time of their death – that the goal is absence qua annihilation), it is a misleading depiction of Buddhism as a whole, and especially of Mahāyāna Buddhism. While buddhahood is the absence of suffering, it is also of course the presence *(mnga' ba)* of every possible good quality *(yon tan)*, and it is especially the presence of an overwhelming desire to help others, a desire that never wavers or wanes. This is not mere verbiage, not a cover for advocating a 'real' goal whose nature is absence. Others are the very reason for buddhahood. There is no progress toward buddhahood without the other, and neither is there any reason for it. As the recipients of the bodhisattvas' charity, and as the object of their patience and kindness, sentient beings are the ground for bodhisattvas' spiritual accomplishments. As beings in need, they are the very reason for bodhisattvas' commitment to the attainment of buddhahood, the state that makes one maximally effective in one's ability to help others. It is true that the Buddha's ethereal Dharma-body *(dharmakāya, chos sku)* is 'unwavering' *(ma g.yos pa)*, that it has no need or wants. It is in part an absence – not of dependence (I know of no text which makes this claim), but an absence of ignorance, of suffering, of limitations and obstacles. It is also, however, in another of its aspects, a presence – of omniscient gnosis, of every positive quality in the highest possible measure. Moreover, buddhas are not only their ethereal Dharma bodies, they are also their form bodies *(rūpakāya, gzugs kyi sku)*, and this aspect of buddhahood exists exclusively for the benefit of others. Hence, a responsibility to others is, as it were, built into the very fabric of what a buddha is. To claim, therefore, that the goal of Buddhism is an absence of dependence on others – to claim that Buddhism is 'a religion of the hole rather than the doughnut' (51) – is at best a partial picture of what the Buddhist texts say about buddhahood.

Paul appears to be committed to portraying Buddhism in this way because he wants to claim that, by contrast to Buddhism, Christianity is a religion of dependence (on God and on others), with its goal envisaged in communal terms. (52) But to make a case for Christianity's commitment to dependence and to communalism it does not strike me as necessary to do so on the basis of a stark contrast with Buddhism – a straw horse Buddhism, I would maintain. I for one am willing to grant that Christianity puts more emphasis on dependence (at least more emphasis on dependence upon a transcendental being). And I would grant that Buddhism (at least in the way that it has developed in the West) is less community oriented than Christianity. Indeed, I believe that Western Buddhism's unconscious adoption of modernist notions of Western individualism has been to its detriment.[15] But even if there is a difference between the two religions in regard to these issues, it strikes me that the difference is one of degrees. In any case, it is inaccurate to claim that Buddhists (even non-Pure-Land Buddhists) believe that enlightenment 'does not require any help from divine intervention'.

On Experiences

Paul has a problem with 'experiences',[16] with 'mystical experiences', and especially 'nondualistic and nonconceptual mystical experiences'. (53ff, 69) Obviously, then, Paul is going to have a problem with Buddhism. There is no question but that elite Buddhism places great emphasis on these types of experiences, though, of course, Buddhism is much more than elite Buddhism, as Paul himself acknowledges.[17] But is it true that 'if the goal is expressed in terms of nondual experiences this must finally be to privilege self-sufficiency – indeed self-absorption – over a position where one's very being is essentially bound up with a community, with others'. (54) Are mysticism and commitment to community mutually exclusive? Paul tells us that 'we can have as a final goal a perfect community or we can have nondual and nonconceptual experiences, but we cannot have both as equal final goals'. (56)

I was once a part of one of the most elite institutions in the Buddhist world – an institution completely committed to training students in the theory and practice of 'nondual and nonconceptual experiences' – a Tibetan Gelukpa monastery. In my 'experience' this was also one of

---

[15] Whether Buddhism in its more indigenous settings is less community and family oriented is, I think, a question to be answered through sociological research. It does *not* appear to me evidently so.

[16] *The Unexpected Way*, 72: 'I seek no more experiences, but only to do your will, O Lord, my God and Saviour'.

[17] There has been quite a bit of discussion among scholars of Buddhism in recent years concerning the centrality of 'experiences' to the Buddhist tradition. Some scholars claim that the category 'experience' is a Western, Protestant importation into Buddhism; see Robert Scharf, 'Experience' in Mark C. Taylor, ed., *Critical Terms for Religious Studies*. Chicago: University of Chicago Press, 1998: 55-69. I (with Paul) side with the view that it is meaningful to speak of experiences in Buddhism – i.e., that it is an emically sanctioned category; see also Janet Gyatso, 'Healing Burns With Fire: The Facilitation of Experiences in Tibetan Buddhism'. *Journal of the American Academy of Religion*, 67.1 (1999): 113-148.

the most positive and vibrant communal settings I have ever lived in. Despite the cultural differences, I felt welcomed and nourished. And the community of which I was a part I continue (to this day) to think of as one of the least dysfunctional I have ever witnessed. I don't want to paint too rosy a picture of Tibetan monastic life. It has its problems. But I cannot deny my experience as a member of such a community. As a community it simply worked.

Now one might argue that, 'as a matter of logic' (56), a contemplative path that has as its goal the cultivation of mystical experiences must be 'self-absorbed' (55) and 'solipsistic' (56), that 'all concern with experiences implicates egoity', (58) and 'involves hedonistic (egoistic) concerns' (58), but the reality of thriving mystical communities (Buddhist and otherwise), I think, belies such a conclusion. True, a radically transformative religious experience – a mystical insight – is something that in the end is private (even when its consequences are not). But of course that does not imply that getting there is private. The experience of one's own death too is private – it is something that is experienced only by oneself – but we would not, because of that, claim that everything that leads up to it (the entirety of a human life) is therefore 'self-absorbed' or mired in 'egoism'. Of course, some extraordinary individuals (Buddhist and Christian) choose the hermit's life, but these are the exception rather than the rule. And in both the Buddhist and Christian cases, I take it, the motivation for living in isolation from the rest of society is not selfish, but rather is to be of benefit to others. Even in these rare cases, a real human community is present to the hermit – in spirit, if not in the flesh.

Christianity (and Christian conversion) too is bound up with – even if it is not reducible to – 'experiences'. Is not love or faith an experience? Is not the feeling of being with others (in the Mass, for example) an experience? Is not the feeling of the vibrant presence of God in nature after taking communion – something that Paul describes in his own work (209) – an experience?[18] Or are love, faith, and the feeling of God's presence to be stripped of their somatic element through reduction to one or another non-somatic cognitive state, or worse, through a mechanistic reduction to bodily actions or social states of being? Is faith really reducible to the verbal declaration of a creed? (21) Is love just 'a way of being with an other' – no references to

---

[18] Paul tells us that 'God as He is in Himself cannot be experienced'. (69) This implies that God *can* be experienced in other ways.

emotion necessary? (76) This is true only, I think, in the philosopher's mind. If Buddhism errs on the side of mind – as it sometimes admittedly does – then surely the type of reductionism being described here errs on the side of matter, for in its attempt to do away with experiences altogether, it reduces them to material acts or social states.

In the end, the simple dichotomy 'Buddhism = experience, Christianity = communal behaviour' (72-76) is just too simplistic to explain the complex views that these two religions have of 'experience' and 'community'. On the one hand, as Paul himself notes, Christian texts speak of – and Christian communities seem to be actively engaged in – techniques, including meditative techniques (75), for achieving 'pureness of mind and thoughts' (73), for cultivating love (74), and so forth. On the other hand, there are many Buddhist examples (both textual and living) that point to the importance of community, and to the communal transformation of behaviour. It is simply not the case that 'reconciliation (confession), prayer, worship and so on' (75) are only to be found in Christianity, as Paul implies.

What, according to Paul, is the nature of the 'experiences' that are constitutive of the Buddhist path? There is at times a tendency in Paul's work to trivialise the Buddhist path and its goal. For example, Buddhist mental transformation is reduced in Paul's analysis to 'becoming a nice person'. (65) And Buddhism itself is at times portrayed as chiefly concerned with pleasant experiences and 'sensations'. (56-57, 62) But the Buddhist goal, of course, is not pleasant feelings or sensations. The Buddha's purpose in teaching was to provide his followers with a roadmap to greater happiness and to less suffering for themselves and for others. But we should not think of 'happiness' here as coterminous with pleasant experiences. The ultimate happiness spoken of by the Buddha – the goal of the Buddhist path – is much more than warm and fuzzy, tingling sensations. Buddhahood is not like having an eternal massage. Likewise, the suffering that is eradicated by following such a path is much more than a lack of feelings of bodily discomfort. According to the Mahāyāna, moreover, those who have cultivated compassion and altruism over their many lives (i.e., bodhisattvas) at the point of their enlightenment become beings maximally capable of helping others. Spurred on by their previous vow to save sentient beings, a buddha then spontaneously *(lhun gyis grub par)* manifests infinite numbers of 'forms' throughout the universe for the spiritual welfare of others. This is the Mahāyāna vision of the goal – hardly the same as achieving 'pleasant sensations' or 'becoming a nicer person'. Is such a vision realistic? Hardly (at least if one's point of reference is scientific materialism). Is it easy? Definitely not. Hopeful? I can't imagine anything more hopeful.

On Love

Paul tells us that:

> Inasmuch as liberation in Buddhism involves nonduality and nonconceptuality it cannot *in itself* involve any relationship of love, and inasmuch as it involves mental transformation its primary concern cannot be with the other... If we can speak here of a relationship of love, or use erotic imagery, it could only be love expressed finally in terms of personal experiences, the Great Bliss (*mahāsukha*) of perfect enlightenment spoken of particularly in Buddhist Tantricism. Love here must be reflexive. It turns back on itself in the infinite play of consciousness, the infinite play of experiences. I wonder if this primacy given to the reflexive play of experiences was what Cardinal Ratzinger... meant when, as I recall, he reportedly referred to Buddhism as 'spiritual auto-eroticism'. (76-77)

For Paul, Buddhism and Christianity engage the other differently. Buddhism's mode of engaging others is inferior. There are impediments – impediments that arise because of Buddhist doctrinal presuppositions – that prevent a liberated being[19] (a) from loving another, and (b) from having the other as her primary concern. Buddhism may speak of love, and may even use erotic imagery – like the Song of Songs does – but we should not be lulled by this into thinking that this is true love (the love of an other). Rather, Buddhist love is narcissistic and onanistic.

Now given the emphasis placed in Mahāyāna Buddhism on love, compassion and altruism, it is not surprising that these statements 'do

---

[19] Paul actually says that 'liberation...cannot *in itself* involve any relationship of love'. And I take it that he means by this that a liberated being cannot, *qua* liberated being, love. What else could it mean? Clearly it does *not* mean that 'liberation itself does not love', for that is so trivial as to be hardly worth mentioning. Liberation is a state, not a being, and only beings can love.

not go down at all well with Buddhists'. (77) But Buddhists are known (or at least should be known) for their forbearance (kṣanti), so let us examine these various claims calmly, one at a time. First, is it true that liberated beings do not love? This is news to both Theravāda and Mahāyāna Buddhism, each of which maintains that even *arhats* (beings who have attained liberation for themselves alone), let alone buddhas, have great love *(mahāmaitri)* for others.[20] But to be fair to Paul, he is probably not arguing that these traditions do not claim that liberated beings love. Rather, he is probably claiming that regardless of what these traditions maintain, liberated beings cannot (because of Buddhism's commitment to nonduality and nonconceptuality) actually love. What they think is love is not real love. Why? Because, (presumably) a commitment to nonduality and nonconceptuality precludes real engagement with a real other. When another is not perceived as real, how can one truly love that person?

It is because Buddhists cultivate nondualistic and nonconceptual mental states (or perhaps because liberated beings experience the world in this way) that true love is impossible in Buddhism. Now the concepts of nonduality and nonconceptuality have a long and complex history in Indian and Buddhist thought. But for a Gelukpa-trained Tibetan Buddhist like myself, they have a narrower meaning, and this is how I propose to proceed, with that narrower meaning in mind. In Tibetan Buddhism the terms 'nonduality' and 'nonconceptuality' are attributes of the direct cognition of reality, and this is probably the sense of these terms that is most relevant to the present discussion. Why should nondual and nonconceptual experiences stand in the way of loving an other? Perhaps because love is a dual experience. After all, in love there is a lover and a beloved. Love requires, or so it would seem, some level of conceptuality – a conceptual notion of a 'self' and an 'other'. These, in any case, are the best reasons I can think of for suggesting that nonduality and nonconceptuality might impede love.

---

[20] See Harvey Aaronson, *Love and Sympathy in Theravada Buddhism* (Delhi: Motilal Banarsdiass, 1999). It is true that arhats, for example, seek a state of personal peace, and that (at least according to the Mahāyāna) they are not *as* concerned with the welfare of others as, say, bodhisattvas or buddhas, but they nonetheless have great concern with the welfare of others. Is the other their primary concern? Perhaps not. But the fact that *arhats* are not principally concerned with the welfare of others has nothing to do with the fact that they are 'involved in mental transformation,' the connection that Paul is trying to make. In fact, it is precisely because they have *not* engaged in a certain type of mental transformation – the type that brings about great compassion and *bodhicitta* – that others are not their principal concern.

To offer a Buddhist response to this version of Paul's argument requires a bit of preamble, so let me offer this now.

Buddhists claim that our conceptions (of ourselves, of others, of our actions) are faulty. When I engage in an act of charity, for example, I think that there is a real José who is really giving a real object to a real Sally. None of these elements – agent, direct and indirect object, and action – exist as they are conceived of by me. To that extent they are unreal. But that does not mean that José, Sally or the act of charity are totally nonexistent. Were I to analyse this action – the action of José giving something to Sally – I might come to the (proper) conclusion that these three elements do not exist as I conceived of them, and if I were really good at this, I might then be able to 'simmer' this conceptual conclusion on the fires of meditative equipoise and eventually come to what the texts call 'a direct, nonconceptual understanding of the reality/nature of charity' *(sbyin pa'i chos nyid mngon sum du rtogs pa)*. That is to say, I might come to an intuitive understanding of the 'emptiness' *(śūnyatā)* or reality *(dharmatā)* of the action 'José gives something to Sally'. At that very moment – when I attain such a nonconceptual cognition of reality – it is true that José, 'giving' and Sally all disappear from my mind. As the mind focuses on the reality of these three things, it becomes 'as if one' *(gcig lta bur)* with that reality. So it is true that at that moment everything goes poof (except for the emptiness/reality, of course), though even then they are not going poof in general, but only in my mind. And it is also true that at that moment I can cognise no 'giving', 'giver' or 'recipient', nor therefore can I at that moment be engaging in the act of giving. This is hardly surprising, given that I am in a state of meditative equipoise! But when I come out of this meditative state, the texts tell us that I experience José, Sally, the gift and the act of giving anew, and this time quite differently. Were I to engage in a new act of charity, I would then experience all of these components of the act of giving 'as if they were illusions' *(sgyu ma lta bur)*. This is considered a much better way to engage in charity, because it corresponds more closely to the way that José, Sally, the gift and the act of charity actually exist. The texts also tell us that ordinary beings (non-buddhas) cannot have a direct, nonconceptual understanding of the reality of charity and be simultaneously engaged in charity. Ordinary beings have no choice but to alternate between the two. They spend some time in the meditative equipoise on the emptiness of (for example) charity, and then they come out of that equipoise and engage in real (or rather 'illusory-like') acts of charity. However, buddhas, it of charity. However, buddhas, it is claimed, can directly perceive the emptiness or reality of charity at the same time as they are engaged in the act. This is one of the great mysteries of the buddhas' nature – that they can directly perceive the ultimate emptiness and the conventional, illusory-like existence of all things simultaneously.

The same, of course, applies, *mutatis mutandis*, to the act of love or compassion. It must be a very different thing to love another when one perceives one's self, the other and the act of love as 'illusory-like'. A buddha's experience cannot but seem even stranger to us. How can one have a vivid insight into the reality of love – into the empty nature of love – while one is loving? For certain brands of Buddhist philosophers (the Yogācāras) it gets even weirder, since for them the 'reality' being spoken of here is actually a 'nonduality of subject and object' *(gzung 'dzin gnyis med)*. Hence, for Yogācāras, when a buddha has love or compassion for another, that buddha experiences love without any notion of a distinction between self (subject) and other (object). As the twelfth century Tibetan master Phag mo gru pa states:

> As soon as you sever the root of self-grasping,
> You realize that self and other are not two.
> To understand self and other as nondual
> Is… the inseparability of emptiness and compassion.[21]

Madhyamakas would not go as far as Yogācāras (or as far as Yogācāra-inspired Tibetans like Phag mo gru pa). Madhyamakas claim that nonduality is an attribute of the *experience* of reality (and not of reality *itself*), so that one *experiences* subject and object vanishing, '*as if* object and subject had become one, like milk being poured into water'. But whether in the stronger (Yogācāra) or in the weaker (Madhyamaka) sense, is this notion of love really *all that* weird? Do we really want to say that love *always and inevitably* involves a sense of duality? Don't we get a glimpse of what nondual love is like when, in those rare moments in life, we lose ourselves in the beloved? Mind you, Buddhists aren't claiming that this is the *only* type of love there is, but only that it is one type of love, an important type of love, a love

---

[21] Phag mo gru pa rDo rje rgyal po (1110-1170), *Sangs rgyas kyi bstan pa la rim gyis 'jug pa'i tshul* [A Method for Engaging the Teachings of the Buddha in Stages]. Bir, 1977: 93: *bdag 'dzin gyi rtsa ba chod tsam na/ bdag gzhan gnyis med du go ba yin/ bdag gzhan gnyis med du go ba des/ bdag med rnam gnyis go zhes bya/ de stong nyid snying rje dbyed med yin/*.

that has the capacity to transform individuals and communities for the better. Of course, one could always define love in such a way that makes having it require a strong sense of duality – of *me* and *you*, where the twain can meet but not meld – and sometimes I get the feeling that this is what strict dualistic theisms (Indian as well as Semitic) are attempting to do: 'There is only one type of love. Don't let go of yourself! Don't lose yourself! Otherwise, it's just *not love*'. But for those who have had a taste of 'losing themselves' in love, this will probably fall on deaf ears, or at least I hope it does.

Of course, if one *assumes* that there is only one way to love – with real *you's* and real *me's* – then we can see why one might claim that the alternative, mystical versions of love found in the Buddhist (and in some contemplative Christian and Hindu) sources cannot be instances of real love. If not real, they must be the figments of the mystics' imagination – purposeless, self-reflexive play, religious self-titillation, 'spiritual auto-eroticism', mental masturbation. But that assumption – that there is only one way to love – is precisely what we hope to have challenged.

Conclusion

After reading The Unexpected Way one cannot help but wonder whether Paul's worldview permits him to see anything of value in Buddhism. Granted that a polemical work is not the place in which to celebrate the virtues of a tradition that one considers an adversary, the tradition that one has left behind in one's conversion. But I wonder what picture Paul would paint of Buddhism if the (now hopefully more moderate) Pope Benedict were to commission Paul to write a follow-up volume entitled something like, 'What I learned in my years as a Buddhist'. Is there anything at all that a Christian might learn from Buddhism? If so, what might that be?

I was both intrigued and moved by Paul's discussion of the fate of his wife Sharon, who is not Catholic. (87-89) Paul's conversion to Catholicism raises for him the very real question of his and Sharon's respective destinies after death, and more specifically, of whether Paul can ever hope to be united with Sharon in the afterlife. He comes to the conclusion that when one partner in a marriage is Catholic and the other is not, 'they shall not be parted. They will be together throughout all eternity'. (88) If God saves the Catholic spouse, then because of the bond of love between the two spouses, 'it must follow that the (non-Catholic) partner is also saved'. Paul then asks:

> And what of others with whom we have a real relationship of mutual love? Is it possible that through love we can perhaps redeem others too, not just our marriage partners? Maybe that is one aspect of the real significance of love. (88)

This suggests to me at least the starting point for a conversation between Paul's brand of Christianity and my brand of Mahāyāna Buddhism. If what Paul says is true – that 'it is love that is truly redemptive' – then Christians have an awesome burden on their shoulders, for in their hands lies the fate of those whom they love and of those with whom they have cultivated loving relationships. This burden is in fact *greater* than that found in Mahāyāna Buddhism, for if what Paul says is true, then Christians have the ability to save others *simply* by cultivating mutual loving relationships with them.

The salvation of all is clearly something that God must wish. If Christians have the power to bring about the salvation of others through their love, then clearly it is incumbent upon them to do so. But despite the awesomeness of this burden, this puts Christians in a position not unlike the one that Mahāyāna Buddhists find themselves in, for, regardless of deep and real underlying differences, the followers of each tradition believe (a) that one's love for others is essential – for Buddhists necessary, for Christians sufficient – to others' salvation, (b) that it is possible to create this bond of love with others, the type of bond that will bring about their salvation, and (c) that it is morally incumbent upon one to do so. If I am right in all of this, it means that even if Buddhists and Christians may have different motivations for loving others, and even if they have different notions of salvation, they nonetheless are embarked on a similar journey – the journey of saving the world through love.

This truth provides us – Buddhists and Christians, each in our own way – with a deep metaphysical reason for engaging in dialogue. For if mutual respect and understanding are preconditions for love, then we are here laying the foundations not only for a better world in the here and now, but for love itself, and therefore for our mutual, interdependent salvation.

PAUL WILLIAMS

Buddhism, God, Aquinas and Morality: An Only Partially Repentant Reply to Perry Schmidt-Leukel and José Cabezón

I am indeed grateful to Perry Schmidt-Leukel and José Cabezón for the attention that they have given to my reflections on the relationships between Buddhism and Christianity in my conversion tale, *The Unexpected Way* and also, in the case of Perry, in a number of my other works as well. They have kindly offered me some space to respond.

1. Perry Schmidt-Leukel

a. Perry and Buddhist 'atheism'

Perry objects to my argument that on the issue of God the Buddhist and the Christian are radically opposed, so radically opposed that just as it is correct to use the term 'theist' of a Christian, the expression 'atheist' would be an appropriate term for a Buddhist. This *is* central to my book, and central to my conversion, for that there is a factual issue at stake here, and that the Christian and the Buddhist are radically opposed on this question such that what the one affirms the other negates is what forced for me the *choice*, the free choice, that was the culminating point of my conversion story. I could no longer be a Buddhist if I believed in God. Perry considers that the word 'atheist' is inappropriate for Buddhism. He prefers, perhaps, 'non-theist', although his exact grounds for this distinction escape me. And while Perry grants that there may be Buddhists (Asian or Western) who are happy to agree that they *are* atheists, he considers they are not true to Buddhist doctrinal history but are rather Buddhist modernists, influenced by Western Orientalism. I note that Perry considers that this is exactly what I was when I was a Buddhist. The fact that as a Buddhist (for over twenty years in the dGe lugs pa tradition of Tibetan Buddhism), in common with so many Western Buddhists, I considered Buddhism to be indeed a form of atheism and was proud of it, holding this to be a distinct advance on theism, which I thought was rather intellectually naïve, Perry seems to take as indicating that I was no Buddhist in a traditional sense, but a Buddhist modernist tainted by Orientalism, perhaps because he seems to think (falsely) that I learned all my Buddhism from textbooks. When, as a Buddhist engaged in Christian-Buddhist dialogue, I tried to explain to Christians who seemed uncomprehending that we Buddhists did not believe in God – that one of the great glories of Buddhism is that here we have a religion which does not need to believe in God, and certainly not the creator God of classical Abrahamic theism – according to Perry I was not fairly representing Buddhist doctrinal history.

Be that as it may, I have argued, and shall argue, that it is wrong to think that the denial of God is not a traditional part of Buddhism. I mean 'God' here in the sense in which the Christian creeds, Christian orthodoxy and, I have to say, the Bible, or Thomas Aquinas, as well as the *Catechism of the Catholic Church*, hold God to exist – indeed alone to have existence in the fullest sense of the word. The Buddhist position is straightforwardly atheist, and Buddhists who are proud of that fact are in no way infected by Orientalism or lacking an understanding of their own religion. I can comprehend their denial, and indeed sympathise with their reasons for it. I respect and admire their pride in that denial. But, although I did, I no longer hold it myself. I believe they are factually wrong, although as Perry notes I am an epistemological fallibilist. That I believe them to be wrong does not entail that I know them to be wrong. I could very easily be quite wrong myself.

Perry states that he 'strongly holds that it is misleading to call Buddhism a form of Atheism. Buddhism is certainly non-theistic but to call it "atheistic" would easily associate it with either the Eastern materialism or naturalism of the Cārvāka-s or with the materialism and naturalism of Western Atheists as we find it since roughly the eighteenth century'. This, it seems to me, is irrelevant. That Buddhism, as a spiritual path to liberation, Buddhahood, or whatever, is not atheism in the sense that Cārvāka is atheism, or in the sense that post-eighteenth century materialists are atheists does not mean that it is not atheism. There are different reasons and contexts for denying God. In ancient India there were many atheistic systems. Jainism, at least in its earliest form, was atheistic as were classical Sāṃkhya and Mīmāṃsā, and yet all these systems taught forms of spiritual liberation. Atheism was a common framework for soteriological paths at the time of the Buddha that grew up earlier than or contemporaneous with the very earliest phases of Indian theistic systems like Vaiṣṇavism and Śaivism.[1] And Perry perhaps misrepresents me when he says that I deny that 'Buddhists too (qua Buddhists) attain true peace'. What I actually say, in a paper on Thomas Aquinas's hypothetical response to Buddhism, is that 'it is not possible to argue in Thomist terms [that is, Thomas, would not hold] that Buddhists too (qua Buddhists) attain true peace' (Williams 2004: 112). And while I do hold that Buddhism in certain central respects is objectively false – I do hold to the existence of God in a sense that I argue it is denied by Buddhists – to link this with the word 'unwholesome' in the way Perry does is again not quite fair. I think that in many ways Buddhism is (or can be) extremely wholesome. Something can be in some respects objectively false and in many other respects wholesome. I do not look back on my time as a Buddhist as a time in which I wallowed in unwholesomeness. I look back on that time with great affection. There was in it, I think – I hope – a great deal that was eminently wholesome. My position is here much more nuanced than Perry suggests. And on all of this I think I simply hold to the position of the Catholic Church, which states that it recognises 'all goodness and truth found' in other religions as preparations for the Gospel, while at the same time also observing that there are 'limits and errors' in them. And the Church teaches that followers of other religions, including Buddhism, 'who, through no fault of their own, do not know the Gospel of Christ or his Church, but who nevertheless seek God with a sincere heart . . . too may achieve

---

[1] It is not clear whether the materialism of the time of the Buddha (the position of Ajita Kesakambalī; see Williams 2000: 19) can be identified in any straightforward sense with the later Indian system known as Cārvāka or Lokāyata. Even if there is a linear connection between that materialism and Cārvāka, it is not legitimate to associate full-blown developed Cārvāka doctrines from later centuries with the age of the Buddha (see here Thomas 1951: 73, who points out that all our sources for Cārvāka as a school are from much later than the time of the Buddha and early Buddhism). That would certainly include specifically Cārvāka atheism. There is no mention of atheism in our early Buddhist sources for Ajita Kesakambalī.

eternal salvation' (Holy See, *Catechism* paras. 843-849). I make it
clear in my *Unexpected Way* (2002: 98), and I want to reiterate it here,
that I think, hope and pray that there are Buddhists who have been and
will be saved – saved in the recognisably Christian sense of 'salvation', for I do not hold that there is any abstract sense of 'salvation' that
is not tagged to the existence of a historical soteriology.[2]

b. Buddhism and the 'transcendent reality'

Perry seems to think that I deny that in Buddhism there can be 'a
transcendent reality'. I have looked back at the section of my *Unexpected Way*, which Perry cites, in support of my supposed denial of a
transcendent reality in this sense. I do not there ever use the word
'transcendent reality', nor am I referring to Perry's Buddhist equivalent, *lokottara*. Perry's reasoning seems to be as follows:

a) I state that Buddhism accepts the existence of *devas*, gods (like In-
   dra, or Brahma). He is correct in adding, although I do not myself
   do so, that for Buddhism *devas* are worldly (*laukika*), and not 'supramundane' (*lokottara*).
b) Perry then takes my statement (2002: 25) that notwithstanding their
   acceptance of worldly gods, '[i]n ancient times Buddhists were quite clear that they denied the existence of a personal creator God as
   taught in rival theistic systems' as entailing that since I assert Buddhists hold devas to be worldly, *laukika*, I must therefore be arguing (he will urge, wrongly) that Buddhists denied the existence
   of the *lokottara*. But this cannot be derived from what I say.
c) Perry is right to think that Buddhism does not at all deny the existence of the *lokottara*, indeed a *lokottara* reality such as *nirvāṇa*,
   since *nirvāṇa* is itself a *dharma* ('phenomenon') and *dharmas* are
   considered in mainstream Buddhism to be fundamental reals.[3] I did

---

[2] I agree here totally with Pope Benedict XVI: 'The Christian can certainly recognize
tentative attempts in the religious images of the world religions that move in the direction of Christianity. He can also find a secret working of God behind them; through the
other religions God touches man and brings him onto the path. But it is always the same
God, the God of Jesus Christ' (Ratzinger 1997: 259).
[3] Though not, note, in systems like Madhyamaka. Hence major systems of Buddhism
would deny that even *nirvāṇa* could be a 'transcendent reality' if it meant something
enjoying the plenum of reality. Since this is precisely what God is supposed to be, fully
real, real in the fullest possible sense, *per se* necessary reality, Madhyamaka Buddhism

not say it did. What I said was that Buddhists were quite clear that they denied the existence of a personal creator God as taught in rival theistic systems. Perry has drawn from what I said something quite false, something indeed quite other than what I think and hold.

I simply do not consider that pointing to the existence of *nirvāṇa* as a *lokottaradharma* is in any way relevant in discussing the question of whether Buddhists accept the existence of God or not. It is simply false to think that because two things (God and *nirvāṇa*) have on a broad reading one characteristic in common (or even two, three or more) – here they are both *lokottara*, 'supramundane' – it follows they are therefore the same thing or even significantly the same type of thing. If a child asks for an orange and she is given an orange football on the basis they are both round – or indeed on the basis they are both round and orange, or round, orange and tactile, or round, orange, tactile and have a smell – she has still been given quite a different thing, and that (I am afraid) is a matter of factual difference.

And *of course* I hold that *nirvāṇa* is also directly relevant in Buddhism to our salvation, in fact as its 'cognitive-object support' (Sanskrit: *ālambanapratyaya*). Perry has derived from my statement (quoted) that 'a God that is not necessary to spiritual fulfilment is not God as taught by Christianity' the conclusion that if in Buddhism *X* is a transcendent reality and is also necessary to our spiritual fulfilment then I am wrong in contrasting Buddhism and Christianity here, and therefore wrong in saying that Buddhism denies God as understood in Christianity. Perry appears to want to infer from my statement that 'a God that is not necessary to spiritual fulfilment is not God as taught by Christianity' that 'if *X is* necessary to our spiritual fulfilment it *is* (plausibly, or at least potentially) God as taught by Christianity'. But if that is what Perry wants to infer then it is simply fallacious. One cannot derive from 'If not-X then not-Y' the conclusion 'If X then Y'. Moreover Perry has ignored the context of my quoted passage. I started by noting that 'it is not difficult to find in Buddhist texts attacks on the existence of an omniscient, omnipotent, all-good Creator of the universe'. I added that there are some who say Buddhism is neverthe-

at least would be ruled out of this aspect of Perry's defence of Buddhism as not atheistic.

less not atheist but agnostic in this respect. They say (Williams 2002: 25):

> Buddhism does not pronounce on whether God exists or not. Buddhists do not claim to know. God is irrelevant to the Buddhist project of (broadly speaking) final freedom from all types of suffering, through the attainment of nirvāṇa, liberation, or enlightenment. Enlightenment is attained through following oneself a set path of morality, meditation, and wisdom. It does not require any help from divine intervention, or any reference to a God.

And immediately preceding the passage Perry himself quotes I state in response:

> Any God as He is understood in a religion like Christianity could not be irrelevant to the path to final spiritual fulfilment. No God as understood by Christians could be irrelevant to final fulfilment. If Buddhism does not teach this God, it either does not teach the path to final fulfilment or it considers that it is not necessary to the path to teach such a God.

I hope it is clear that in spite of what Perry says I am not at all trying to say that in Buddhism *nirvāṇa* as the cognitive-object support of the spiritual path, indeed the cognitive-object support that is also a 'transcendent reality', is not (in Perry's words) 'immediately relevant in our salvation'. What I am saying is that the 'agnostic strategy' will not work with the God of Christian orthodoxy. Buddhism is not agnostic on *that* God, Buddhism is atheist on that God.

Perry states that for me 'the main emphasis lies with the first aspect of the supposed atheism, that is, the purported irrelevance of God as a precondition of our salvation'. He is wrong. He has drawn from what I said, in the specific context of a strategy of appealing to 'Buddhist agnosticism' rather than atheism, a general conclusion he thinks I want to make about Buddhism, that of the irrelevance of God in Buddhism to salvation. He then continues by showing that *nirvāṇa* is directly relevant, indeed a condition, of our salvation and hence considers that he has countered my 'main emphasis'. Let me repeat: What Perry sees as my main emphasis is so far from being my main emphasis that I did not even know I was making it. And I was talking specifically about 'God as He is understood in a religion like Christianity', 'an omniscient, omnipotent, all-good Creator of the universe'. To point to *nirvāṇa* as the cognitive-object support of enlightenment – in other words to point out that if there were no *nirvāṇa* it would not be possible to have an enlightenment-experience (because in these Abhidharma contexts if X is a cognitive object it is thereby a condition of its own cognition, and if X can be a cognitive object then X must exist, and hence *nirvāṇa* must exist as a condition, although emphatically not an instrumental cause, of its own cognition) – is utterly irrelevant to my argument for Buddhism as a form of atheism.

c. Does Buddhism deny a creator God? – Some Thomist reflections

I want now to move to an issue that I consider to be far more central to my case for Buddhist atheism, the critique offered throughout Buddhist literature of a creator God. I have recently published a more detailed paper on precisely this topic (Williams 2004). I want here to outline my argument in that paper, and make some comments on Perry's response in his current work to the issues I think it raises. Much more detail, and supporting textual references, can be found in my published paper.

a) I hold to the existence of God in the sense that Thomas Aquinas does. Buddhists, I contend, deny the very possibility of God in that sense. For Aquinas God is, *inter alia*, the source of all things and that to which they aim as their teleological end, their fulfilment (*principium rerum et finis earum*). For this reason God is said to be both the *alpha* and the *omega*, the beginning and the end. And Aquinas considers that we can show plausibly that God exists precisely through arguing back from the existence of things, all things, to their need for a creator. Thus God is for Aquinas creator, and He is the creator in the sense that He answers the question 'Why is there something rather than nothing?'. This question would stand even if there were no beginning. It applies at each and every point in time (I shall return to this topic below).

b) Hence if Buddhists refute the possibility of a creator then they refute the possibility of God understood as creator and thereby in the sense of Christian orthodoxy, the creeds, and the *Catechism*.[4] Other issues to do with what God might be are irrelevant. And Buddhists do refute the possibility of a creator, repeatedly. In my paper I go into detail on one such refutation, that by Śāntideva in his *Bodhicaryāvatāra*. Perry considers that such refutations of God from the specifically Madhyamaka tradition of Buddhism are irrelevant here, since they only occur in the context of what is there called 'ultimate analysis', in which case all causes including everyday causes are also refuted. But in this Perry is really quite wrong. If that were true it would follow that Madhyamaka texts are not denying God as conventionally existent, as the conventional creator (perhaps as the Hindu Śaṃkara holds *saguṇa brahman* to exist as the conventional but ultimately illusory (*māyā*) creator of the world), but only saying that God does not exist ultimately. This is wrong not just because in that case their arguments would not serve as a refutation of God (*Maheśvara*) understood in the sense it is by someone like Śaṃkara, but also because Madhyamaka texts themselves distinguish between things that can exist conventionally, but are not found under ultimate analysis, and things that if they are to exist at all can only exist ultimately and therefore if they are not found under ultimate analysis they are complete fictions. God, like the Self (*ātman*), is an example of the second. I deal with this in my paper. It makes no sense in Madhyamaka terms to say that God, the creator of everything, exists but not *sasvabhāva*, i.e. intrinsically. If a thing is of the type that could exist only intrinsically then its refutation in ultimate analysis entails its lacking existence *even conventionally*. This is because it is agreed on all sides that it simply could not exist merely conventionally. A conventionally existing God needed to create all things is simply not accepted in Buddhist tradition. In other words the Buddhists are correct here in stating that if God existed God would have to exist with the absolute plenum of existence. That is what God for a theist is, a most really real thing.[5] This is part of what we mean in Christian philosophy when we spe-

---

[4] The *Catechism of the Catholic Church* points out (para. 290) that in the Hebrew Bible the verb 'create' (*bara*) always has God as its subject. God does not create necessarily – it is a free act of generosity on His part. But God is, at least for us, essentially creator. This is important, for Perry is going to adopt a position that entails that God for Aquinas is simply not a creator at all.

[5] Ignoring here any philosophical or theological problem with the word 'thing' as attributed to God.

ak of God as a 'necessary existent'. In Madhyamaka terms that is existing inherently or intrinsically (*sasvabhāva*), in theistic and hence Thomist terms it is existing as a *per se* necessary being. Perry is saying that Madhyamaka does not refute the (conventional) existence of God as a creator, but only God as a *per se* necessary being who is a creator. That is simply wrong as an interpretation of Madhyamaka, and Perry gives no grounds to support it. Any God who is the answer to the question why is there something rather than nothing could only be a *per se* necessary being. Thomas holds that, and effectively the Buddhist holds that too. On such points Buddhists and Thomas are in agreement. So in my detailed use of Śāntideva I am right in holding that it is God as a creator that is being refuted.

c) God is defined by Śāntideva as pure, worthy to be worshipped, permanent, one only, and creator of everything. This characterisation (as far as it goes) would be perfectly acceptable to Thomas and Christian orthodoxy. It is this being that Śāntideva argues simply cannot exist, period. Madhyamaka texts, but many other Buddhist texts too, refute God as creator by showing that an eternal being cannot exert causal efficacy. An eternal cause could not exert causal efficacy, or if it did its effect would be eternal too. Hence everything in the world would have to be eternal. Now it is true, as Perry points out, that there are some Buddhist traditions such as Theravāda and Sarvāstivāda that would hold that a permanent reality, *nirvāṇa*, could act as a condition, the cognitive-object support of attaining enlightenment. But first this is a view that is by no means held by all Buddhists. It would not be held by Sautrāntika-s, or by Mādhyamika-s. Nor would Dharmakīrti, who is by far the most influential Buddhist philosopher in these discussions of God and causation, hold it. Dharmakīrti considers that to be (*astitva*) is to exert causal efficacy (*arthakriyāsāmarthya*), and causal efficacy can only be exerted by a momentary, and definitely not by a permanent, being (see, for example, Dreyfus 1997: 65-7). But either way, to be a cognitive-object support is simply to act as a condition of cognition. It could not possibly be to exert the efficient causal activity required for creating the actual existence of everything.[6] A cognitive-object support requires the occurrence of co-operating

---

[6] In Sarvāstivāda Buddhist terms to be an *ālambanapratyaya* is not to be an *adhipatipratyaya*, that is, a *kāraṇahetu*.

causes and conditions to bring about a result. The answer to the question 'Why is there something rather than nothing?' has to be an efficient cause, not a cognitive-object support, since a cognitive-object support requires that there are other co-operating causes and conditions already in existence. Thus I want to argue that when Buddhists refute the existence of a creator of everything, considering it to be incoherent and unnecessary, they are refuting the existence of God as an efficient cause and as such God as understood by Thomas Aquinas and also by the vast majority of the Christian tradition.

d. The creative function of God, for Aquinas, is not only that of teleological, or final, cause

But strangely, and radically, Perry seems to think that for Aquinas God is only the teleological aim of creation, what in Aristotelian terms would be called not the efficient cause but the final cause. This is indeed quite astonishing, since Thomas refers to God as both the source of all things *and* their end (e.g. *S. Th.* 1a 2, preamble; 1a 45, 1; 1a 93, 4 ad 1), the alpha *and* the omega.[7] For Thomas the very expression 'creation' is used to refer to God as creator. That is, God is *inter alia* the efficient cause of all things. Aquinas speaks of 'the emanation of all being from the universal cause, which is God; and this emanation we designate by the name of *creation*'.[8] Moreover to say that God as creator is not the efficient cause but only the final cause of all things would not only be quite literally a contradiction for Thomas, it would also be wildly out of line with Christian orthodoxy which maintains that 'in the beginning God created heaven and earth' (not to mention all commentators on Aquinas both mediaeval and modern). While some of Thomas's propositions were indeed initially condemned (later reversed) in 1277 after his death, it is never suggested that Thomas

---

[7] On God as *alpha* and *omega* in Aquinas see e.g. Torrell 2003: 53-8. This, Torrell points out, is in many ways the very basis of Thomas's theology and the very structure of the *Summa Theologiae*. It is the model, in a way Platonic, of creation as coming from God and through the activity of the Trinity returning to God.

[8] *Summa Theologiae* 1a 45, 1, in Pegis (1945) vol. 1: 433. Thomas is using 'emanation' in a technical sense that can be taken here as simply indicating that from which things come. It should not be associated with some Hindu or Buddhist ideas of emanation as transformation (i.e. *pariṇāmavāda*), so that God becomes literally the material cause of the universe.

held such an astonishingly heretical view that God was not the efficient cause of all things. Also, Thomas holds that it is from the need for an efficient cause that one can argue back to God as creator, and God as creator is a *prerequisite* for God to be a teleological goal. Finally, Thomas actually says at the conclusion of his second *via* to God in *Summa Theologiae* 1a 2, 3, an argument he says is based on 'the nature of an efficient cause' (*secunda via est ex ratione causae efficientis*): 'Hence it is necessary to posit some first efficient cause, to which everyone gives the name "God"' (*ergo necesse est ponere aliquam causam efficientem primam, quam omnes Deum nominant*). Many, many more examples could be given, but this ought to be enough. Thus it is quite wrong to think that Buddhist arguments against the existence of God as the actual efficient cause of things do not touch Thomas Aquinas's God since Thomas holds that God is not the efficient cause of the universe but only its final cause, its teleological goal.

What are Perry's grounds for thinking that Thomas holds a view that he patently does not and cannot hold? The first seems to be that Thomas does not hold creation to be an act in time. And there he is quite correct, for Thomas does not (see, for example, his *Quaestiones Disputatae de Potentia*, translated in McDermott 1998: 263-70). Thomas holds that there is no contradiction in thinking that God can cause the universe and all events in it timelessly. It is for this reason that I think the Buddhist causal arguments against God do not touch Thomas's position. Having said this, Buddhists would simply consider that to be an efficient cause of anything, let alone each individual thing, actually acting couldn't entail that the efficient cause is outside time. In other words, Buddhist thinkers would simply deny that there could be a creation by an eternal cause, God, which is outside time. And they may well be right, but that is a different point. Perry seems to infer from Thomas's denial that creation by God is an event in time that *this* is why Thomas holds that the world could also be everlasting, without beginning or end. He hence concludes that since Thomas holds that the world could be eternal in time he cannot be referring to God as the first cause in time who started everything off. Thus Thomas cannot hold that God is an efficient cause at all, but only the final cause.

So, according to Perry Thomas holds that the dependence of the universe on God:

is, according to Aquinas, not the sort of dependence that we
find within the chain of chronological events which are linked through efficient causal connection. God is not the cause of the world in that way, in which innerworldly efficient
causes function.

Perry is here quite right. God for Thomas is indeed not an efficient
cause in the sense of 'innerworldly' chronological events that are linked through efficient causal connection. But Perry seems to think that
for Thomas God is therefore not an efficient cause at all. God is the
cause (presumably of the universe):

in the sense of Aristotle's idea of the unmoved mover, that
is as the ultimate goal of the world, God as its teleological
cause (*causa finalis*). Everything exists – even if it would
exist without beginning in time – because it is ordered towards God. To call God 'creator' is in a sense subservient
to calling God the final goal and highest good of the world.

But in saying this Perry is simply wrong. For Thomas, God as the unmoved mover is not at all the same in meaning as 'the ultimate goal of
the world'. Aristotle's unmoved mover is indeed God, and is hence
the teleological goal of our striving. But at least for Aquinas He is not
the teleological goal of our striving *qua* unmoved mover.[9] *Qua* unmo-

---

[9] Aristotle is indeed very unclear about the causal status of God, the Unmoved Mover,
although it is at least plausible that he thinks of God's causal function solely in terms of
being a final cause. If so, this is certainly bound up with Aristotle's thinking that, since
the universe does not need a beginning to start it all off, he should not refer to God in
that way but rather as that which draws all movement towards Himself. But this would
not at all apply to Thomas, who as a Christian is quite aware that God has to be more
than simply the final cause since God as creator has to be responsible for the actual
existence ex nihilo of the world and not just for its teleological direction. God is the
alpha and the *omega*, and Aquinas knows perfectly well that 'in the beginning God
created the heavens and the earth' (even if 'beginning' here is not to be understood in
time). As we shall see, for Thomas God would be the creator, responsible for the existence of something rather than nothing, *even if the universe were, with Aristotle, eternal* (although Thomas does not think it actually is so). It is not clear whether Aquinas's
use of the 'unmoved mover' argument in the first of his five *via*-s is an argument that
eventually moves from God as efficient cause to God as final cause, partly precisely
because of the unclarity of Aristotle on this point. But in his authoritative study Wippel
(2000: 458) argues for it, too, remaining in the *Summa Theologiae* at the level of God as
efficient cause. Either way, Aquinas also has other arguments to God that clearly are not
arguments to God simply as the final cause. Moreover Aquinas is quite explicit at *S.Th.*
1a 105, 5 ad 3 that when we speak of God as not just the cause of the universe but also

ved mover God is creator of all things inasmuch as He is creator of all change from potency to act. Aquinas makes this quite clear by his specific use of the idea of the unmoved mover in the first of his five *via*-s. That God is the teleological goal of our striving *qua* unmoved mover might be Perry's view of God, but as we have seen it is not that of Aquinas. Perry devotes some space to demonstrating his broad agreement with Buddhist objections (such as moral objections) to the existence of God as creator, as efficient cause. And of course morality is still, as Buddhists argue and Perry has shown, apparently perfectly compatible with such a denial. I am sure Perry himself finds these arguments plausible, perhaps convincing. But they would not be plausible to, let alone accepted by, Thomas, or to the history of orthodox Christian philosophy. That Perry might himself hold that God (perhaps understood solely as a transcendent reality that acts as the cognitive-object support for particular types of liberating experience) cannot be creator, but only the teleological end of our spiritual striving – our *omega*-point if not our *alpha* – I can grant. Perhaps he does. But it is emphatically not the view of Aquinas, the Bible, the creeds, Christian orthodoxy or the Catholic *Catechism*.

Aquinas discusses the Aristotelian view that the universe is simply eternal (a view also held by Buddhists) a number of times, notably in his late (1271) work *De aeternitate mundi*. There he states quite categorically that he is (McInerny 1998: 711):

> in agreement with the Catholic faith, and contrary to what some philosophers [such as Aristotle] mistakenly have thought, that the world has not existed eternally, and that its duration has a beginning, as Holy Scripture which cannot deceive attests.

Thomas's point, however, (in disagreement with many others, including his Franciscan friend St Bonaventure) is that this cannot be shown conclusively by reasoning. Reasoning cannot *prove* that the world had a beginning. There is no contradiction in the world not having a beginning. But, and this is crucial, since Thomas holds that it can be shown through reasoning that God exists, the existence of God

---

as the cause of each act of an agent we are using 'cause' with reference to all four senses of 'cause' and not just with reference to God as the final cause, the ultimate teleological goal, of each act of an agent.

cannot be incompatible with the logical possibility that the world is eternal. As we have seen, Aquinas thinks that God can be indeed plausibly shown to be the efficient cause of the universe, since in the case of God Thomas thinks He is a *sui generis* type of efficient cause. Hence for Thomas being an efficient cause of each and every thing is perfectly compatible with the universe being eternal (see also *Summa Theologiae* 1a. 104, 1, and Davies 1992: 35). God, for Thomas, as the answer to the question 'Why is there something rather than nothing?' would be the answer to this question at each and every moment, and such would be the case even if the world were eternal (which Thomas thinks we know firmly – but only on the basis of faith – it is not). If everything exists simply as ordered towards God only as its final cause, then God would precisely *not* be the *creator*, that on which the very existence of things depends. This is because in order for things to exist as ordered towards their goal they *first of all have to exist*, full stop. And it is the very existence of things full stop, their radical contingency, which for Thomas suggests the need for a necessarily existent cause, a creator. If I may quote the distinguished Dominican Thomist M.-D. Chenu (2002: 87), for Thomas (italics original):

> when creation came about, at the heart of the being that it receives from God is placed an ontological link – a pure relation where the poverty of the created one is expressed – and the creature is thus bound to God even as it is set forth in existence. To be created is first of all to *be*: the being is of one who is dependent, always linked to its source of being, but whose dependence only has significance because it is something that *is*. This fact has real priority in the order of being: what is created *is* by reason of its relation to its creator.

Perry's interpretation precisely rests on denying that Thomas holds that God is actually the creator. This is because for Thomas to be creator is indeed to be the efficient cause, the *alpha*, as well as the *omega*, the final cause. It rests on denying this ontological link, this eternal dependence of creation on the creator. It hence rests on denying *inter alia* the radical gratitude that flows from realising that one owes God *absolutely everything*. That is wrong for Thomas, but also, if that is what Buddhists hold – that there is no God as creator in that sense (and hence we do not need to show God any gratitude for our being, any worship, any thanks) – then my point is established. I too think that Buddhists hold that there is no God as creator. Perry also seems to think that there is no God as creator, and he thinks Aquinas would agree with him. Aquinas would of course be horrified. Thomas certainly thinks that God exists as creator. So do Christian orthodoxy, the Bible, the creeds, and the *Catechism*. In denying that God exists as creator the Buddhists deny God, at least a creator God, and are thus atheist. And, let me emphasise again, as far as I know Buddhists traditionally have always been happy to accept that.

e. Thomas does indeed think that words can be applied literally to God

Now for another point, still related, I am afraid, to the understanding of Aquinas and hence, I argue, of Christian orthodoxy, the Bible, the creeds, and the Catholic *Catechism*. Perry considers that for Thomism no concepts or words can be applied literally to God. This is often stated of Aquinas, usually backed up with one or two quotations taken out of context, and used to base a framework for some sort of argument that God as described in Aquinas *et al.* should be taken merely as a useful, perhaps pragmatic, descriptive tool but not intended to be actually, factually, true and certainly not to be urged against religions like Buddhism that prefer not to use such language. But again, while that may turn out to be true, as an interpretation of Aquinas it is quite wrong, and demonstrably so.

Aquinas talks of God and language at numerous points in his writings (see for example Wippel 2000: chapter 13). Perry cites a fragment from *De potentia*: 'The utmost of human knowledge of God is to know that we cannot know God' (*illud est ultimum cognitionis humanae de deo quod sciat se deum nescire*). Perry holds that for Aquinas no words and concepts apply to God literally, they 'are useful analogies that bring us into the right existential disposition when we approach the holy mystery'. This may be Perry's own view of language about God, but as an interpretation of Thomas it is far too heavy a burden to be borne by such a poor little quotation from *De potentia*. I shall return to it soon.

In *Summa Theologiae* 1a. 13, 3 Thomas asks 'whether anything can be said of God literally' (*utrum aliquod nomen dicatur de Deo proprie*)? Of course this is quite simply what Perry says Thomas holds

cannot be done. But Thomas says that it can. He explains that some
words are used of God metaphorically, words like 'rock'. But there
are other words that refer to certain perfections, like 'being', 'good',
'living' and so on. These words can indeed be applied to God literally
(*op. cit.*, ad 1). Thus to say God exists, to say God is good and so on
are to make statements that for Thomas are *literally* true of God. They
are not intended metaphorically. Nor for Thomas are they intended as
useful analogies to bring one into the right existential disposition towards the holy mystery. I assume that in referring to 'analogies' Perry
is thinking here of Thomas's view that language used of God is used
analogically. Well first, *pace* Perry, for Thomas language used analogically of God is nevertheless language used literally of God. And
Thomas does not mean by *analogia* what we mean in everyday English by 'analogy', certainly not simply Perry's 'useful analogies' (see
Summa Theologiae 1a. 13, 5). What Thomas means is that when we
use words quite literally of God, such as 'God is good', we are not
using the word 'good' in a univocal sense with other everyday uses, in
exactly the same sense. God is not good in exactly the same sense that
a medicine is good. But equally we are not using words in an equivo-
cal sense, such that words about God have literally nothing in common with their everyday senses save their phonic shape. It is not like
'bat' in a flying mammal and a part of cricketing equipment. There
has to be a third use of language when it is used, nevertheless quite
literally, of God. Thomas adds that when we say God is good, or wise,
we are referring to perfections which in the order of reality are not
only applied literally to God but are used *primarily* of God, and only
derivatively of creatures (*S. Th.* 1a. 13, 7).[10] Thus, to quote the relevant definition of the analogical use of language from a recent manual
on Thomas's philosophy (Pasnau and Shields 2004: 116; italics original):

A and b are analogically F = df (i) a is F; (ii) b is F; (iii) a
and b are literally F; and (iv) a and b are neither univocally
nor equivocally F.

---

[10] Although that is not the case in the sense of our order now of using these terms, we
might say it is in our order of learning their meaning. Discussions of the analogical use
of language in Aquinas can be found in any of the standard introductions to Aquinas's
philosophy, such as Davies 1992: chapter 4.

Hence Thomas does hold that language can be used literally of God, albeit analogically. And speaking analogically of God is a perfectly proper way, indeed necessarily the only possible way, of speaking literally of God. Let me repeat: it is not simply a matter of 'useful analogies'. From Thomas, and also from other works of orthodox Christian theology, we can find many expressions that Thomas would hold can be applied literally, although of course, analogically, to God. Thus we can say that God is literally the creator, active, desirable, eternal, omnipotent, omniscient, omnipresent, good, immaterial, perfect, unchanging, just, merciful, loving, the ultimate end, was incarnate in Christ, is trinitarian, is simple, His being is His essence, and so on, and so on. Let me note in passing that the trinitarian nature of God is not for Thomas incidental and disposable. Trinitarian is actually what God is, from all eternity, timelessly, in the Holy Spirit, the mutual love of Father and Son. But Thomas does not consider that reasoning can show God is trinitarian. Philosophers bereft of the Revelation that comes through faith will only ever come to a bloodless God that simply exists, but never discover that God actually is the infinite richness of the Trinity. Reasoning can show plausibly that God exists, and what must, and what cannot, follow from that. But it cannot reveal the actual nature of God, which is that God is trinitarian. We know this from Revelation, not as simply some sort of analogy in order to orient our minds (see *S. Th.* 1a. 32, 1; for a survey see e.g. Davies 1992: chapter 10). God really is trinitarian. And from the Trinity, Thomas thinks, springs the whole of Christianity as a religion. In Buddhism *nirvāṇa*, or indeed the *dharmakāya*, are not trinitarian in the Christian theological sense.[11] As such they simply could not be, and never could be, for Thomas God. And if they are not God they are completely, radically, utterly other than God, for all that is not God is other than God and to take that which is not God as God is quite simply idolatry.

---

[11] The *trikāya* ('three bodies [of the Buddha]') in some traditions of Mahāyāna Buddhism is irrelevant. For its details see Williams 1989: chapter 8. To take just one example in passing: even on a charitable interpretation of similarities between the Trinity and the *trikāya*, since the Son and the Incarnation are not the same it follows that one could not equate the multifarious transformation bodies of the Buddha in Mahāyāna Buddhism with the Son. Moreover for Thomas and Christian orthodoxy trinitarian is the very nature of God. This means that God is timelessly trinitarian, 'throughout all eternity'. The trinitarian nature of God is the very nature of 'ultimate reality', the necessary Being that is God. If there were nothing in existence, God would still be trinitarian. None of this could be said of the enjoyment bodies or the transformation bodies in the *trikāya* theory. It is as if, in *trikāya* terms, one were saying the *dharmakāya* (or, for some systems, specifically the essence body, the *svabhāvikakāya*) is trinitarian.

Seen from our side their concepts may have some features in common with that of God. They may be intimations of God. They may be preparations for the Faith. They may even be the witness to God where God is otherwise absent. But for Thomas, and indeed for orthodox Catholic Christian tradition, not to mention the other Abrahamic religions, to take that which is not God as God is idolatry. To say that God, the living trinitarian God, is finally unnecessary and something else can be taken as the *summum bonum* instead, or there is simply no difference between the two, would also be considered sheer idolatry. As I understand it, Buddhists for their part would deny that there is a single reality for which expressions like is *per se* necessary existence, creator of all, just, merciful, loving, the ultimate end, was incarnate in Christ, is trinitarian, is simple, His being is His essence, would be literally (even if analogically) true. To think there is would be an example of particularly vicious *avidyā*, ignorance, something that could not be true *even conventionally*, and could not lead to enlightenment. And I have absolutely no objection to Buddhists thinking that. That *is* after all (traditional) Buddhism, and I respect that they are Buddhists in the traditional Buddhist way. Indeed, respect for their being Buddhists in the way that Buddhists traditionally are Buddhists is the very prerequisite for meaningful dialogue with them. The same respect must be surely be shown by a Buddhist for a Christian who is to enter into meaningful dialogue with a Buddhist. The Christian is respected as being a Christian in the way that Christians are traditionally Christians.

For Thomas we can indeed plausibly infer that God exists, and is truly good, for example, from the goodness of His creation. But, and this is crucial, while it is true that God is (for example) good we cannot know what the term 'goodness' means when applied to God Himself. In other words, for Thomas, we cannot know in this life, or indeed perhaps ever fully, the quiddity of God, what God in Himself actually is. We know these expressions truly apply to Him literally, albeit analogically. But what they mean from His own side, as it were, is not known by us. This is because of the sort of 'being' God must be – or in an overwhelming sense what He cannot be – if He is to be who He is, the answer to the question 'Why is there something rather than nothing?'.

We know these expressions are literally true of God. They are not just a matter of 'existential orientation' but are actually true of Him. Those who deny them of God (including those who deny God's existence) are for Thomas actually, factually, wrong. But just because God, as the answer to the question 'Why is there something rather than nothing?', actually exists it follows that when we unpack what this answer must entail of God we discover that what these true expressions mean concerning Him in His own quiddity, His *quid est*, is something of which we have not the faintest idea.

Perry has taken his quotation from *De potentia* out of context. I want to quote from a standard modern translation of the whole passage (McInerny 1998: 316; my italics):

> It should be said that from the fact that our intellect is not equal to the divine substance, the substance of God exceeds our intellect and thus is not known by us [now comes the sentence quoted by Perry]; what is ultimate in human knowledge of God is that one knows that he does not know God, *because he knows that what God is exceeds everything that we can understand of him.*[12]

In other words Thomas is not saying that there is no literal language of God. That what God is exceeds everything that we can understand of Him does not entail that we can understand nothing literally of Him. Quite the reverse is the case. To say that God exceeds everything we can understand of Him is to say that we can indeed understand some things of Him. Moreover Thomas is referring here to the substance of God, in other words what God is in Himself, His quiddity, His *quid est*, as what is not known by us. It is realising that this is the case that is said by Thomas to be ultimate in the human knowledge of God. It is in this sense too that we have to understand Thomas's famous statement in *Summa Theologiae* 1a 2 that 'concerning God we are not able to know what He is but only what he is not' (*sed quia de Deo scire non possumus quid sit sed quid non sit*). As Anscombe and Geach pointed out many years ago, Aquinas is simply saying here that we do not have *quid est* knowledge of God: 'Aquinas is not saying that we cannot make true predications concerning God' (1961: 117; cf. also Davies 1992: 41). Thomas had already said earlier (McInerny 1998:

---

[12] *De potentia* 7, 5 ad 14: *(Ad decimumquartum dicendum) quod ex quo intellectus noster divinam substantiam non adaequat, hoc ipsum quod est Dei substantia remanet, nostrum intellectum excedens, et ita a nobis ignoratur: et propter hoc illud est ultimum cognitionis humanae de Deo quod sciat se Deum nescire, in quantum cognoscit, illud quod Deus est, omne ipsum quod de eo intelligimus, excedere.*

314) that 'when the intellect attributes . . . [appropriate] . . . names to
God . . . they signify the divine substance – not perfectly according as
it is, but rather imperfectly as it is understood by us. . . . each of these
names signifies the divine substance, but imperfectly, not as compre-
hending it . . .'.[13] As Thomas states in the *Summa Theologiae* (1a. 13,
6), as regards signifying what God is words referring to perfections
can be literally used of God. In terms of the way they signify, their
primary usage for us is with reference to our world and *in that sense*
they cannot be used with strict literalness of God. But in terms of what
God is, while they can be used literally – really, quite literally, and
truthfully – providing we are not misled by their ordinary worldly
meaning, we nevertheless cannot know what these expressions mean
of God Himself (i.e. *quid est*). We can say a great many true things of
God, but we simply have to say that these terms apply to God 'supera-
bundantly', or 'super eminently', and be aware that we do not now
know what they mean of God's own essence. As Thomas says in the
De potentia, we have to say truthfully and literally that God is wise,
for there is some likeness in Him to the wisdom that flows from Him
to creation.[14] In other words, God is the creator of wisdom, which is a
perfection, and therefore it must be true (literally true) to say of Him
too that He is wise. But wisdom could not be in God in any way that
we could really understand or indeed describe (say, scientifically, *per
genus et differentia*). Hence in this specific context we could also deny
wisdom of God. But we should not think that this entails literally denying wisdom of God, as if such language cannot be used literally and
truthfully of God, as Perry seems to think, but only orients us appropriately to the divine mystery.[15] For, Thomas says, '[w]isdom is not
denied of God because he falls short of it, but because it is in him mo-

---

[13] *De potentia* 7, 5 co.: *et ideo licet huiusmodi nomina, quae intellectus ex talibus con-
ceptionibus Deo attribuit, significent id quod est divina substantia, non tamen perfecte
ipsam significant secundum quod est, sed secundum quod a nobis intelligitur. . . . quod
quodlibet istorum nominum significat divinam substantiam, non tamen quasi compre-
hendens ipsam, sed imperfecte.*
[14] See, for example, McInerny 1998: 314-315, following in this respect the Pseudo-
Dionysius; see also Torrell 2003: chapter 2 esp. 40-42.
[15] How could it orient us appropriately if such language were not actually *true* of 'the
divine mystery'? Torrell 2003: 39 points out (following T.-D. Humbrecht) that for
Thomas, correctly, negative theology presupposes prior positive theology and cannot
eliminate the need for literal positive affirmation concerning God.

re super-eminently than it is said or understood, so we must say, "God is super-wise"".[16]

f. A final point

I concede that I am indeed open to criticism for speaking in too unqualified terms about 'the Buddhist', and 'the Christian'. There are Buddhist traditions, such as the *gzhan stong* ('other-empty') versions of *tathāgatagarbha* ('Buddha-nature') thought that are arguably somewhat closer to a Christian idea of God in some respects than other Buddhist traditions. Likewise I have to accept that there are many divergent views within Christianity. I thought it was obvious in my book that I was speaking from the point of view of mainstream orthodox Catholic Christianity. When I say Buddhism is atheistic I am speaking of God as found in the creeds, the Bible, Aquinas, Christian orthodoxy and the Catholic *Catechism*.[17] Perry's view is clearly different. It is of course always possible for someone so to define 'God' that any putative atheist group is no longer atheist. Thus it is never possible to show that any group is atheist against a sceptic who insists on urging otherwise. All one can do is locate theism within a particular tradition that gives the concept of 'God' meaning and say that from the point of view of that tradition a particular person or group is indeed atheist. I have argued that Buddhism is atheist from the point of view of Aquinas *et al.*, and it seems to me that Buddhists, certainly in India

---

[16] *De potentia* 7, 5 ad 2: *Rursum quia sapientia non negatur de Deo quia ipse deficiat a sapientia, sed quia supereminentius est in ipso quam dicatur aut intelligatur, ideo oportet dicere quod Deus sit supersapiens.* Or, to quote from that influential modern Thomist Herbert McCabe (2002: 57):

> But didn't I say that we have no idea what God is? How then can we say what She is? We can use language to say what God is so long as we always realize that we do not know what our words mean. We can say that God is love, so long as we recognize that this love is incomprehensible. We can say God is wise and good and happy, just as so long as we are not trying to classify God amongst the wise and good and happy things we are familiar with, so long as we recognize that when used of God these words have a meaning beyond anything we can understand of wisdom or happiness or goodness. But we mean these statements quite literally. It is quite the opposite with images and metaphors.

[17] And while one might dispute that we find a totally unified view of God in these sources, there is there a view of God that is unified enough to contrast with Buddhism – all forms of Buddhism – such that what the former affirms the latter explicitly or implicitly denies. If the former is theistic – and it is – then the latter is atheistic.

and Tibet, but now too in the West, have always been proud of being atheists and consider it to show the definite philosophical superiority of Buddhism

2. José Cabezón

a. My concern is that of 'balance of rationality', not proof

José wants to debate with me on the existence of God. Which is strange if Perry is right, since according to Perry there should be no fundamental disagreement of fact concerning the existence of God between me as a Christian, and José as a Buddhist. Perhaps I should sit back and let José and Perry debate the matter before then returning to the fray on the basis of what they decide.

But of course I think it is José who is right here. José is a Buddhist, and he happily confirms that *qua* Buddhist he is an atheist. He does not believe in God. What Christian orthodoxy etc. affirm concerning God, the Buddhist denies. We do indeed thus have a basis for debate, and I would argue that such a debate – rather than polite platitudes or watered-down agreement – is what Buddhists and Christians should be doing. But I am not going to have a full-blown debate with José now (even when he and Perry have finished their discussion). The arguments José uses against theism in his paper are by and large ones with which I am familiar – I wrestled with them for years before returning to theism. And they are very powerful arguments. Contrary to what José says, in my book I really did want to put to my Buddhist friends only the fairly modest claim that Christian theism is at least as rational as the Buddhist position of atheism. In other words, there is a very genuine debate that can occur between them. For I notice that there are many in the modern world that do not think this, but who think that Buddhism is much more rational than the 'blind faith' that is Christianity.

b. A Thomist context for debating the existence of God [18]

What I argue in my book is that it can be shown that *belief* in God is rational, as rational as the Buddhist denial of the existence of God. Belief in God is not the same as knowing that God exists, for it is perfectly compatible with belief in something that such a thing turns out not to be the case. Hence belief in God does not necessarily require complete *proof*. Nevertheless I want to argue that believing in God is not irrational, and it is not a matter simply of 'blind faith', as some seem to think. That is not the view of Thomas, and it is not my view.

There are those who think that Thomas holds one can indeed prove the existence of God, and that this is what his famous 'five ways' is all about.[19] I am not convinced that this is true of Thomas. He talks about demonstrating the existence of God, making it evident, but it is not clear to me that he talks about actual *proof*. In *Summa Theologiae* 1a. 1, 8 ad 2 Thomas states that theology, even on issues where philosophers have been able to discover the truth through their own natural reason, treats these conclusions as such as probable rather than certain. Now, the existence of God is considered by Thomas to be just one of those issues. Thus I suggest that for Thomas the existence of God inasmuch as he considers it can be demonstrated by our natural reason remains for us an issue of probability rather than certainty. Be that as it may, it seems clear to me that Aquinas does not consider that his arguments to demonstrate the existence of God are to be taken as proofs in the conclusive deductive and mathematical sense that we have come to expect since, perhaps, Descartes.[20] Thomas himself con-

---

[18] In my 2004 paper I introduce the term (with slight tongue-in-cheek) 'Thomas-ist' rather than 'Thomist'. This is because 'Thomist' within Catholic theology comes with a lot of historical and philosophical baggage. While I would want to acknowledge an enormous debt to Thomas Aquinas I am not sure at the present time whether I would want to associate myself too closely with the total 'Thomist package'. For an excellent outline of the position of Thomas on God that I am indicating in what follows, written with his usual wit and clarity and covering also most of the other aspects of God that I have mentioned in the present paper, see Davies 2002b: chapter 8. This piece would be a good place to start for anyone completely unfamiliar with Aquinas's theology, followed by Davies (2002a) and Davies (1992). On ways of reading Thomas, including the current state of play, see Ker (2002).
[19] For a recent case, see Pasnau and Shields 2004: chapter 4 which is full of talk, without any justificatory evidence, of Thomas's 'proofs' of the existence of God.
[20] Even Anselm's version of the so-called 'ontological proof', similar in some ways to Descartes', is arguably not really thought of as a proof by Anselm, in the sense of something that might stand independent of faith but enabling a necessary (or even inductive) derivation of elements of it. It is, he says, 'faith seeking understanding' (see Anselm's

siders that the existence of God is certain, but that is because he accepts revelation, not because he holds it to be a necessary logical derivation from his arguments in the five ways.

The God that Thomas considers can be demonstrated through reasoning is God as the answer to the question 'Why is there something rather than nothing?'. This question is emphatically *not* as such the question 'What chronologically started everything off?'. That is a question to which as a matter of fact revelation gives an answer, but it is a different question from the one treated in his five ways. And Thomas is not asking a similar, but really rather different, question 'Why is there everything – understood as the totality or the bundle of things – in addition to each individual thing?'. Thomas considers his question would apply at each and every moment: 'At each and every moment, why is there something rather than nothing?'. Thomas considers the question 'Why is there something rather than nothing?' to be a genuine question, and he holds that any answer we give to this question 'is what people call "God"' (e.g. *S. Th.* 1a 2, 3: *hoc dicimus Deum*). He does not consider that there is a range of possible answers to that question, and the correct one is 'God'. Rather, whatever it is that is the answer to that question, he wants to say, is what we all call 'God'. But a great deal of Thomas's work, in the earlier sections of the *Summa Theologiae* for example, is devoted to what must be true – and of course more often than not what cannot be true – of whatever it is that can be the answer to the question 'Why is there something rather than nothing?' if it is indeed to be an adequate answer to just this question and not another one. Thus, for example, whatever it is that answers this question cannot be in time, and in answering the question and as necessarily being therefore the cause of all things it cannot operate in time. Moreover whatever it is that answers this question must necessarily have created *ex nihilo*, from nothing at all, for it is part of the meaning of any answer to the question 'Why is there something rather than nothing?' that there can be nothing else in existence out of which it could cause everything. Thomas does not claim to know what it can be like to have the various qualities that such a creator must have, and in a very real sense he thinks these cannot be *qualities* as such (inhering in, but logically separable from, a substance) at all. He

---

Proslogion 1: 'I do not seek to understand so that I may believe; but I believe so that I may understand' [Anselm 1998: 87], based as Anselm says on *Isaiah* 7: 9). That is, it presupposes a faith in God he already holds and seeks to explicate rationally.

does not know, for example, what it can be to be a timeless cause, or how one could possibly create *ex nihilo*. For Thomas God is truly, literally, a *sui generis* creator. He is a timeless cause, but what that can possibly amount to Thomas has not the faintest idea. He is merely saying that *if* there is an answer to the question 'Why is there something rather than nothing?', the causal activity of that answer (for example) must be causal activity that is compatible with being outside time. How these things can be are, for Thomas, mysteries not in the sense that they are irrational – let alone contradictory – but in the very rational sense that this must follow from God as the answer to the question 'Why is there something rather than nothing?'.[21]

So from this Thomist perspective the framework for the atheist is already determined. The atheist can argue one of the following: A) The question 'Why is there something rather than nothing?' is an illegitimate question, either because it is meaningless,[22] badly framed, or

---

[21] Thomas would certainly hold that if any of these conclusions are literally self-contradictory then they couldn't be true. *That* is one crucial and central way by which the atheist can attack our theism. A Buddhist, for example, might seek to show that the concept of a timeless cause operating is simply a logical contradiction. But the Buddhist has to demonstrate that it *is* contradictory, not just assert it (let alone simply assert that it is impossible, or does not occur).

[22] There can be no doubt that in terms of philosophical grammar this is a very strange question. It looks as if both 'why?' and 'something' are losing the grip of their moorings in meaningfulness. If 'why?' appeals to the Principle of Sufficient Reason then it is hard to see what sense can be given to the 'why?' when its reference is to 'something rather than nothing'. And while it seems to play the grammatical role of a quasi-name in the question, 'something' cannot be taken as if it were a name of a particular thing. It is hard to see that it can be taken as a name at all. Of course, Aquinas did not think it should be. So such metaphysical questions cannot be operating according to their apparent grammar at all. In what sense, then, are they meaningful questions? Now, I think the question 'Why is there something rather than nothing?' in this context can be defended against the accusation of meaninglessness (and hence not really being a question at all). But I shall not do so now. I might add that *for one who actually already believes in God* the meaning floods back into the question. This, perhaps, is one dimension of Augustine's and Anselm's 'faith seeking understanding'. These arguments are for one who already believes, clarifying and deepening one's understanding, as far as is now possible for us, of the concepts involved. It underlines again my suggestion that for Aquinas too 'Why is there something rather than nothing?' is not intended as anything like (what we would expect to see in) a *proof* of the existence of God. It is an explication for one who believes of what we *mean* by 'God', an explication that Aquinas subsequently continues in showing what can and what cannot be said of what the term 'God' must therefore intend. But to be an explication of what the believer *means* by God, rather than a logical proof, does not entail that the explication could not also function in another context as part of an argument (perhaps a cumulative argument, rather than a logical proof) for *belief* in God.

perhaps because it simply could not have an answer;[23] or B) The question 'Why is there something rather than nothing?' is a legitimate question, but I do not know the answer, I cannot know the answer, I do not care about the answer, and/or any answer is utterly irrelevant; or C) It can be shown that any answer that is being proposed to the question 'Why is there something rather than nothing?' cannot be correct. The force of the word 'cannot' here could be based on 'not fitting with the wider tenets of a particular system', for example it contradicts scripture, but otherwise the force of 'cannot' has to be that of 'is contradictory'. In other words, the opponent could argue that Aquinas (for example) has proposed an answer to our question 'Why is there something rather than nothing?' that involves a logical contradiction. On the other hand note the reverse of this. If a proposed answer here does *not* involve a logical contradiction then it has not as such been shown to be false by the critic, atheist or otherwise. Moreover that it is rational actually to ask our question rather than sidestep it can also be bolstered by versions of the 'fine-tuning argument', a modern version of the old argument from design, that recently convinced the philosopher Anthony Flew after a lifetime of defending atheism that a minimal deistic form of God is more likely than not. Here, as a recent exponent of the argument has put it, 'the initial conditions of the universe and the basic constituents of physics must be balanced on a razor's edge for intelligent life to evolve . . . [and this] . . . offers us significant reasons for preferring theism over atheism' (Collins 2003: 133, 145). Arguments for the plausibility of theism – that the existence of God is not only rational but also more likely than not – do not have to rely on just one argument, but can be mutually reinforcing.

So Thomas wants to argue that there is a question 'Why is there something rather than nothing?' and that it is a legitimate question, and as such we are free to give it an answer. Whatever that answer is, is what we call 'God'. Because God is the answer to this question we can deduce from it many things that such a God could not be. And of the things that we can say quite literally would be true of God as the answer to that question, we also have to say that we simply do not know what they could mean of something in itself (we cannot really even use the expression here 'some *thing*') that would be the answer to that question.

---

[23] Wittgenstein, for example, says at one point in his *Tractatus Logico-Philosophicus* (6.51) that if a question has no answer it cannot be a question.

For example, I have pointed out both in my *Unexpected Way* book and in my paper on the *Kun byed rgyal po* (Williams, forthcoming) that 'mind' in any recognisably meaningful sense is not going to be adequate as an answer to the question 'Why is there something rather than nothing?'. José disagrees. He seems to agree with me that while each and every mental act individually may be contingent, and could have not existed, a world in which there were no mental acts at all could not exist: 'The Buddhist', José says, 'would deny that there could *exist* a possible world in which there are no mental acts whatsoever' (José's emphasis). But what he has to show is not that such a world is inconceivable but that it is *logically contradictory*. The 'could not' in 'could not exist' has to have the force of logical necessity in order for José to be able to make his point successfully. He has to argue that it is logically impossible for there to be a world without mental acts, and hence without consciousness. Otherwise the very existence of consciousness is simply an actualised possibility. If only that were the case, then the very existence of consciousness would come within the range of the question 'Why is there something rather than nothing?'. Why is there consciousness, rather than not? There *could* have been no consciousness, no sentience, whatsoever.

There is the issue of the existence of consciousness, which I argue is a contingent fact. There is also an allied issue that José introduces, an issue that is an integral part of a great deal (if not all) of Buddhism. That is the dependence of states of affairs (that is, everything) on mental acts. In Prāsaṅgika Madhyamaka, for example, all things – absolutely everything – exist in dependence upon the imputing mind. Their very existence is mind-dependent. This includes the existence of the mind itself. All this seems to me highly implausible, but even if it were the case I would argue that its turning out to be the case is itself no more than yet another contingent fact. First, I simply reject as irrelevant José's example of trying to *conceive* what a world would be like with no consciousness in it to do the conceiving. It is tautologous that one cannot conceive of a world, which seems to mean here to 'picture' it, without consciousness or consciousness-dependent conceptual schemes. But it seems clear that I can certainly state without contradiction 'There exists a world even though there exist no consciousnesses'. Indeed, as I understand it, in one way or another this is actually the view of most scientists. It is not possible to argue convincingly that the following is a logically necessary truth: 'If all consciousnesses went out of existence tomorrow nothing would then exist'. And even if this hypothetical proposition were contingently true, which it seems clear it is not, it would still come within the range of the question 'Why is there something rather than nothing?'. There were many, many millions of years prior to the evolution of consciousness in which things – natural kinds such as trees, quartz, or amoeba, or the sun and moon, rather than artefacts such as tables or chariots – genuinely existed although there were no minds to impute them. Certainly, they were not *called* 'quartz', 'trees', 'amoeba', or 'sun' and 'moon'. They were not at that time *'pictured'* as 'quartz', 'trees', and 'amoeba', or 'sun' and 'moon'. They were not *conceptualised* as 'quartz', 'trees', and 'amoeba', or 'sun' and 'moon'. And they no doubt cannot enter into our language and planning without conceptual schemata that depend upon consciousness. But that is a different issue – we are talking about the referents of our concepts, not the concepts themselves. Of course, the Buddhist – notably here the Prāsaṅgika Mādhyamika tradition from which José stems (and on these issues holding a view that is by no means universal in Buddhism) – differs. But it is not obvious to me that the Buddhist is right, or indeed who on this issue can claim to be the most rational. The Buddhist position requires a deep level of faith that is at least as strong as that attributed to the Christian.

It seems to me that the world exists, contingently, with many facts in it, the existence of which, while contingent, is independent of consciousness. And consciousness itself is a contingent fact about the way things are and not a necessary fact. Moreover any suggestion that the existence of consciousness is a logical necessity would contradict, I think, what must be the Prāsaṅgika Mādhyamika position that no statement attributing existence to something can be an example of a logically necessary truth. All statements attributing existence, if true, can only be true due to contingent states of affairs, that is, due to causes and conditions. Hence the truth of such statements must be a matter of contingent, and not logically necessary, truth. But all contingently true statements could have been otherwise. That they are true is due to the way a contingent state of affairs has turned out, and that requires first of all contingent states of affairs. They therefore all come within the *range* of the question 'Why is there something rather than nothing?', and cannot be appealed to as part of the answer.

But to repeat: Both José and I consider this question 'Why is there something rather than nothing?' nevertheless to be a question worth asking. Or at least, neither of us considers it to be a badly formed or meaningless question, a question that on principle could not have an answer. This is because both of us think there is indeed an answer. We differ as to what might count as an answer to our question. For me, following Aquinas, whatever the answer is we call it 'God'. But Thomas also indicates what, he wants to argue, can and cannot be said of that answer if it is to be adequate as an answer to just that question. Thus what José suggests as being a plausible answer, for Thomas could not fit with what must be the case if it is to be adequate as an answer. 'Mind', if the term is to be used in any relevant or meaningful sense, as tagged to the mental events of sentient beings, simply cannot be the answer to the question 'Why is there something rather than nothing?'.

But note that none of this anyway *proves* the existence of God. I want to say (and I think Thomas would also want to say) that it is not *irrational* to refuse to ask our metaphysical question. It is not *irrational* to say that it cannot have an answer, or that it is meaningless. And perhaps I should add that it seems to me, and I notice to José too, that it would not be *irrational* to argue that even though it is a question that can be asked, and answered, nothing follows from that. The 'God' that we have reached has no religious content or implications.[24] To ask

---

[24] After a lifetime of defending atheism the philosopher Anthony Flew has recently conceded on the basis of a version of the 'fine-tuning' argument – broadly, the unlikelihood that it could be a mere coincidence that the universe is so finely tuned for life – that a cause of the fine tuning, a cause that therefore can be called 'God', is more likely than not (see his interview with the Christian philosopher Gary Habermas at http://www.biola.edu/antonyflew/flew-interview.pdf [last checked 23/9/05]). Flew has grudgingly accepted what he himself calls a form of deism. But Flew appears to consider that nothing religious follows from this, and certainly not anything that we might call 'institutionally Christian'. It is as if having been convinced that God is more likely than not, Flew looked for the fewest concessions he could make. His God is an uninterested God, like that of Aristotle. And from a religious point of view it is also an uninteresting God. One might expect that having come to theism Flew would ask 'What must I do to be saved?'. But he does not, for he makes it clear that he hopes for salvation in death, a complete cessation for himself. Flew's God might explain the mere existence of the universe, but nothing else. This, I think, is because he does not move to the universe *as intended* by God. Yet surely this move is a rational one. I think I might now want to argue as follows:

a.   'Why is there something rather than nothing?', if it has an answer, entails (with Thomas) that there is a God. That it has an answer, or that there is simply no answer, are equal.

b.   Modern teleological arguments (i.e. arguments from design) for God, such as the fine-tuning argument, entail that it is more likely than not that there is an answer to 'Why is there something rather than nothing?'.

c.   Thus it is arguably more reasonable to believe in God than not. But such teleological arguments also enable us plausibly to suggest that God *intends* the universe.

this question, to answer it, and to become a theist in an institutional sense, say, as a Christian, all involve leaps. I want to argue these leaps are not themselves irrational. But equally it is not irrational either to refuse to make those leaps. It might be a failure of imagination (as the philosopher Denys Turner has urged at a number of points in his recent writing) but it is not irrational.

c. Good deeds, happiness and necessity

I want now to make some similar points about my comments, objected to by José, on God, Buddhism and morality. I accept (at least for the purpose of argument here) that it may be the case for Buddhists that it is a necessary truth that good deeds bring about happiness, because it is true by definition. In other words, it would be contradictory within Buddhist discourse to say that good deeds do not produce happiness. Good deeds are defined as 'deeds that bring about happiness'. That may be the case. Of course, the actual acceptability of this definition does require appeal to reincarnation, and to reincarnation in a sense that can preserve personal identity over (if necessary) infinite lifetimes. Otherwise it would appear to be counterintuitive (to say the least) to define good deeds as deeds that bring about happiness. There are many deeds that we would normally think of as good deeds that do not appear as far as we can tell, in this life, to bring about happiness. Conversely, there are many deeds that we would normally want to class as wicked deeds that seem to bring great joy and happiness to their perpetrators. I will leave it to you to think of examples. To define good deeds this way is at least open to debate. It may indeed, without relying on reincarnation with personal identity, have severely morally unwelcome consequences. Hence I would argue that if it turns out to

---

If God is responsible for the universe, and intends it, then we are entitled – expected – to ask the question 'What behaviour should follow from this?'. And I argue that the behaviour that should follow is that arising from gratitude. But the expression of gratitude is a culturally conditioned phenomenon, and the 'culture' that makes the expression of gratitude to a *creator* possible is religious culture. And the great theistic traditions (i.e. those traditions that recognise a creator) have all shown that gratitude expresses itself in worship. I should add that I consider gratitude to a creator to follow morally, not as a matter of logical implication. If someone says that they accept a creator but do not think that gratitude follows I could not say that was logically contradictory. But I might urge that it is ungrateful, and hence is *immoral*. And since Flew's deism does not entail any behavioural changes, any worship, I suggest that his deism is still religiously (i.e. practically) equivalent to his former atheism.

be deeply counterintuitive it might well be unreasonable (and perhaps even *immoral*) to define good deeds that way.

Be that as it may, there is, I think, a more significant problem with José's position. If good deeds are simply defined as entailing happiness this would appear to leave us without any basis for producing a typology of good deeds, and hence a moral code. Take the case of good deed X, let us say giving donations to the monastic order. I perform an example of X: I give donations to the monastic order. If José is right, according to the Buddhist, X is a good deed *because* it brings about happiness for me. This is by definition what makes it a good deed, as José puts it 'this is simply the way "good" [is] defined'. In order for it to be logically necessary that good deeds produce happiness the association of good deeds with happiness has to be *simply* a matter of definition. But in that case we cannot say that acts of type X are good deeds by virtue of their *type*. This is because we cannot ever know in advance of it actually happening in individual token cases that acts of *type X* will produce happiness for their perpetrators. Since they are good *because* they lead to happiness, there is nothing about the actual *acts themselves* that makes them good. Hence we can never know that an act is good in advance of its karmic results, and thus we are never warranted in saying that acts of *type X* are good by virtue of the type they are. At the most we could say that acts of type X have always in the past been good because it so turned out that they led to happiness. Moreover since they have been defined as good because they bring about happiness, it follows that the fact that acts of *type X* have in the past been good – that is, they have led to happiness – is a purely contingent matter since there is nothing *in the acts themselves* that makes them good apart from the contingent matter that they turned out to lead to happiness and are hence by definition 'good'. There is no necessary connection between the act itself and the resultant happiness. The element of necessity appealed to here is between the happiness and the act that caused it being, by definition, good because it turned out that it produced happiness. It is the necessity of definition, not a necessity of causal connection. Hence we cannot say in advance which acts will turn out to be good acts, but we can say after the event (after their producing happiness) that it turned out to be those acts, and they were of type X. But then, using an argument familiar from Hume's critique of induction, this gives us no grounds whatsoever for arguing that acts of type X will in the future be good. The future is new. Hence there can be no grounds for recommended conduct, and no grounds for precepts or any other moral code. 'Do good and avoid evil' may still be recommended, but if José is right it becomes impossible *by definition* – and hence necessarily impossible – to derive from this any prescription as to what should be done and what should be avoided.

But of course Buddhists do not think it is actually like this. Buddhists do think that there are acts of particular types that lead to happiness, and other acts of particular types that lead to suffering. That is the way it is, and they always do so 'whether Buddhas arise or do not arise'. They might define the first type of acts as 'good', and the second as 'bad' (or whatever). But the point I make in my book is that it is a logically contingent matter that these actual acts *do* lead to happiness, or lead to suffering. That they do is not itself logically necessary. The Buddhist claims nevertheless that this is how it is, not just in the past but will be so into the future as well. It is how it is in all actual worlds. But, I suggest, this is still not itself necessarily true. That acts of type X lead to happiness in all actual worlds will not make it a necessary truth. It is perfectly logically possible to say that an act of type X – giving donations to the monastic order – does not lead to happiness. There is a logically possible world – although not, the Buddhist urges, an actual world – in which that is the case. That giving donations to the monastic order leads to happiness in all actual worlds is hence a contingent matter. One simply cannot argue as an implication from its being true by definition that good deeds lead to happiness, that deed X is in itself a good deed, let alone that throughout all time and space acts of *type X* are good deeds. These are contingent matters to which relating good deeds and happiness by definition is irrelevant.

But, *pace* José, actually I do not use this as an argument to a necessary cause, God. At least I do not if the suggestion is that this is yet another attempt by me to *prove* the existence of God. What I actually say is that 'if it is rational to believe that this [deeds of type X produce, and always will produce, happiness] just happens to be the way it is, it seems, to say the least, equally rational to believe it is like this because it is the product of a Creator' (2002: 42). My argument again is that granted the truth of the Buddhist contention that throughout all time and space acts of *type X* are good deeds, it is at least as rational to believe this can be anchored in the intention of a creator than that this just happens contingently (but apparently causelessly) to be the case. If the Christian submits to 'blind faith', so too does the Buddhist.

d. Have I simply ignored the centrality of love and compassion in Mahāyāna?

It is suggested that my picture of Buddhism is almost entirely that of a
'Hīnayāna', and that I deny or neglect the centrality of love and compassion in Mahāyāna Buddhism. I reject the charge. Throughout the
book I make ample positive reference to love and compassion in Buddhism, including Mahāyāna.

I have a great deal to say about these issues, including a defence of
my view that Buddhism is pessimistic in the very specific sense in
which I use the word 'pessimism' in my 2002 book. I do not have
time to do so here, however. There are certainly those who in the past
have argued from a view of Buddhism as pessimistic that this entails,
or is entailed by, the fact that the goal of Buddhism is to abandon the
world. Hence, they have argued, compassionate and good deeds are
not possible for enlightened beings given what the goal of Buddhism
is all about. José explains at length, and very lucidly, how it is that in
the Mahāyāna Buddhism of his own tradition a Buddha is fully
capable, indeed supremely capable, of engaging with the world and
benefiting sentient beings. I am happy to hear it. I agree with José
completely that this is indeed the dGe lugs view. And I make it quite
clear in my book that I hold and accept that Buddhas, for example, are
considered by Buddhists to be eminently compassionate. I am delighted to repeat it here too.

Looking back at the relevant section of my book (2002: 52-56) it
seems to me that I am in context not talking much about Buddhism at
all. I am actually talking primarily about *those fellow Christians* who
may think that the *Christian summum bonum*, in other words the post-
mortem heavenly state, might be one of simple nondual and nonconceptual awareness of God in some sort of so-called 'mystical experience'. My criticism here is actually of Christians, not Buddhists
(2002: 52-56). If this is taken as the goal of Christianity then it clashes
with *inter alia* a venerable tradition in Christian eschatology that goes
right back to Hebrew roots that would see the final goal in terms of
relationships, our relationship to God and also our relationships with
each other. I wanted to suggest in my book that a relationship of love
with God, which I do see as integral to the Christian *summum bonum*,
is not compatible with being in an eternal state of nondual and nonconceptual mystical experience the content of which is God. Perhaps
more importantly, I wanted to say that an integral part of the Christian

summum bonum is also being in community with other persons, and this too is quite incompatible with *the final goal* being one simply of nondual and nonconceptual mystical experience the content of which is God.

José suggests that I am talking about the impossibility of love of significant others given one is a Buddha who sees things nondualistically and nonconceptually. He explains how this is considered to be possible in dGe lugs thought, and praises it as a particularly deep and intuitively satisfactory way of being with others and being moral with them. I am impressed with what he says, although I do still have philosophical doubts about whether even a Buddha could relate to others if he or she were having experiences that were not just nonconceptual but were *intrinsically nonconceptualisable*.[25] What I actually say (2002: 55; italics original) is that 'perfect love involves recognition of and respect for difference in perfect harmony. . . . Difference is *by definition* dualistic, and its expression *by definition* involves conceptuality'. And I add (*op. cit.*: 56) that '[w]e can have as final goals a perfect community in a relationship of love with God and our fellows, or we can have nondual and nonconceptual experiences. But one cannot have both as equal final goals'. These are philosophical and theological issues. I thought I was criticising here particular ways of reading the *Christian* final eschatological goal.

But looking back at it – yes, I admit that in my book I am not sufficiently clear in this. I now think that generalisation from the context of the Christian *summum bonum* in which I was writing, which I make and on which José takes me up, was inappropriate. It does indeed invite just the response that he has so clearly given. Of course, it all depends what one means by 'nondual' and 'nonconceptual'. I am delighted to hear from José that there are ways of understanding these expressions that render it plausible that this is indeed how Buddhas see and are. I concede to him.

My point in all this was to play off a Christian goal that is one of love of God, and of other persons, in a state that (I should add, for Thomas Aquinas) is embodied in 'a new heaven and a new earth' – a Christian goal that I would argue is primeval in Christianity – against a vision of the Christian goal that sees it in terms of a post-mortem state of nondual and nonconceptual mystical experiences. There are

---

[25] For more on what I see to be the problems involved in intrinsically nonconceptualisable experiences see Williams (1992).

some who would thence argue that since this is also a Buddhist goal, the *summum bonum* of Buddhism and that of Christianity ultimately converge. It was that view of Christianity that I was contesting, not a view on Buddhas and morality. It seems to me love of God is not possible in a permanent post-mortem state of nondual and nonconceptual mystical experience. I also add that the element of communal relationships with other persons that is part of traditional Christian eschatology also entails that this cannot be right as a description in Christianity of our absolutely final post-mortem goal. The absolutely final Christian goal is a community of persons in love. My argument here is really with Christians, not, *pace* José, with Buddhists.

3. Final concluding points:
Some repentance, continued defiance and flight!

To summarise: To Perry, I am still entirely unrepentant. I am more convinced than ever that it is appropriate to call Buddhism 'atheist', in any sense in which one speaks of 'God' in the creeds and Christian orthodoxy. Perry and I hold radically different positions, and I have noticed that it is a certain type of Christians who have been among the most unremitting critics of my book. Perry describes it as an opposition between the light versus darkness model, and a model of 'looking through a dim mirror'. I confess I find the latter a strange image. Any mirror, dim or otherwise, simply shows a person his or her own face. It looks very much like the self-obsession that I have been criticised for drawing attention to in my book. It is not at all the same as 'looking through a glass darkly', where one does indeed see through the glass truly if dimly to something beyond. But perhaps that is the image on which Perry really wanted to draw. Be that as it may, these two models are his (no doubt relying on St Paul), not mine. I see it simply as a matter of the leap of faith, and the logic of what follows from that. I believe that something is actually, objectively, true. But I do not know it is, and that enables me to be open to the possibility that other perspectives may turn out to be actually, factually, true either as well as, or instead of, mine. Truth may for all I know turn out to be black or white, but that does not mean that I am now justified in claiming that I know which it is. I simply believe it. That is different, and to conflate them is to misunderstand the logic of belief.

I am enormously grateful to José for his sensitive and courteous nuancing of a great deal of the very black-and-white writing that I do in my conversion tale. He appreciates, at one point, I think, that it is a conversion tale and this is the way conversion tales are constructed. He is right, of course, in his nuancing and I accept it without personally thinking that it fundamentally alters what underlies my black-and-white story. Still, I apologise to José and to other Buddhists if there has been any lack of relevant and sufficient subtlety in the telling of my story. And I should add that I am delighted to hear from José too that having broken all my tantric vows, not to mention the other wicked things Buddhists will hold I have done, it still does not entail as very likely if not inevitable that I shall be reborn in the lowest hell for a very long time. This is what I was always told (both in texts and by my lamas) followed from breaking one's tantric vows. It is widely believed that this is the case. That it is not should be better known, and I hope that knowledge of it also reaches down to Yama.

As a leading authority on the great dGe lugs pa philosopher and debater mKhas grub dGe legs dpal bzang (1385-1438), José will be very familiar with the (admittedly sectarian) story of mKhas grub rje's debate with a rival Tibetan Rong ston pa Shākya rgyal mtshan (1367-1449). After some time it is said Rong ston pa simply fled from mKhas grub rje and in order to escape Rong ston pa used his powers to dissolve himself into a statue of the Buddha Maitreya.

Each of us, I think, should also know the right time to flee and dissolve into our icons. For me that time has now come.

BOOKS CITED

Anscombe, G.E.M., and P.T. Geach (1961) *Three Philosophers*, Oxford: Basil Black-well.

Anselm of Canterbury (1998) *Major Works*, edited with an Introduction by Brian Davies and G.R. Evans, Oxford and New York: Oxford University Press.

Aquinas, St. Thomas, *De potentia*, Latin text available online at http://www.corpusthomisticum.org/qdp7.html. Last checked 7/6/05.

Aquinas, St. Thomas (1964-80) *Summa Theologiae* (London: Eyre and Spottiswood; New York: McGraw Hill Book Company). 61 volumes. Contains Latin text.

Chenu, M-D, O.P. (2002) *Aquinas and his Role in Theology*, translated from the French by Paul Philibert, O.P., Collegeville, Minnesota: The Liturgical Press.

Clément, Olivier (2002) *The Roots of Christian Mysticism: Texts from the Patristic Era with Commentary*, London, Dublin, Edinburgh: New City. Seventh edition.

Collins, Robin (2003) 'The teleological argument', in Paul Copan and Paul K. Moser, ed. *The Rationality of Theism*, London and New York: Routledge.

Davies, Brian, O.P. (1992) *The Thought of Thomas Aquinas*, Oxford: Clarendon Press.

Davies, Brian, O.P. (2002a) *Aquinas*, London and New York: Continuum.

Davies, Brian, O.P., ed. (2002b) *Thomas Aquinas: Contemporary Philosophical Perspectives*, Oxford and New York: Oxford University Press.

Dreyfus, Georges B.J. (1997) *Recognizing Reality: Dharmakīrti's Philosophy and its Tibetan Interpretations*, Albany, N.Y.: State University of New York Press.

Holy See (1994) *Catechism of the Catholic Church*, London: Geoffrey Chapman.

Inwagen, Peter van (1995) 'Non est Hick', in Peter van Inwagen, *God Knowledge and Mystery: Essays in Philosophical Theology*, Ithaca and London: Cornell University Press.

Ker, Fergus (2002) *After Aquinas: Versions of Thomism*, Oxford: Blackwell.

McCabe, Herbert, O.P. (2002) *God Still Matters*, edited by Brian Davies, London and New York: Continuum.

McDermott, Timothy (1998) *Aquinas: Selected Philosophical Writings*, translated with an Introduction and Notes by Timothy McDermott, Oxford and New York: Oxford University Press.

McInerny, Ralph (1998) *Thomas Aquinas: Selected Writings*, edited and translated with an Introduction and Notes by Ralph McInerny, Harmondsworth: Penguin Books.

Newman, John Henry (1994) *Apologia Pro Vita Sua*, edited by Ian Ker, Harmondsworth: Penguin Books.

Pasnau, Robert, and Christopher Shields (2003) *The Philosophy of Aquinas*, Boulder, Col. and Oxford: The Westview Press.

Pegis, Anton C. (1945) *Basic Writings of Saint Thomas Aquinas*, edited and annotated, with an Introduction, by Anton C. Pegis, New York: Random House. Two volumes.

Smart, J.J.C., and J. Haldane (2003) *Atheism and Theism*, Second Edition, Oxford: Blackwell.

Thomas, Edward J. (1951) *The History of Buddhist Thought*, London: Routledge and Kegan Paul.

Torrell, Jean-Pierre, O.P. (2003) *Saint Thomas Aquinas: Volume 2 – Spiritual Master*, translated by Robert Royal, Washington, D.C.: The Catholic University of America Press.

Williams, Paul (1989) *Mahāyāna Buddhism: The Doctrinal Foundations*, London and New York: Routledge.

Williams, Paul (1992), 'Non-conceptuality, critical reasoning and religious experience: Some Tibetan Buddhist discussions', in Michael McGhee, ed., *Philosophy, Religion and the Spiritual Life*, Cambridge: Cambridge University Press. Royal Institute of Philosophy Supplement: 32.

Williams, Paul (1998) *Altruism and Reality: Studies in the Philosophy of the Bodhicaryāvatāra*, Richmond: Curzon.

Williams, Paul, with Anthony Tribe (2000) *Buddhist Thought: A Complete Introduction to the Indian Tradition*, London and New York: Routledge.

Williams, Paul (2002) *The Unexpected Way: On Converting from Buddhism to Catholicism*, London and New York: T&T Clark/Continuum.

Williams, Paul (2004) 'Aquinas meets the Buddhists: Prolegomenon to an authentically Thomas-ist basis for dialogue', *Modern Theology* 20, 1: 91-121. Reprinted in Jim Fodor and Frederick Christian Bauerschmidt, ed. (2004) *Aquinas in Dialogue*, Oxford: Blackwell.

Williams, Paul (forthcoming) 'Some theological reflections on Buddhism and the hiddenness of God', forthcoming in a Templeton volume of studies on the hiddenness of God edited by John and Margaret Bowker.

Wippel, John F. (2000) *The Metaphysical Thought of Thomas Aquinas: From Finite Being to Uncreated Being*, Washington, D.C.: The Catholic University of America Press.

KAJSA AHLSTRAND

Boundaries of Religious Identity: Baptised Buddhists in Enköping

Enköping is a municipality in Uppsala County, in east central Sweden. The municipality has a total population of 38211 (1 Nov 2004), fairly equally distributed between the town and the rural area. The town itself dates its history back to the 12th century. Enköping is situated by the rich farmlands close to lake Mälaren. The town has been a major crossroads for commerce and has several manufacturing industries, a hospital and the Army Signalling Regiment. The municipality used to be the main producer of horseradish for the Swedish market and the monkey wrench was invented and first manufactured in Enköping. Enköping today is a pleasant, even if a somewhat unexciting town, which in 2003 won the international award 'Best small town in the world/most liveable community' in the 'Nations in Bloom' contest.

Enköping is the focus of a locality study, inspired by the Kendal Study (Paul Heelas and Linda Woodhead, Lancaster University) and carried out by the Church of Sweden Research Unit between 2004 and 2006. As part of the Enköping Study the Church of Sweden Research Unit sent out 2000 questionnaires in September 2004 to randomly selected inhabitants (16-76 years of age) in the municipality. We received 1045 replies, which is a satisfactory return rate considering the nature and size (18 pages and 45 questions) of the questionnaire. Women, people over sixty and Swedish born people are slightly over represented.

In this paper I will take Q 27 as my point of departure. We asked:

To what extent do you regard yourself as…
(Tick one box for each alternative)

	Completely	Fairly much	Moderately	Fairly little	Not at all
a Christian	164	109	303	204	191
b Muslim	9	4	4	8	860
c Jew	2	3	4	9	861
d Buddhist	4	4	13	24	837
e Hindu	2	1	3	5	859
f Believer	75	80	176	174	387
g Spiritual	36	47	133	133	530
h Religious	24	33	129	162	533
i Seeker	24	60	86	84	632
j Atheist	43	49	40	49	698
k Doubter[1]	24	66	110	97	587

The table invites reflection and a lot of cross tabbing. In this presentation I will focus on those who identified themselves as 'Buddhist' in the questionnaire. The distinguishing feature of this group are the two lower categories of engagement: there are more people who identify 'moderately' and 'fairly little' with this religion than what we find in the other religious groups (apart from Christianity). In the following I will identify two categories of Buddhists which I call 'strong Buddhists' and 'mild Buddhists'. The strong Buddhists are those who identify with one of the two upper categories ('completely' or 'fairly much'), the mild Buddhists those who identify with one of the two lower categories ('moderately' and 'fairly little').

---

[1] A note on terminology: The designations 'believer' and 'doubter' are fairly common in the Swedish language. A 'believing Christian' or just 'believer' is often a member of a Free Church. It can also mean that a person is not 'just' a cultural or nominal Christian but has a personal relation to the faith content of the religion. A 'doubter' is usually seen as having a more positive relation to religion ('doubting Thomas') than a sceptic or agnostic, but agnostic would be the closest synonym. 'Spiritual' (*andlig*) has a narrower connotation in Swedish than in English. The expression 'I am spiritual but not religious' is virtually unknown in Swedish.

We thus have a group of 'mild' Buddhists, persons who are attracted to Buddhism and who, when given the opportunity not to choose between the world religions, chose both Buddhism and Christianity – in mild forms.

In the survey, Buddhism appears as the second-largest religion in Enköping. Is Enköping a centre for Buddhism in Sweden? No, there is in fact very little visible Buddhist presence in the town. There is no Buddhist monastery or temple. The closest Buddhist Centre is an FPMT (Foundation for the Preservation of the Mahayana Tradition – Tibetan in the tradition of Lama Yeshe and Lama Thubten Zopa Rinpoche) Centre in Västerås, some 30 km west of Enköping.

There are very few 'cradle Buddhists' in Enköping. Thailand is the only Buddhist majority country represented in the survey; three of the respondents were born in Thailand. A recent census gave the number of persons with Thai origin in Enköping as about 100. From other Buddhist majority countries, Enköping has received 35 persons from Sri Lanka, 25 from South Korea (if South Korea is to be regarded as a Buddhist majority country), 15 from China, 15 from Taiwan and 12 from Vietnam. Many children adopted by Swedish families were born in Sri Lanka, South Korea, China and Vietnam. It is highly likely that many (maybe even the majority) of those who have listed these countries as their countries of origin were adopted by Swedish (Christian) families. Many of the Thai people are either in the restaurant business or Thai women married to Swedish men.

There is, of course, also the possibility that there are some second or third generation Swedish Buddhists, but it is not likely that they make up a significant proportion of those who have identified as Buddhists in the survey.

We can safely assume that most of those who identify as Buddhists are Buddhists by choice, not 'cultural' or 'ethnic' Buddhists. Furthermore, they have to a large extent had to create the Buddhism with which they identify, as Buddhism is almost totally invisible in Enköping. Apart from a few small shrines in Thai restaurants, some books by the Dalai Lama in the bookshop and possibly a few CDs with guided meditations in the health food stores, the Buddhist presence is hardly noticeable. The Christian presence, on the other hand, is both visible and taken for granted. Circa 80 per cent of the inhabitants in Enköping belong to the Church of Sweden. The main church in town is an impressive twelfth century stone church dedicated to Our Lady. There are two Free Church congregations: one Pentecostal-

Baptist and one Reformed-Baptist, each of them has about 200 members. There is also a group of Syrian Orthodox Christians, but no Orthodox church. The Roman Catholics borrow one of the Church of Sweden churches for regular celebrations of the Eucharist led by a priest from Uppsala.

Weekly church attendance in Enköping is 3.4 per cent (all Churches), monthly church attendance 9.5 per cent. 75 per cent of the children are baptised (CoSw) within one year of their birth and 36 per cent of the 15 years old are confirmed (CoSw).

In this rather massively Christian environment we find 44 persons out of 1,045 who call themselves Buddhists. In the following we must remember that we are talking about very few people and no claims can be extrapolated beyond the very people who have answered the questionnaire. There are thus no claims to representativity, but we can read the figures as testimonies from individuals who have chosen to call themselves Buddhists: what is their Buddhism like and how do they negotiate their chosen Buddhism with their Christian environment?

Firstly, we can see that the majority of those who identify as Buddhists also identify as Christians:

	Comp. B	Fa much B	Mod. B	Fa little B	Not B
	4	*4*	*13*	*24*	
Comp. C	1				
Fa much C	1		3	6	
Mod. C		1	6	5	
Fa little C		2	2	10	
Not C	2	1	2	2	

Many of those who call themselves Buddhists have not chosen Buddhism instead of Christianity; they have chosen both. We can see that it is far more common to be Buddhist *and* Christian, than to be exclusively Buddhist. Even some (the majority, in fact) of the 'strong' Buddhists combine their Buddhism with Christianity (5 out of 8). This is even more evident when we turn to the 'mild' Buddhists: 32 combine Buddhism with Christianity, while 4 chose Buddhism only.

Among the strong Buddhists we find 5 women and 3 men, among the mild Buddhists 18 women and 18 men (with the men in majority 15/8 in the lowest category 'fairly little'). Education-wise, the Strong Buddhists are not university educated (only one of them has a university degree) whereas there are 12 university educated persons in the 'fairly little' category. This is in line with the general picture that there is negative correlation between university education and strong religiosity.

Almost all the Buddhists make use of the Church. Not only were they baptised, confirmed and married in the church; their children are also baptised and confirmed.

	Comp. B	Fa much B	Mod. B	Fa little B
	4	*4*	*13*	*24*
Baptised	3	3	12	23
Confirmed	3	2	12	15
Church Wed	3	3	3	11
Child Bapd	2	3	5	11
Child Confd	1	2	3	5
Other rel. rit.	2	1	1	29

One person has stated that they had a 'Buddhist wedding'. This is the only instance where a specifically Buddhist rite is mentioned. The high figure for 'other religious rituals' among the 'fairly little Buddhists' should not be interpreted as religious rituals in religions other than Christianity. The majority of those who gave specifics (not only Buddhists) wrote things like 'attended funeral', 'received communion' or 'helped a neighbour'.

If the Buddhists in Enköping are so Christian, what are their specific Buddhist traits? There is one activity that is closely linked to defining oneself as a Buddhist, and that is meditation. Of all the 1045 responses 15 persons stated that they meditate regularly, out of these nine identified as Buddhists. The practice of meditation is thus a distinguishing feature of the Buddhists in the study. Two 'completely Buddhists' meditate regularly, the other two have tried meditation. All who identify as Buddhists have at least heard of meditation. The majority of the Buddhists, however, do not meditate regularly and a third of those who meditate regularly are not Buddhists. The more a person regards herself as Buddhist, the more likely she is to practice or have practised meditation. Among the 'fairly little Buddhists' (24 persons) 14 had only heard of meditation but never tried it, 2 practised regularly and 8 were no longer practising meditation.

In Q 23 we asked about religious experiences:

23. Have you experienced anything of the following?
0 That you have received the help in life that you have needed as a direct answer to prayer
0 That you have felt God's presence
0 That you have felt the presence of some kind of spirit
0 That you have been filled with infinite peace
0 A strong spiritual experience in nature
0 A strong spiritual experience in connection with the birth of a child
0 A strong spiritual experience in a Church, Mosque, Synagogue etc
0 A strong spiritual experience in connection with the death of someone
0 That you have been in contact with a deceased person
0 That you have had an out-of-body experience
0 Near-death experiences of some kind
0 That you have had telepathic contact with someone
0 That you have been able to predict the future in a supernatural way
0 That what has happened in your life seems to have been pre-ordered

Those who identify as Buddhists tend to have many spiritual experiences:

	Comp. B	Fa much B	Mod. B	Fa little B
	4	*4*	*13*	*24*
Answer to prayer	2	3	2	4
God's presence	3	1	4	4
Presence of spirit	4	2	5	11
Infinite peace	2	2	6	8
Nature	3	2	5	12
Childbirth	1		2	9
Place of worship	2	1	4	1

Death	2	1	1	3
Out-of-body	2	2	2	3
Near-death	1	1		1
Telepathy	2	1	3	2
Premonition	2	1	2	3
Pre-ordered events	2	3	3	4

The strong Buddhists score highly when it comes to religious experiences. To experience the presence of some kind of spirit and to have strong spiritual experiences in nature seem to be the most common kinds of spiritual experiences for all the Buddhists. The Swedes are 'nature mystics' (shown in other studies), and to have a strong spiritual experience in Mother Nature is the most common type of spiritual experience in the survey (about 20 per cent of the respondents reported having had such experiences). Experiences of infinite peace together with experiences of the pre-ordering of events come in as the second most common spiritual experiences in the survey – and this is also the case with the mild Buddhists, but not with the strong Buddhists. The strong Buddhists lean towards a theistic spirituality, they report answers to prayer and experiences of God's presence.

This, of course, cannot be taken as being representative of the Buddhists in Sweden, or even in Enköping – the sample is far too small. But it does show that it is possible to identify strongly as a Buddhist and hold views and interpret experiences in ways that are not traditionally part of normative Buddhism. If we turn to the two questions where we explicitly ask about beliefs in God and the after-life, we find the following:

Q 40. Which of the following statements is closest to your own view? *(Tick one box only)*

0 I believe in a personal God with whom you can have a personal relationship
0 I believe in an impersonal higher power
0 I believe that God is rather something within every human being than something without
0 I don't believe in a God or a supernatural power
0 I don't know what to believe

	Comp. B	Much B	Mod. B	Little B
	4	*4*	*13*	*24*
Personal God	2		1	2
Impers. Power	1	1	6	5
God Within	1	2	3	9
No supernat.		1	1	2
Don't know			1	6

Q 41. What do you think happens to us after death? Tick one box only in front of the alternative that is closest to your own view.

0 There is something after death but I don't know what
0 We go either to heaven or to hell
0 We all go to heaven
0 After death we are reborn again and again into this world
0 We reach an eternal state of enlightenment/light/bliss
0 Nothing, death is the end
0 I have no idea of what happens to us after death
0 Own alternative……..

	Comp. B	Much B	Mod. B	Little B
	4	*4*	*13*	*24*
Something	1		4	9
Heaven or hell				
Heaven for all				
Reborn		1	6	4
Eternal bliss			1	
Death is the end		1	2	3
Don't know	2			6
Own alt.	1	1	2	4

A little play with statistics: 50 per cent of those who identify themselves as 'completely Buddhist' believe in 'a personal God with whom you can have a personal relationship', but only 42 per cent of the 'completely Christian' believe in such a God. Is it surprising that the Enköping Buddhists are fairly Christian? Or is it more surprising that Enköping Christians call themselves Buddhists? When given the possibility to tick more than one box, Buddhism was an attractive alternative to 44 persons.

What kind of Buddhism is it that they know and have encountered? The survey does not provide us with an answer. But if we draw on knowledge of Swedish culture and combine that with interviews with some of the respondents to the questionnaire, we can suggest three main sources of knowledge about Buddhism in popular culture.

The first source of knowledge about Buddhism is from religious studies, which is a compulsory subject on all levels in the Swedish schools. Buddhism is portrayed as a peaceful, rational way of life. It is suggested that Buddhism is a phenomenon that is more of a philosophy than a religion, that it draws on experience rather than dogma and that peace and happiness for all living beings is at its heart. Buddhism appears to be a religion that has never been involved in violent conflicts. Another source of inspiration or knowledge is the Dalai Lama, especially his *The Art of Happiness: A Handbook for Living* which has sold (2003) 300,000 copies in Sweden. The impact of an international bestseller can be questioned – do people read the books that they buy, and if they do, what do they mean to them? Thomas A. Tweed has coined the term nightstand Buddhists for Western people who read Buddhist inspirational books. Carl Bielefeldt in his article 'Divisions and direction of Buddhism in America today'[2] uses the term 'Buddhist sympathizers' and describes their nightstand reading as 'public Buddhism' or 'media Buddhism'.

The second source of knowledge comes from holidays in Thailand. Thailand has become the new favourite holiday destination for the Swedes. In 2003 54,693 Swedes visited Phuket and 46,986 Bangkok (as a comparison Las Palmas had 73,807 visits and Palma de Mallorca 54,863 visits in 2003). Many travellers have given testimonies of the kind, friendly, generous and truly spiritual people they have encountered in holiday resorts in Thailand. This has come to the fore especially in the aftermath of the tsunami in December 2004 (approx. 600 Swedish citizens on holiday in Thailand died in the tsunami). Many found comfort both from the team from the Church of Sweden that came to

---

[2] (http://www.american-buddha.com/carl.bielefeldt.stanford.htm?signup)

the site of the disaster and from the ministering of the local Buddhist people.

The respondents have presumably encountered a friendly, fairly undemanding Buddhism, a Buddhism that gives room for spiritual experiences and affirms human life. But the Christianity they grew up with wasn't too bad either. It connected them to the past (the beautiful medieval churches) and to people around them. If they are not forced to make a choice between the two religions there are no reasons why they shouldn't choose both. This might well be what religious identity may look like even beyond Enköping.

RUBEN L.F. HABITO

Being Buddhist, Being Christian: Being Both, Being Neither

Being Buddhist

My path as a Buddhist began in my early twenties as I was introduced to Zen Master Yamada Koun in a formal encounter known as *shōken* (literally, 'illuminating and seeing') at San-un Zendo, or 'The Zen Hall of the Three Clouds', in Kamakura, Japan in October of 1971. 'Three Clouds' stands for the three founding Teachers of the Sanbō Kyōdan Lineage, Harada Dai-un (Great Cloud), Yasutani Haku-un (White Cloud), and Yamada Kōun (Cultivating Cloud). On this occasion, I was being initiated into the Zen Buddhist community that practised according to the guidelines of this lineage as established by these three Zen Masters (Rōshi).

To the Master's question, 'What is your aspiration in Zen practice?' I responded, taking cue from the various options presented by the instructor at the preparatory talks leading to this encounter: 'I wish to discover and realise my True Self'. And based on this response, the Master gave me the Koan MU to guide my Zen practice from that point on.

A Koan is a practical device, usually involving an anecdote of an exchange between a Zen Master and a Student or Monk, a question, or a phrase, given to a practitioner to 'work on' in seated meditative practice (*zazen*). It provides a way of derailing the activity of the discursive intellect, and goading a practitioner toward an experiential moment of awakening.

This famous Koan MU goes like this:

> A monk asked Zen Master Jōshū (Chao-chou in Chinese): Does a dog have Buddha nature or not? Jōshū answered, MU.

The Chinese character that corresponds to this curt reply 'MU' literally means 'No!' or 'No way!'. Read in this manner, the Koan would seem to be negating a widely held doctrine in Mahayana Buddhism. This is the doctrine to the effect that 'All sentient beings are endowed with Buddha nature'.

Accepting the proposition, and recognising that a dog belongs to the class of sentient beings, the logical conclusion would be: 'Yes, of course, Q.E.D., a dog IS endowed with Buddha nature'.

However, in this Koan, Zen Master Jōshū seems to be either challenging this doctrine (that all sentient beings are endowed with Buddha nature) or denying that a dog is a sentient being, which of course goes against common sense or accepted convention. In any case, in responding 'No!' to the question, 'Does a dog have Buddha nature or not?' – the Zen Master is throwing out established Buddhist doctrine, or common sense altogether, or both.

The point of the Koan, however, as explained to the practitioner who receives this from the Master, is neither about accepting or denying the proposition about sentient beings having Buddha nature, or not. Rather, the point, it is emphasised, is to invite the practitioner to engage in seated meditative practice (*zazen*) in a way that enables him or her to go beyond the dualistic opposites of Yes and No, of having and not having. The practitioner is enjoined simply to breathe in and out in a natural way, to be fully aware of each movement as one breathes, and let each outbreath be accompanied by that inscrutable word-sound MU. Just put your whole being in MU, the practitioner is told, until one becomes totally absorbed, or better, dissolved, in MU.

Having been given these instructions, I then plunged into my practice, taking time (usually about half an hour to an hour daily, and an all-day group *zazen* twice a month at the Zendo) in my regular schedule, which at that point was devoted to learning the Japanese language at the Jesuit Language school in Kamakura, to sit in a cross-legged posture, with the back straightened, breathing in and out, with the outbreath accompanied by MU. During the rest of the time apart from sitting, one is advised to be mindful of one's breath, and occasionally, in the midst of some routine activity like walking, sweeping the floor, or relaxing during a break between classes, one is also advised to let the outbreath be accompanied by the silent sound of MUUUUU, and then go on.

It was not more than a few weeks since being given this Koan for my practice when, one afternoon, coming home after group *zazen* at

San-un Zendo, and sitting on an easy chair in my room, it suddenly dawned on me. 'Aha! This is it! Of course!'. In that instant I *knew* what this MU was all about. This sudden realisation made me laugh out loud, leap from my chair in exuberant joy, and rush out of my room, looking for my Jesuit spiritual director, Fr Thomas Hand, to tell him, 'I got it! I got it!'. Fr Hand was then also practising Zen under the same Zen Master Yamada, and it was he who had encouraged me and introduced me to the Master.

What did I 'get'? The image I recall that provoked convulsive laughter, verging on tears, was that of the Buddha with the half-smile, an image I had previously seen in pictures. In that flash of an instant as I sat on my chair, I *understood* from inside, what that half-smile was all about. The half-smile was the Buddha's way of answering the question 'Who am I?' 'What is the nature of the universe?' 'What is this matter of being born, getting sick, getting old, and dying, all about?'

I could not contain myself with the laughter and tears that ensued, and at Fr Hand's urging, I phoned Yamada Rōshi's residence, and requested an appointment for an interview. After two successive visits over the next few days, wherein he asked me the usual checking questions related to the Koan MU, he affirmed that I had indeed experienced what in Zen is known as *kenshō*, literally, 'seeing into one's true nature'. He then gave me directions for further Zen practice, and handed me a small booklet that was to be my 'syllabus' for continuing Koan work under his guidance. This was in early December of 1971.

The ensuing years found me doing graduate studies at the Department of Indology and Buddhist Studies of the University of Tokyo. I had the privilege of studying with internationally known Japanese scholars as my mentors in the various subjects, including seminars reading Sanskrit, Pāli, Chinese and Japanese Buddhist texts. My graduate dissertation was on the understanding of the Absolute in Indian Buddhist thought, focusing on the notion of *dharmakāya* as expounded in the Sanskrit treatise (*Ratnagotravibhāga Mahāyānottaratantra Śāstra*, said to be by Sāramati). This was a fifth-century elaboration on the keynote Mahayana notion of Emptiness (*śūnyatā*), presented in affirmative ('kataphatic') terms that contrasted with the negative ('apophatic') logic of second-century philosopher Nāgārjuna.

Concurrently, incidentally, I was also allowed to take subjects in Christian scripture and theology at the Jesuit Theologate at Sophia University, in preparation for ordination to the priesthood in the Roman Catholic Church. I was ordained in March 1976, and continuing my Buddhist studies, completed the doctoral program at Tokyo University in 1978. I was subsequently assigned to teach at the Philosophy Department of Sophia University, focusing on introductory and advanced undergraduate courses in Buddhism.

Through these years, with my ongoing practice of Zen meditation, with my academic studies in various historical and doctrinal aspects of Buddhism, and then especially with my work of introducing and elucidating aspects of Buddhist thought to the Japanese college students who came to my classes, I myself came to a deeper and deeper understanding and appreciation of Buddhist perspectives on the world, on human existence, on spiritual practice.

The three marks of Dharma, consisting of Dissatisfactoriness (*dukkha*), Impermanence (*aniccā*), and the Selfless (*anattā*), as presented in the Pāli scriptures, have served for me as very clear guidelines for understanding our human situation.[1] The Four Ennobling Truths, a cornerstone of the Buddha's presentation of his enlightened outlook to those around him, has continued to serve as a structural map for me in looking at our ailing human condition and seeking ways toward healing. It also offers a framework we can follow on a communal level toward the healing of our global malaise.[2] Those who have heard me give talks on spiritual practice as related to socio-ecological engagement will be able to recognize this structural map as an underlying framework in my view of the world.

A central Buddhist notion that continues to inform my outlook on the world and on our human existence is that of 'Emptiness' (*śūnyatā*). In our group sittings at our Zen community we regularly chant the Heart Sutra in English translation, and the constant refrain highlighted here is the statement, 'Form is no other than Emptiness, Emptiness no other than Form'. 'Form' is whatever can be seen, heard, smelled, tasted, touched, or conceptualised, in short, all that exists in this universe of beings.

---

[1] I have developed this in my *Experiencing Buddhism: Ways of Wisdom and Compassion*. New York: Orbis Books, 2005: 40-51.
[2] I have addressed this in an essay published in a collection in honour of the late Bhikkhu Buddhadāsa on his 84th birth anniversary, entitled 'The Four Noble Truths as a Buddhist Spirituality of Engagement'. Sulak Sivaraksa, ed., *Radical Conservatism: Buddhism in the Contemporary World*. Bangkok: International Network of Engaged Buddhists, 1990: 498-511, as well as in *Healing Breath: Zen Spirituality for a Wounded Earth*. Dallas: MKZC Publications, 2001.

To say that all that exists in this universe 'is no other than Emptiness' is indeed to make a major declaration about the nature of the world and of reality. But this is only one side. The other side is that this Emptiness is 'no other than Form (that is, everything that exists in the universe).' These two sides are equally affirmed with full force, as expressions of this view of reality that unfolds from Zen practice and experience.

I have found a work by Nishitani Keiji[3] to be a very helpful and effective presentation of the worldview centred on the notion of Emptiness. I had begun to read some essays in this collection as I was just finishing my first year of language school, about the time I had formally begun my practice of Zen. I recall that as I sat in *zazen* with the koan MU, I took the hint from the Master that it was not a matter of answering 'yes' or 'no' to the question of whether the dog had Buddha nature or not, and also not a question of 'having' or 'not having'. It was a question that pointed to a realm beyond the duality of 'being' and 'nonbeing', or 'something' as opposed to 'nothing'. Nishitani's essays in this collection sought to elucidate 'the standpoint of Emptiness' as that which transcends these dualistic oppositions. These essays gave me an important hint in what I sought to realize in my Zen practice. My search came to be focused on the question: What is that which is neither 'being' nor 'nonbeing'?

This is the question that was in the background of my mind, as I sat on my easychair that afternoon after the group *zazen*.

Nāgārjuna's Verses on the Middle Way (*Mūlamadhyamaka-kārikā*), particularly XXIV, 18, 19, also offer a hint on understanding this:

> Whatever is dependently co-arisen
> That is explained to be emptiness...
> Something that is not dependently arisen,
> Such a thing does not exist.[4]

What this is saying is that to affirm all existent things as 'empty' is not to take a stance of nihilism, but to affirm that whatever exists does not do so as an independent substance (it is devoid, or 'empty', of substantial nature of itself) but precisely exists only as it is intimately

---

[3] Nishitani Keiji, *Shūkyō to wa Nanika?,* a collection of essays translated as *Religion and Nothingness*, by Jan van Bragt. Berkeley: University of California Press, 1982.
[4] Translated By Jay Garfield, *The Fundamental Wisdom of the Middle Way.* New York: Oxford University Press, 1995: 304.

interconnected with everything else that exists. In other words, this is an affirmation of a vision of the interconnectedness of all things in the universe.

What I 'saw' in that flash of an instant, as I saw the image of the Buddha's half-smile, is this world of emptiness *qua* interconnectedness. And this 'I' is right there at the heart of it! This is the realization that made me burst into laughter and tears at the same time.

To 'see into one's own nature' is simply to realise this interconnectedness with everything in the universe, not just in conceptual terms, but truly, intimately, as the Truth (Dharma) that makes me who I am, the Truth that makes everything what it is, just as it is. This is to take on the mind of the Awakened One, to see things with the Buddha's eye of Wisdom. And this way of seeing things as they are, as interconnected with everything, is what grounds a life of compassion. The joys and hopes, the pains and sorrows, of each and every sentient being in this universe, is no other than one's very own joys and hopes, pains and sorrows.

This compassion is embodied in a powerful way in the figure of Kuan-yin, or Kannon in Japanese pronunciation. Kannon, also known as Kanzeon, is the 'Hearer of the Cries of the World', that is, the cries of pain and suffering of sentient beings. She is also depicted as with a thousand arms, reaching out in all directions to help those in need in their particular ways and situations.

It is the cultivation of this Wisdom of Emptiness, that is, the realization of one's intimate interconnectedness with all beings, leading to a way of life grounded in compassion, that is at the heart of the Zen Buddhist practice that I have learned from my Teachers in this tradition. This is what I also seek to convey to all who seek my guidance, as I take on the tasks of Zen Teacher at our Maria Kannon Zen Center in Dallas, where I have been since 1989.

In this capacity, I have been attending the annual meetings of the American Zen Teachers' Association, a group of those with authorisation to teach Zen in their respective lineages who are currently leading their own practice communities. As we in our own different ways endeavour to embody the spirit of Zen Buddhism, specifically in the context of North American culture and society, through our annual gatherings and regular communications, we learn from, support, and challenge one another in our shared tasks and responsibilities.

I have also been inspired and supported by my association with the Buddhist Peace Fellowship, on whose Board I served for a number of years, and I continue to be a supporting member. This is a group founded in the 1960s by Robert Aitken, an esteemed Elder dharma brother in the Sanbo Kyodan lineage, and associates, an association whose primary mission is to embody the ideals and take on the concrete tasks of a socially engaged Buddhism in contemporary society. We have continued to maintain connections of solidarity with Buddhist groups in different parts of the world, notably through the International Network of Engaged Buddhists (INEB) initiated by Sulak Sivaraksa, a prominent social critic and lay Buddhist based in Bangkok, Thailand.

Reflecting on all I have received and continue to receive as I continue in my Buddhist path, I bow in deepest gratitude to all the Buddhas and bodhisattvas of the ten directions, in the past, present and future, and in particular to my Teacher, Yamada Kōun, all my Sanbō Kyōdan dharma brothers and sisters, to my co- practitioners at Maria Kannon Zen Center and to my Zen Teacher colleagues, and the numerous persons I have met through the years who also follow the Buddhist path in their own particular ways, and who continue to be sources of inspiration for me as I tread my own.

Being Christian

When I embarked on the Buddhist path described above, I was in my early twenties, a Jesuit seminarian preparing for ordination to the priesthood. Born and raised in a devout Roman Catholic household in the Philippines, since childhood I learned to pray daily with family, in the morning and at bedtime, and before meals. I felt deep devotion to the Blessed Mother Mary, and kept a rosary in my pocket, praying with it daily over a number of years up to my early teens. I loved going to early Sunday mass, when the choir would lead the congregation in Latin chants, with the uplifting aroma of incense all around.

Then I began to feel some stirrings in my mid-teens that led me to question basic things I assumed while growing up. Does God really exist? If so, and if we are to believe that God is a loving and all-knowing God, how can there be so much suffering in the world? My reading of the existentialists, notably Albert Camus' works, heightened these questions all the more.

I recall being in a classroom in my senior year of high school, half-listening to the Literature teacher explain the intricacies of a poem, when my gaze was drawn outside the window to the empty blue sky. At that moment a curious thought came to me: if I could flash a beam of light from where I was and send it across the universe (based on what had I read of the laws of physics at that point), given enough time, it would come right back to this place where it is beamed off. The universe, I understood from my readings of those books on physics and relativity that had fascinated me since my fifth grade in elementary school, was 'finite, yet unbounded', and 'curved', that is, in such a way that a beam of light does not go in a straight line but along the curvature of the universe. Hence this notion of the return to the place where it started, given 'enough' time (maybe trillions of light years?) came to mind. And with this thought came another one: this makes the idea of a god up there, separate from the universe itself, 'managing' all this, listening to prayers of us puny humans on earth, answering some, and not answering others, and so on, a totally redundant idea! The white-bearded grandfather god that I had imagined as a child disappeared from my horizon from that moment on.

What remained in view was this wondrous universe that functions with its own in-built laws, wherein every element is interconnected with everything else. But then with the demise of the grandfather god, new questions came on the scene. What then of human destiny? What are we here for? How do we humans live in a way that is most fulfilling and meaningful, facing the fact that we are all going to die anyway?

These questions escalated as I entered college and lived in a boarding house all by myself, now away from family. With a full scholarship provided by the Philippine government toward a degree in physics at the state university, I was to be a scientist who would help take my country on the road to technological advancement, along with some dozens of others selected from all over the country in competitive examinations. However, instead of paying attention to my math and physics homework, I would rather spend my time in the library for hours poring over books in philosophy and religion, trying to get some light into those questions that were now burning in my heart. This questioning was also spurred by conversations with new friends I was privileged to meet at the Student Catholic Action Centre of the university, where the names of Sartre, Camus, Dostoevsky, as well as Joyce, D.H. Lawrence, and a host of other writers and thinkers I came to know about for the first time, came up not infrequently.

At the centre wall of the main hall of the Student Catholic Action centre, where I hung out most of the time when not in class, was a portrait of a smiling priest, Fr John P. Delaney SJ, who had died some years before I came to the university. More senior students and others who had been around longer kept mentioning him in conversation, also often citing the motto that this Jesuit priest had himself lived by and had inspired those who met him during the years he was chaplain at this student centre: 'Give until it hurts'. Somehow this man had become an icon and ongoing inspiration for the different kinds of people who found their way at the Student Catholic Centre for various reasons, whether to participate in the liturgy, attend open lectures, join in volunteer activities, or like myself, just hang out and spend the time chatting with friends or looking out for some pretty young lass to befriend and hopefully go further. The life and words of JPD, as he was endearingly called, continued to be cherished in this student community. I found myself also nodding, and saying, 'that is the kind of life I would like to live, that is the kind of person I would like to be'.

At the end of my first year in college, auspicious events led me to a visit to the Jesuit Provincialate in Manila, and to an unscheduled face-to-face conversation with the vocation director, Fr Benigno Mayo SJ. In the course of this conversation, a moment of clarity and on the spot decision led me to ask him, 'how do I apply for admission?', and before I realised what I was getting into, I found myself going through the interview process over the next few weeks, and several months later I was admitted as a novice in the Society of Jesus.

Even as a Jesuit novice and then as a scholastic (this is the term used to refer to those in studies in preparation for ordination as a Jesuit priest), I was still struggling with the basic issue of God's existence. The white-bearded grandfather god was already dead for me, since that incident of seeing the wide empty sky while looking outside the window in senior high school. But, also during that year of senior high school, on my way to a dance party while talking with a friend who was describing an experience during anatomy class in medical school, I was graced with momentary experiences that gave me a glimpse of an inscrutable, 'unthinkable' kind of Wisdom, as I considered the intricate workings of the human body, of subatomic particles, and the movements of the stars.[5]

Yet, situations of chaos and unpredictability on different levels, and the realities of evil and of human suffering and injustice in the world, kept me in a state of intellectual struggle even through the years of my Jesuit formation. These realities continued to present for me a major challenge to such notions as Omnipotence and Omniscience, Justice and Love, attributes of the God of classical theism. I found these attributes hard to reconcile with the overwhelming sense of evil and suffering in the world that I had grown more and more sensitive to through the years, all the more as I was exposed to these realities directly in my visits to grassroots communities in the Philippines and in other Asian countries.

What kept me going through all this time was the inner nourishment received through the Spiritual Exercises of St Ignatius, founder of the Jesuit Order. Sometime during the initial two-year novitiate, each Jesuit goes on silent retreat for thirty days to undertake these Spiritual Exercises, and continues with a shortened, eight-day version annually. Outside of retreat period, on a daily basis, an hour of meditation or contemplation in the spirit of the Exercises is included in the schedule, in addition to other devotions and communal worship that are part of Jesuit community life.

The crowning point of these Exercises is a form of practice known as the Contemplation on God's Love. After going through four phases ('four weeks') with their given themes and directions, which in different and complementary ways usher the exercitant through the purificatory, illuminative, and unitive stages of the spiritual journey, one is invited to this form of contemplative practice with concrete directives.

This exercise can be described in summary form like this: 'Consider inanimate objects like rocks and pebbles'. Then, 'consider plants, such as trees and grasses'. Then, 'consider animals, like dogs and cats and salamanders, birds and bees, and the like'. And then, 'consider human beings, in particular, certain human beings close to you'. At each consideration, the exercitant is enjoined just to breathe and stay in respectful silence, beholding with one's mind's eye whatever is presented before one, as outlined above.

---

[5] I wrote about this experience in an essay included in a collection edited by Harold Kasimov, Linda Keenan, and John Keenan, entitled *Beside Still Waters: Jews and Christians Encounter Buddhism.* Boston: Wisdom Publications, 2003.

This for me was a powerful kind of practice that brought in with new intensity those glimpses of the inscrutable, unthinkable Wisdom I was graced with in senior high school on the way to a dance. It would usher in repeated experiences of seeing everything around me, the stones on the walking path, the shrubs and hedges and flowers, the mice and cockroaches and dogs and cats, each and everyone of these persons around me that I get to meet daily, as suffused with that inscrutable, unthinkable kind of Love and Wisdom that I realised also enveloped and embraced myself in totality, unconditionally. I could not conceptualise what this was, and it remained in that realm of the Unknown, but yet I also felt Its immediacy in every breath and in every beat of my pulse.

Yet even these experiences of being enveloped and embraced by this inscrutable, unknowable Love and Wisdom did not give sufficient basis to make the affirmation, 'God exists'. The question of suffering and injustice and evil continued to nag at me, objecting: 'If God, who must be a loving and all-wise and all-powerful Being, *does exist*, how can such a God allow all this to happen?'.

A Jesuit in formation, preparing for ordination to the priesthood, yet not able to affirm the existence of God! I was a living contradiction, a condition which I felt less intensely on some days than others, when I had my daily rituals, my studies and my volunteer activities to keep my mind and body occupied, generally in ways fruitful and satisfying in themselves.

It was mid-afternoon on a day when I felt this contradiction rather intensely, and I could not settle down and concentrate on anything, so I just kept pacing the long corridors back and forth, at the seminary, Loyola House of Studies in Quezon City, Philippines, where I was doing my studies and living in a community with about 80 other Jesuits. In the middle of all this walking about, I stopped in the middle of the corridor, and my gaze fell upon a wooden crucifix that was hung on a wall at the end of the corridor. Stopping for a brief moment with my gaze on that image of the wooden Christ upon the Cross, I saw, in that figure, the children in the neighbouring *barrio* (village) where I helped out as a volunteer, who were suffering from malnutrition, who had acute skin disease, who would die of some illness aggravated by their malnutrition; the workers at the nearby factory laid off due to economic recession, parents of those malnourished children, trying their best to make ends meet but always left short; and my mind's eye travelled from those whom I had some acquaintance with, to those I did not, including all the people who were ever born and lived and suffered on this Earth, and those who continue to live and suffer, and those who will be born and will thus suffer, each in their different ways, many of them crying out, 'My God, My God, why have you forsaken me?'. All of these people were right there, in that Figure on the Cross.

As I beheld that Figure, and all that it represented, all the people who were ever born and lived and suffered and died, across centuries of time and across cultures and countries and continents, suddenly a voice came, gently yet clearly, from within, addressing the Figure on the Cross, saying: *'You are My Beloved, in whom I am well-pleased'*.

At that moment I was enveloped by a deep, deep peace and inner assurance, which I could not, and still can not, fully explain in words. I can only say that, upon hearing those words from within, I realised that I could live with the fact of evil, and suffering, and injustice, not in a way that condones these, nor in a way that allows myself to be taken in by these forces, but in a way that enabled me simply to accept the fact that they exist. And at the same time, I realised that in the face of all this evil and suffering and injustice, there is 'something' more convincing, more reassuring, more overpowering, than all this evil and suffering, and that made it all worthwhile undergoing this, and even dying as a consequence of it. That 'something' remains for me a totally inscrutable Mystery, but I can only refer to it as the Source of that voice that I heard, saying, to all those who were ever born and lived and died, and who will be born and live and die, my own puny little self included, that *no matter what, 'You are My Beloved, in whom I am well-pleased'*. It was, and is, a voice of unconditional acceptance, of all that was, is, and ever will be, *no matter what*, that I can still hear in varying degrees of intensity every now and then even up to now.

It would take me many more years to be able to sort out what happened in that moment, as I continued with my studies as a Jesuit in the Philippines, then as I was sent to Japan to study some more and to join the work of the Jesuits there, as I was ordained priest (in 1976), and continued in priestly and educational work in the Japan Province of the Society of Jesus. My theological studies in preparation for ordination gave me the opportunity to read and reflect and ponder over basic questions I had been asking through the years, and enabled me to connect basic terms and concepts in Christian tradition with the inner assurance I had received.

I have been led to understand that to be 'Christian' is to live in the Spirit of Christ, the Anointed One of God, and at the heart of this is to live as affirmed by that unconditional Love that says, 'You are My Beloved, in whom I am well-pleased'. And in finding one's whole life, one's entire being so affirmed, and affirmed unconditionally, one is thereby empowered also to embrace, and affirm, just as unconditionally, each and everyone that one encounters in this life, each and every being that was ever born and lived and died, and will be born and live and die. At least, this is how I am trying to live.

All the individual encounters and events, all the decisions big and small that I have made in my life, including those in my work as a Jesuit scholastic and then as an ordained priest, and including my decision to ask for a dispensation from my Jesuit and priestly vows, my departure from Japan, my transfer to Dallas, Texas, to take up a teaching position at Perkins School of Theology, Southern Methodist University, my marriage to Maria (Reis Habito), the ways we have tried to bring up our two boys, Florian and Benjamin, the ways I try to relate to each and everyone I meet at work and in other social contexts, all find a connecting point in that voice, heard clearly as I was pacing the seminary corridors, and then again and again in many different ways through the years. *You are my Beloved, in whom I am well-pleased.*

It is my continuing hope that before I breathe my last, perhaps after I retire from my 'day job' that keeps my family sheltered and fed, I would be able to reflect somewhat more systematically on all of this, taking cue from each article of the Nicene Creed, beginning with *I believe in God*, down to *...the resurrection of the body, and life everlasting, Amen*, seek to articulate how I am able to join the Christian community through the ages in making these affirmations, though I am only able to get a glimmer of what these 'articles of faith' imply, as 'through a glass darkly'.[6]

---

[6] I have made an initial attempt with the last article in the Creed, in an essay, 'The Resurrection of the Body, and Life Everlasting', published in *The Sound of Liberating Truth: Essays in Buddhist Christian Dialogue, in Honor of Frederick J. Streng*, ed. By Paul Ingram and Sallie King. New York: Curzon, 1999.

Being Both?

If I am asked, 'are you Buddhist?' my response would be, 'By the merit of the countless Buddhas and Bodhisattvas throughout space and time, I aspire to continue in this path of Awakening'.

I take refuge in the Buddha, the Dharma, and the Sangha.

By this, I identify and place myself with those who take the teachings (Dharma) of the Awakened One (Buddha) as a guide in their lives, the community of sentient beings like myself, who seek to cultivate wisdom and embody compassion in their life (Sangha). In doing so, I acknowledge my gratitude to the numerous individuals in my life who have inspired me to continue on a Buddhist path, and seek their inspiration and guidance.

If I am asked, 'are you Christian?' my response would be, 'By the grace of God, with the guidance of the Holy Spirit, I aspire to live following the way of Jesus the Christ.'

In the name of the Father, and of the Son, and of the Holy Spirit. Amen.

By this, I express infinite gratitude and total surrender to that Unknowable Mystery, that whom Jesus called Abba, Father, in whose Motherly Love I find myself embraced every moment together with the whole of creation; to the Beloved who, begotten of the Divine, became emptied of this and took on the form of our humanity, revealing to us our own divine source; to the Consoler who manifests to all people throughout all ages and in all places, all that is good, true, holy, and beautiful.

I identify and place myself with all those who have followed, or who seek to follow Jesus as their model in life, seeking to be on the side of the marginalised, the poor and oppressed of this earth in the way Jesus was, to witness to the *kindom* of God in our midst (I emphasize here the word *kindom*, the circle of those bound together as kin, as explained by Mujerista theologian Ana Maria Isasi Diaz, and not 'kingdom', which implies a vertical hierarchical rule). I continually seek the help and inspiration of all the Christian saints, canonised and yet to be canonised, who have lived selfless lives in the service of others, following Jesus in the way of the Cross, toward the newness of life in the Resurrection.

Yet in proclaiming such a lofty ideal, I also confess my sinfulness in not always being able to live up to it. I can only continue to aspire to do so.

But if asked, 'are you then *both* Buddhist and Christian?' – I hesitate and am unable to answer for now. My hesitation has to do with this important disclaimer: I do not consider myself 'part Buddhist, part Christian', or 'sometimes Buddhist, sometimes Christian'.

In saying that I aspire to live as a Buddhist, my intent is to be Buddhist through and through, living according to the Precepts, taking the Dharma as a guide, and the Sangha as my support. In our Zen community, we chant the Three Refuges, the Sublime Attitudes, the Heart Sutra, the Four Vows of the Bodhisattva, and many other Buddhist chants. We also recite the Verse of Atonement, acknowledging our failings, owning up to and taking responsibility for 'all harmful karma ever committed by me since of old, on account of my greed, anger, and delusive ignorance', and yet ever seeking to continue walking the path of Awakening.

In acknowledging that I seek to live as a Christian, my hope is that I am able to live thoroughly in the Spirit of Christ Jesus, in a way that does not and will not compromise anything that is involved in Christian life and understanding. Again I also confess my sinfulness in not always being able to live up to this ideal, but continue to pray and ask for guidance in mending my ways and living a bit more closely to the path Jesus opened to all of us.

Being Neither?

There is a saying in Japanese, to the effect that 'Those who chase after two rabbits will catch neither'. So perhaps in declaring my aspiration to live as a Buddhist, and my aspiration to live as a Christian, as I have described above, I am thereby contradicting myself, and rendering myself unable to live up to either in a faithful and authentic way. This is what lies behind my hesitation to answer with a flat Yes to the question of whether I am both (Buddhist and Christian).

In my hesitation, or better, my current inability to say that I am Buddhist *and* Christian at the same time, perhaps it would be more fitting to say, I am *neither?*

After all, when I sit in Zen, either by myself facing a wall, or at Maria Kannon Zen Center with the small community of those who join us in our regular sitting, just *being there*, fully present in each moment, with every breath, with every sensation, with every thought, with every pain, there is no Buddhist there, there is no Christian either.

There is just Mary, at the foot of the Cross of Jesus, bearing in herself all the pains of her own beloved Son, who in turn bears the all the pains of this our sinful world in his own body. There is just Kannon, Hearer of the Cries of the world, who hears the voices of suffering of all sentient beings caught up in greed, ill will, and delusion, and who responds to these cries and voices, reaching out in all directions with her thousand arms, to teach, to advise, to chastise, to console, to heal, or just to be there with the pain.

Michael von Brück

A Theology of Multiple Religious Identity

1. Remarks on the Notion of Identity

The notion of identity may be considered in our context in two ways, first as a philosophical or epistemological term, second as a psychological and sociological term. Philosophically identity is established in case something refers to itself. The problem lies in the term 'itself'. Something is given as representation to itself in as much as an objectification of a subject happens. If this is so, the identifier and the identified are the same and not the same at the same time. Interestingly enough, time comes into play here. Between the subject and the object in the process of cognition there is no difference in space, but in time. Identity implies identification, and this is a temporal process. In other words: identity is not a fact but a process in the making. Much more would have to be said here, but this may suffice.

Secondly, psychologically identity means a cluster of dependencies: we depend on relations established during the process of maturing, relations to the parents, to language and environments etc., generally speaking: psychological identity is a function of social processes which are continuously interpreted and reinterpreted in a changing identity matrix. The relation is not symmetrical: 'my' identity depends on given relations, and my own interpretation is always some reformulation, representation of what has been experienced. Identity is a shift of a 'something' into a new context, and this context is my present experience. Since this experience is shaped by fields of relations that differ during my life and in several social contexts, I naturally live in different psychological identities which are marked and shaped by different social contexts. To give an example: As a Saxonian living in Bavaria I have an identity as a Saxon, remarkably recognisable by my accent in German. As a German living in Europe I have an identity as German, remarkably recognizable by my German accent when I try to speak English or another European language. As a person living, say, in Africa, I will easily be identified as a European and not as an American – especially in these times, i.e. assume an identity that is not only given but partially chosen for obvious reasons. And if some extra-terrestrial (ET) would visit planet earth I would be easily identified as human, as being different from ETs.

Thus, the construction of identity has two notable marks: first, it is a process which leads to ever changing results; second, identities overlap and can be simultaneous like defined systems such as Chinese boxes, where one includes the other. But sometimes and in certain contexts identities may exclude each other – such as the gender difference when identity is an identifying process in gender relations, which however do not exclude the different subjects from being identical as humans.

What has been said so far holds true for religious identities. Consider the term Hinduism. We know that Hinduism comprises different religions in terms of typological definitions of religion used by scholars in religious studies. But for those looking from this side of the Indus river all those behind the other banks were called Hindus (Buddhists included, by the way). Later the term became more refined, and Buddhists were excluded, but even today Hindus often regard Buddhism as an aspect of their own religion, namely 'Export-Hinduism'.

It is a similar case with Christianity. Are Protestants and Catholics both 'Christians'? In a sense yes, but under other considerations 'no', as Cardinal Ratzinger may want to have it. In certain Asian languages different terms are used to translate the difference, and all depends on the psychological, political and social circumstances. In times of persecution in Japan all the different Christian religions were one subject of persecution, i.e. one identity. But in terms of organisational structure, self-definition and also theological identity – which was and is historically constructed – we have perhaps to speak of different identities.

Thus, already the notion of identity shows that identity is a construct in multiple relationships which are to be interpreted in a host of multiple or plural parameters. Thus, if we look into identity we cannot avoid facing reality as a pluriform and pluralistic field of references. Identity constitutes 'I' and 'we' in facing and interpreting something or somebody as 'other'. Thus, identity is pluriformity. But how to understand pluriformity or plurality or, taking this descriptive term in general terms as the fabric of religious reality: religious pluralism?

2. Remarks on the Notion of Pluralism

2.1 Historical Developments

Historically, religious pluralism is a political and intellectual attitude developed after painful historical experiences of religiously justified wars in the seventeenth century in Europe. Christianity was divided confessionally and politically. Therefore a first step was a *pragmatic pluralism* in politics which politically acknowledged the claims of different forms of Christianity in view of the impossibility of implementing any further a monolithic form of culture based on the monotheistic principle 'One God, One emperor or pope, One rule, One society'. This concept never was political reality but since the times of the Roman emperors it remained the ideological claim of centralised power based on religious monotheism. The modern liberal and pragmatic principle of a division of power (executive system, legislative system, juridical system) is the basis for the freedom of the individual (Locke, Montesquieu) and as such the acknowledgement of a pluralistic structure of human relations over against a monistic system.

This pragmatic pluralism did not yet have a sharp theoretical foundation, because truth was still regarded as being one, based on a precritical theory of correspondence of fact and true expression. The truth of science and the truth of religion had not yet been clearly separated. This changed with the age of enlightenment in the eighteenth century. Here a *theoretical pluralism* was developed, though with different and ambiguous political consequences. The argument was based on a distinction between the truth of reason and the truth of faith. Faith was not any more subject to rational proof, because Kant's critical investigation showed that we know what we know through the categories of the limited human mind which are both innate (time, space, causality) and culturally conditioned (language). Religion became a matter of practical reason, and the best example of the consequences was Lessing's Nathan who states that the true ring cannot be known theoretically but should be tested practically. This allows for a suspended judgement and gives space to tolerance in the limits of the requirements of reason. Theoretical pluralism has different connotations which need to be distinguished and which have had different historical consequences:
- *Logical pluralism* (Christian Wolff, Immanuel Kant) which makes the distinction between knowledge and opinion. Mathematical truths

cannot be compromised because they are subject to the rational distinction between true and false, but opinions wherever they occur are based on factors of pro and con, they are provisional knowledge and need not be exclusive, i.e. the other opinion can be appreciated and tolerated, even if one has good reasons not to share it.

- *Pragmatic pluralism* (William James, *A Pluralistic Universe*, 1901) in the context of a theory of knowing argues against any monistic presuppositions which want to establish one metaphysical principle only, but tries to understand religions and their ideas on the basis of their specific history.

- *Political Pluralism* (H.J. Laski, *A Grammar of Politics*, 1925) is the product of nineteenth century social developments and requires that individuals be free to organise themselves in order to express their differing interests and to fight for them in legally organised form. Not only the plurality of political parties but also the organization of unions, cultural movements, pressure groups etc. are part of the principle that the social consensus is being negotiated in the discourse and civilised antagonism of group interests.

- *Historical Pluralism* (O.F. von Gierke, *Das deutsche Genossenschaftsrecht*, 1868-1913) is a modern development based on the sociological insight that different groups (economic classes, milieux, religious denominations etc.) have different historical experiences in one and the same historical context which should have legal consequences, in so far as between the private sphere of the individual and the public affairs of the state there is the *Genossenschaft*, i.e. freely organised groups (family, societies, churches) which differ in perception of, and interests concerning, the social process so that a specific perspective of a 'social law' could mediate the pluralities into a workable pluralism. This debate provoked the wider insight that the history of a society is pluralistic in itself both in terms of historical experiences and in terms of the perception and construction of historical identities.

The present concept of a *pluralistic society* within the framework of a market economy and the organization of society in a democratic setting is based on all these aspects and historical developments. It is the organised exchange and balancing out of different (and even contradictory) interests of individuals and groups based on the principle of equal or just *participation*: Ideally, each individual as such or in organized groups should be able to participate economically in the 'free market' and politically in the process of communication and opinion-making in a society. Therefore, the law is to guarantee fair play and access to all possible resources. The question is not a question of truth but of equal access to the means of participation in the social processes of a civil society. All religious truth claims should be subordinated under this principle.

Religions, however, in most cases have a different agenda: They claim the possession of truth *and* salvation due to special revelation and – in the case of proselytising 'world religions' – propagate their way of life as the *only* way to human fulfilment. Thus, a pre-critical unity of cognitive and existential truth is innate in most theological systems. Modern 'protestant' movements (in Christianity as well as in Judaism, Buddhism, Hinduism, even Islam and other religions) may try to apply Kant's critical distinction to argue for a separation of the questions of *truth in terms of knowledge* and *salvation in terms of existential conviction*, but the so called 'fundamentalist' reaction denies this disentanglement because of the fear of loss of identity and values. The present debate about a pluralistic theology of religions is by no means only a matter of intellectual clarification but has much to do with this political and institutional setting.

2.2 Systematic Distinctions

The question of a multiple religious identity is directly connected with the factual plurality of religions in a shared space of living and the theoretical recognition of this plurality as a consciously recognised pluralism. Based on these historical developments certain logical distinctions in the notion of theological pluralism might prove to be useful. First, we need to recall that the pluralistic theology of religion(s) is a reaction against exclusivism and inclusivism. Without this background the thrust of the argument of the pluralist theory would be missed. We cannot go into the details of the development and typology of these views[1] but want to highlight only some special implications.

Exclusivism has a twofold basis first in a theological argument and second as a claim of social power. Theologically, exclusivism is based on the exclusive claim to a specific revelation which is is to be recogni-

---

[1] A very comprehensive overview dealing with nearly all possible options of a theology of religions with historical details and systematic expositions has been presented recently by M. Hüttenhoff, *Der religiöse Pluralismus als Orientierungsproblem. Religionstheologische Studien.* Leipzig, 2001.

sed as divine intervention and is thus beyond rational arguing. This is a supranaturalistic claim which historically appears in different forms. It is an abstract claim because it cannot avoid stating that any transcendental or supranaturalistic 'content' needs to be mediated by a set of semiotic structures which are culturally relative. Any exclusivistic claim is made in language, and symbols of language are particular, related, changing and subject to interpretation, i.e. language is a net of communication which is to be disclosed in hermeneutical discourses. In other words, this net of communication is inclusivistic of differences in semantic notation and connotation. Therefore, in cognitive terms exclusivism is a self-contradiction. As a claim of social power exclusivism is collective self-aggrandisement and historically often has been a cover for greed and political power. It is the attitude of clerical systems which cling to structures of power, and exclusivism in the political and the religious arena is the ideology of the establishment. Psychologically speaking exclusivism is often based on fear and uncertainty, because it avoids the open argument and vulnerability in meeting opposing views and the claims of the other. Religious reformers such as Gautama, Jesus, Nanak, Ramakrishna, Gandhi and others opposed those exclusivistic claims by pointing out that they are an expression of idolatry: the limited symbol is being idolised as absolute.

Inclusivism is a form of paternalism. It tries to include the other into the own. In cognitive terms this is unavoidable, as I will argue at the end of this paper, but in social terms it is dangerous, because here the otherness of the other is negated, and acceptance of differing views and values is possible only in as much as it can be argued that the other finally is not other at all – difference is negated or declared to be unimportant, and the claim is that all is the same. Here it is important to investigate the motivation of the argument. Two options seem to occur: (a) If the other is regarded as the same but not equal, the position is a kind of cynical denial of the rights of the other; (b) if the other, however, is taken to be equal in all aspects of life (soteriological, economic and social) the position would lead to the acceptance of mutuality. And as a position of *mutual* inclusivism it is in a certain way an unavoidable option.

The argument of the *pluralist* concerning the theology of religions is to point out the problem of inclusivism (a). The pluralist option here is a principal theological option for the possibility that the other in his or her otherness can reach the fulfilment of life. This does not mean that all the other claims is to be taken as truth. It means that in principle his or her view and/or values for principal theological arguments *may be valid or true*. The theological option for a pluralist position needs to be looked at in an analytic way, because under this 'theological option' a number of different aspects of pluralism are often being discussed without a proper distinction between

- metaphysical pluralism
- philosophical pluralism
- epistemological pluralism
- cultural pluralism
- theological pluralism.

These aspects cannot be established on the same level of theoretical consistency, and they need to be treated briefly in order to enhance our analytic tools for an operational set of arguments concerning a possible pluralistic option (or options).

Metaphysical pluralism might be a theoretical option, but to me it seems to be unsatisfactory because the human mind seeks unity, simplicity (elegance) in the explanation of the world and finally a unified world view. Looking into the history of metaphysics as well as the history of physics this is obvious: Thinking looks for the unity of knowledge.

Philosophical pluralism is a logical question. Whether different logics are possible or not is debatable. In principle, different worlds can be imagined, and they might have different philosophical principles. If it is being argued that even the laws of nature are subject to historical change (in macro-spheres and macro-times) different principles of different worlds can be envisaged. However, we need to be aware that even these different imageries need to be interpreted in our present languages and logical systems, otherwise they could not become subject of our cognition. Thus, a strict philosophical pluralism would be irrelevant, to say the least.

Epistemological pluralism is impossible because any cognition needs to be expressed in a semantic framework that is given, for it is the basis for intersubjectivity. But since the intersubjective system of language is the precondition for mental consistency of the individual, it is not only a matter of communication between individuals, but a matter of mental stability of the individual itself. Any new cognition is related to what is already known. Otherness is relational alterity. These relations follow patterns of historical contingency, thus the other is a related aspect of one's own identity – in terms of notions as well as attitudes – and always in the making. In the making means that new impulses or experiences are interpreted in terms of known ones. That is to say, all 'newness' can be known as such only in so far as it is not totally new or other but related. Even if a person would be strictly bilingual he or she may certainly change perspectives, but at a given time he or she needs to operate under the perspective of one semantic system in order to construct a consistent experience. And both perspectives need to be and are correlated in the process of a continuous translation. Therefore, epistemological pluralism is a contradiction in itself.

Cultural pluralism is a matter of political ethics. It has to do with fairness and justice. Natural diversity and cultural diversity are something given before humans have an option to argue for or against it. Even if one would hold the view that different cultures and languages are a hindrance to the development of humankind and that the difference of forms of life should be overcome, one would have to express this view and argue for it in different languages and cultural patterns of communication. Cultural pluralism is a historical datum, and to acknowledge it is to give rights and empowerment to marginalised groups. Therefore, it is an ethical imperative.

Theological pluralism is the position that differences in the interpretation of the world do not imply that the other is excluded from salvation. The question of truth and the question of salvation are distinguished. It does not claim that any other religion (or one's own religion for that matter) is 'true' as such, but that truth and untruth might occur everywhere, whereas salvation is not dependent on a specific expression of truth. Truth claims need to be justified according to criteria which are subject to intellectual analysis and debate on the basis of coherence and consistency, irrespective of their belonging to any tradition. From a Christian perspective, it is argued, to accept such a pluralism is necessary because plurality is empirically given in the order of creation. Another example is the religious history of India: philosophical positions can be contradictory and mutually exclusive, but all those positions are not decisive for salvation (*mokṣa*). Rather, *mokṣa* is a matter of seeing the relativity of any possible view and transcending it existentially. In Indian parlance, truth (*satya*) is not only acknowledged but realised or experienced (*anubhava*). Here, you can be wrong but saved.

3. General Observations on the Present Cross-cultural Discourse

The present debate on cross-cultural relations and, as an important part of it in terms of theory, the debate on a pluralistic theology of religions, is a multi-cultural and multi-religious undertaking. No religion can express the tenets of a particular view in a purely self-referential way with regard to a made up 'single indigenous' tradition, but the actual discourse discloses the interconnectedness of needs, motivations and notions and allows us to see that our traditions themselves are products of cross-cultural processes. Therefore, the plurality of perspectives is a given fact when one looks at these perspectives materially. This has consequences:

1. We need to be aware that any discourse on cross-cultural questions such as pluralism and the quest for truth is bound to use a specific language, in this case English. This determines the rules of the debate. We would play a different game if we were to talk in Chinese or German or Hindi. This is not only a linguistic question including the acknowledgement of the relativity of language, but a question of power: the language being used is the language of the one who determines the rules. We cannot avoid talking in one language, and for many historical and political reasons this is English. But we need to be aware of the problem, for here we are already dealing with a major difficulty of the cross-cultural discourse on normative questions such as truth.

2. Religion as a stabilising factor for social identity and as a basis for ethical orientation is not a matter of the past but a very important social factor in the present political situation worldwide. In fact, during the last twenty years or so religions seem to have become more relevant than at any other time during the earlier decades of the twentieth century. Thus, even in India, where at least among the urban youth a trend towards Westernisation and Secularisation can be observed, the well known secular journal *India Today* (Oct 5, 1998) reports, on the basis of a comprehensive survey, that religion might be considered to be the 'new opium of the young' (37) which would give the restless in the country stability and orientation in an unsettling world. The result of the investigation has it that precisely the youth believe in God (94%), that most young people pray (97 %) and that religions offer a substitute for the authority of parents, who would no longer be trustworthy as guides and resources for a value base.

3. Today, there are no geographical areas left which would be closed culturally and religiously, i.e. there are no cultural spaces with clear boundaries and a rather consistent cultural background which would be based on just one tradition. Rather, we have more or less mixed cultures which are shaped by historical influences of different religions and various cultural systems of the past. On the other hand, constructions of social identity as well as religious socialisations are being established through influences from within and from without. The results of these developments are specific processes of amalgamation which all the time produce structures of an ever higher degree of complexity. Especially the modern means and ends of worldwide communication systems make it possible that different value systems, which may or may not have religious backgrounds, are communicated in rather uncoordinated ways. At the same time ever more disparate religious, cultural and linguistic patterns of socialisation, i.e. social and ethical values, are selectively mixed (consciously or unconsciously) and shape the pluralistic structures of our societies which at base are fundamentally orientated towards a consumerism that is made possible by technological developments. However, 'religion' is not only a pattern of behaviour according to old traditions that would give stability by having recourse to a coherently constructed past, but religion more and more seems to become an important force and factor in shaping the identities of individuals and groups in new ways.

4. Different language systems and cultures organise their perception of reality in remarkably different ways and construct different systems of categories. Therefore, we need a meta-discourse on the conditions of cross-cultural communication which requires that no one model be a player and a rule-maker at the same time. That is to say, *the rules of communication are to be created in the process of communication itself.* Such a discourse will not only reveal the multiplicity of foundations of values in different cultures but will also show how the dialectics of dissent and consent is being shaped in a cross-cultural process of value-creation. To acknowledge this dynamics is to establish the value of justice in the rules for the communication process itself.

4. Classical Philosophical Issues in View of the Problem of Pluralism: Perception, Reality, Consciousness

Theological debates on the pluralistic theology of religions are built on such notions as reality, truth, knowledge, consistency, values, relativism versus absolutism etc. However, these notions themselves are hardly investigated, they are handled as an exchange that seems to be fixed. But this is not the case. If theology has a twofold task, namely to express hermeneutically what the tradition might mean in its contents, and relate these findings apologetically to ever changing contexts, it is this 'apologetical framework' which needs to be looked into when old metaphysical notions such as the ones mentioned above are reformulated under present day post-ontological conditions of a critical epistemology, a hermeneutics of suspicion and a bewildering plurality of truth claims. Therefore, the following remarks are intended to be a kind of prolegomena to the semantics of a pluralistic theology of religions.

4.1 Perception

During the 1960s the Club of Rome issued warnings concerning the limits of economic growth both in the ecological and social field. This has changed the perception of economic and cultural value structures on a worldwide scale, first in the developed countries, but later also in developing countries. However, today we know that what was being talked about was a limit of quantitative growth, whereas the question of qualitative growth has not been really tackled yet on the agenda of international organisations. The problem of quality, however, is a philosophical and ethical problem, because the categories of quality are mediated through cultural und religious values which are different in different areas of the world.

Human beings strive for realisation of values and ideas on the basis of the difference between what should be and what is. Balancing out the difference is a matter of justice. Justice, therefore, is not one value among others, but it is the participatory right of all partners in the process of societies in balancing out all possible values.

In the context of today's historical experiences of globalisation there are new social diversifications which interpenetrate each other. This challenges traditional patterns of identity and value-orientation. As a result one can observe on a worldwide scale the loss of social and emotional stability of groups and whole societies which formerly were grounded in rather clearly defined traditions. Here, the horizon or the space which human beings map out and work out through their historical perspectives and political actions is being changed: *human beings live in a limited ecosphere which they form and by which they are formed.* That is to say: *Human beings are both subject and object of their own economic and cultural acting.* They are actors and the result of their own actions. What follows is that human beings are fully responsible for their own well-being and their historical catastrophes respectively. This, it seems to me, is the real change in the perception of reality during the last few decades, and all religions and traditional cultures do need to adapt to this different situation. Cultural acting and economic acting appear to be in a much closer relationship than has ever been recognised before: *Humans shape themselves in producing, and in doing so they produce their own shaping.*

4.2 Reality

Reality is not an ontological entity in itself which would exist apart from human consciousness. At least we cannot know anything apart from perception and reflection as a process of consciousness. The real is what we perceive as real. Our modes of perception, however, depend on patterns of values which have been shaped by previous cultural behaviour. Human beings perceive as real primarily what is relevant, i.e. what influences human interests and survival positively or negatively. That is to say, reality is the result of interactive processes of perception between individual, society and the eco-spherical environment. Therefore, not only culture but also nature is a construct of the processes of culture, religion and politics, which are conditioned historically. Again, we have to add that in history we do not have a single culture or a single history, but different histories which have produced different languages, religions and value-systems. Those cultures have interpenetrated each other in processes of mutual formation, but at times they have also stayed apart to some extent.

The other consequence of our reflection here is that the human being is not a stranger to nature but rather a part of a net of communication in which is created what we call reality. The responsibility of man, therefore, is an answer to his fate that in being conscious of himself he is already a question to himself, a question of his own existence. This insight has the consequence that the values through which we perceive reality are being created always anew in historical processes of change. But such processes both create themselves and at the same time presuppose themselves in a systemic way. What is real is determined by a social consensus on values. As we have demonstrated, this consensus depends on cross-cultural and interreligious processes of communication about the structures of perception.

These methodological reflections – which may seem to be somewhat abstract – demonstrate without doubt that the real question is not so much which kind of reality we are living in, but which kind of reality we *want to* live in. To say it in other words: Which basic values are necessary so that we can limit the drive to unlimited economic growth in a limited system of resources in such a way that society would still be able to provide standards of living which enable humans to live in dignity, for instance in providing enough jobs so that a certain minimal amount of social justice is guaranteed? Is not a kind of 'ascetic culture' (Carl Friedrich von Weizsäcker) necessary, at least in ecological terms? But would such an 'ascetic culture' make sense in economic terms? To answer these and similar questions we have to be aware that 'dignity', 'ascetic culture', 'ecology' are concepts which are culturally conditioned and need to be re-asserted and reinterpreted in processes of cross-cultural communication. Hence, since there are no unconditioned abstract terms which, once decontextualised, could claim universal validity, there are also no abstract answers either.

4.3 Consciousness

The patterns of perception of reality are what we call consciousness. Yet, on the basis of what we have been discussing so far it is clear that consciousness cannot be defined either as an individual entity or as a social one, or as a global holistic system; rather, consciousness is a process of communication between the human being, other human beings and the environment. However, even the term 'environment' may not be appropriate, for as we have seen, reality, which human beings do change and create, is nature, but a nature which the human being himself is part of. In view of the basic principle that all phenomena in the world are interrelated (including economic, cultural and political processes)[2] we have to concede, that a hierarchical model of structures of perception, structures of power etc. has to give way to a more cooperative model of structures of communication.

It is the economic and cultural globalisation as such that calls for a networking of political and intellectual processes of organisation in which the polarisation of individual and nation-state as well as the contradiction of nature and culture (and technology) is overcome. This would imply a change of consciousness which would also bring about a radical change of many a traditional cultural-religious identity. Religions as the traditional basis for social identities are immediately challenged by this process of the change of structures of tradition, because under the conditions of modern pluralism the very matrix of shaping identities is being changed through simultaneous participation in different traditions, in different value systems and value communities. This has a bearing on our understanding of what religions are, what cultures are, what different languages are, and it would have tremendous implications for a different mediation of tradition and values. In other words, such an understanding would change our ways of handing down tradition; it would certainly have an effect on schools and universities.

5. The Problem of Truth and Religious Constructions as the Foundation of Values

Theological concepts depend on a community which accepts those concepts intersubjectively. Thus, the community seems to be the presupposed basis for any debate on values. On the other hand a community is formed as a coherent structure only because of a specific identity. Identity, however, is shaped both by delimitation from other identities and by building up structures of a worldview which is the basis of tradition, collective memory and a consistent structure of rules. Therefore, it seems to be this set of assumptions and beliefs as collective memory which is the presupposed basis for any community. In other words, we cannot focus on either of the two factors without looking at the other factor at the same time: *Community comes into being becau-*

---

[2] This, of course, is an application of the standard Buddhist concept of *pratītyasamut-pāda* (interdependent co-arising), see M. von Brück, *Buddhismus. Grundlagen, Geschichte, Praxis.* Gütersloh, 1998: 99ff.

se of a shared set of collective ideas, and those ideas live only in a specific community.

Here we will focus only on one aspect of the complex matter, i.e. the problem of the consistency of a set of values which seem to shape a certain culture, country, continent or tradition. The philosophy implied here could be expressed in one sentence: *It is as it should be for things are what they are precisely in being expressed that way.*

However, such unquestioned ideas, paradigms or sets of rules are taken for granted only as long as there is no alternative and no need for comparison and a selective process of acquiring the tradition. As soon as a society is confronted with alternative models of living and different rules, it needs to construct a new identity, for even a conscious foundation or philosophical reasoning for a certain standpoint is qualitatively new over against a tradition which had been taken for granted. As soon as there are competing ideas it is also (but not only) a matter of consistency to formulate a religious value system which is convincing and acceptable to a society. Thus, the question of truth comes in.

5.1 Truth

But what is truth? Here, we cannot go into the details of the philosophical problem of truth as it has been discussed in Western and other philosophical traditions.[3] It suffices to keep in mind that any discourse on this question needs to cultivate an awareness that the question itself is culturally conditioned: there is not one universal question of truth which might be answered in different material ways through cultural conditioning, but the very *structure* of the question of truth or the whole *concept* of truth is different in different cultures, both diachronically and diatopically. Thus, Indian Buddhism developed the concept of *satyadvaya*, the two levels of being or truth (*satya*), viz. the conventional or relational level and the absolute or holistic level.

This was modified in China where the model is not a hierarchy of levels but an organic harmony of the interplay of mutually dependent

---

[3] I have discussed some basic methodological points concerning a cross-cultural debate on 'truth' in: M. von Brück, 'Wahrheit und Toleranz im Dialog der Religionen'. *Dialog der Religionen* 1 (1993): 3ff.

forces. This Chinese concept of 'truth' as the balanced harmony of mutually dependent forces or powers found its specific expressions in Confucianism, Taoism, Chinese Buddhism etc., but it was always there and is a distinct paradigm compared to the Indian model of hierarchies and levels.[4] Very different from the Indian and Chinese concept is the Greek and European model of truth. But even one culture develops different models of truth in the course of its history. So 'truth', i.e. the construction and methodology of truth, is also subject to historical change.

Let us look briefly into the European tradition in order to substantiate the point. As has already been noted, both the notion of truth and the methodology for finding truth are historically conditioned. Where European history is concerned, I shall distinguish three models which differ from the models of other cultures as I have just mentioned:

- an *onto-theological* model which lasted from the pre-Socratics until the Realists in the Middle Ages;
- a model centred on *subjectivity* which lasted from Nominalism until German idealism;
- *language analysis* ever since.

Most thinkers of Greek Antiquity and the Christian tradition until Nominalism believed in an ontology which could express general notions about reality. Parmenides, Plato and Aristotle held the view of identity, continuity or at least of correspondence between being and thinking in the concept of *logos* or *nous*. Unchanging and 'true' structures as well as things could be known in their suchness. How? By participating in these eternal structures. That is to say: to attain the proper knowledge of reality is the basis of the ethical quest and the foundation of certainty. A statement which has been proved true once was true for ever. Aristotle[5] holds that the relation of each being towards truth is the same as its relation to being as such. Therefore, the congruence of being and knowing makes possible the *theoria* of philosophy, i.e. the possibility of talking truth. In this line of thinking Thomas Aquinas[6] defines truth as *adaequatio intellectus et rei*. This theory of correspondence has been developed and refined in different

---

[4] See M.vonBrück and WhalenLai, *Buddhismus und Christentum*. München, 1998: 621ff.
[5] Aristotle, *Metaphysics* 993 a 30.
[6] Thomas Aquinas, *De veritate* q. 1, 1.1; *Summa theol.* q. 16, a. 2 ad 2.

ways, but in any case it presupposes that, without doubt, the 'thing' or the matter can appear to reason as it is. Christian theology added that the basis for the correspondence of the knowing and the known is nothing else than God. If the divine *logos* were not present in human thinking, nothing could be known as true. Participation in truth is participation in the Divine. Hence, what became known as true was divine, beyond any doubt. However, in human history this participation in the Divine was made difficult (or nearly impossible) due to human freedom and striving for independence from God (the *hybris* of the Greeks) which Christianity called sin. The paradox is that humans, in using the freedom given by God, unavoidably deviate from God at the same time. And this is why human history is the struggle and fight for truth, for positions, claims and values. The paradox could be solved only by an act of highest freedom of God himself: his self-sacrifice.

This structure of thinking was convincing as long as its foundations were generally accepted: the correspondence of divine and human *logos*, or the ontic order and the order of thinking. However, at the height of the Middle Ages and especially during the Renaissance the eternal divine order had a competing realm to deal with: the reality of matter, which was held to be 'objective', whatever could be known through senses and experiment. But even here we still have the basic structure of the old view: things change temporally, but in space they exist eternally, they change in time, but this change follows a course which is predictable as long as all the initial conditions were known. Now it was the world that was limitless in time and space and thus 'the world' (or matter and nature) inherited what before were the characteristic marks of God. Therefore, even in this model the traditional ontological structure remains the same: truth once known remains constant in a given system.

These ideas and ways of thinking were shattered by Nominalism, by later sceptical theories and, in our century, by modern physics and recently by the neurosciences. Now, all notions, ideas and concepts which we are using are no longer grounded in a superhuman realm of ideas, but in the human mind. All we can think is a construction made by our own mind. That is, ideas do not refer to God or some immovable order beyond but to the human being itself. Therefore, the foundation of truth can be sought only in human subjectivity – *cogito ergo sum*. Finally, there is no longer any assumption about a correspondence of being and thinking, but only the self-affirmation of the human subject. To shorten a long philosophical development we can summarise and comment on the consequences of this view: *Truth does not become subjective, but it rests on an intersubjective process of communication.*

Whatever this may mean for other fields of experience and thinking, here it suffices to note that this development led to the relativity of truth and the relativity of all criteria for truth, the relativity of values and the lack of an 'ordering centre'.[7] This had and has consequences for the search for identity – not only for the individual and its 'meaning of life', but also for the coherence of societies. In other words, relativity means also plurality of truths and values, of ethical principles and ideas.

Here I cannot go into a discussion of truth in different Asian traditions. In Asia, too, we observe processes of pluralisation, both in India and in China, but the consequences have not been the same.

5.2 Truth and Language

Summarising what has been discussed so far we can say: any concept of truth depends on language. All human language is metaphorical, i.e. the concepts of space, time, causality, matter, being, consciousness, truth and so on are metaphors which are mutually dependent and related to each other. They are not just descriptive but imply reflections which depend on the social construction of a trans-individual communication of consciousness and contexts. Language – and concepts – not only communicate information about something given, but evoke images and motivations. Those motivations are communicated in structures of communication which form the matrix of a social pattern. This pattern is not a pre-stabilised harmony, but it is historically contingent and needs to be called a product of cultural processes.

Therefore, there is nothing like 'the' Asian values (or even Chinese values) or 'the' Christian European tradition, but there are complex *historical* processes which construct precisely those concepts for the sake of social and political coherence of a given society. Expressed in a different way: *Tradition is not something given in the past, but a process of construction in the present.* And today, no doubt, it can be

---

[7] Werner Heisenberg, *Wandlungen in den Grundlagen der Naturwissenschaft.* Stuttgart 1959: 139.

said that those processes – be it in China or Europe – follow pluralistic patterns.

6. Christian Faith, Truth Claims and the Question of Multiple Religious Identity

The possibility of a multiple religious identity depends on intellectual, emotional, social and institutional concerns and decisions. *Intellectually* the consistency of different views on God, humankind and the world needs to be attained, at least in principle, because it would be difficult to combine totally contradictory views without losing intellectual integrity. *Emotionally* it is most difficult to combine different religious identities because religious emotions are formed uniquely during childhood. If during this period of life different emotional religious identities are combined it may be possible to belong emotionally to different traditions, but in most cases there is one religious formation during childhood and the other ones are added later during adolescence and/or adulthood. This implies an emotional difference towards the different traditions which cannot be bridged later in life. It is similar to having acquired a mother tongue and added knowledge of different languages in later life. Like languages, religions are learned differently during different periods in life. Thus, one may develop later in life multiple religious identities, but the emotional belonging is not the same and the relationship to the respective traditions is different in each case. *Socially* it is certainly possible to belong to different religious groups at the same time, though, as history shows, in most cases by combining allegiance to different religious groups individuals in exchange and cooperation with other individuals form a new group identity which may emerge as a new religion. *Institutionally* the problem depends entirely on the regulations of the institutions which may or may not allow belonging to other religious institutions. In the cases of Christianity, Islam and Orthodox Judaism this is hardly imaginable; in parts of Christianity (Quakers), Liberal Judaism, Hinduism and Buddhism it is possible or might become possible. It depends on the ideological structure which legitimises the institution, and in most cases this is the question of *theology*. I want to share some reflections only on a possible Christian answer.

1. Different identities do not necessarily exclude each other but can complement each other. Therefore, local, regional and global identities can be related to each other. This holds true for political identities as well as languages, i.e. dialects, regional languages, communication in a 'world language' etc. In similar ways religious identities can be related to each other. Different identities influence each other through processes of amalgamation and exclusion. Identities are shaped in ever changing contexts and they are always a process.

2. Economic and cultural globalisation requires a networking of political and mental processes which transcend individual as well as national structures; even the difference between nature and culture (technology) is being challenged. This process implies a dramatic evolution of consciousness which changes traditional identities. Traditionally religions have been central sources for identity, and that is why they are challenged by those processes in their very structure as traditions. Under the condition of modern pluralism the formation of identity is different than in the past, i.e. more than ever a simultaneous participation in different identities is not only possible but more and more the rule. This implies simultaneous participation in communities of tradition and values which have been different or even separated before. This has consequences for the claims and reclamation of tradition by institutions which form their identity in clinging to and constructing traditions. Such institutions are churches, theological communities etc.

3. Human history is the struggle for truths under the condition of contradictory truth claims. This implies that each perception and the consequent knowledge necessarily remain relative and particular. Cultures and religions which have reached beyond regional boundaries have established their identities in competition with each other and stabilised themselves in excluding the claims of the other – constructing the other as the stranger or the enemy. Truth is conditioned by language, and language is metaphorical, i.e. notions such as space, time, causality, matter, being, consciousness, truth etc. are metaphors related to each other and conditionally interdependent. Those notions are not merely descriptive but they imply a contextual reflection which is dependent on processes of consciousness formation. Language not only communicates information about given facts, but it evokes images, motivations etc. The result is that when we talk about truth the problem is that we are not talking only about the possible congruence

of thinking and facts (*adaequatio intellectus et rei*), but about a communication of experiences.

The claim to have the truth more adequately than other traditions has led to violence in the past, because truth claims were established by force so as to achieve not only political dominance but also psychological stability of the subject who absolutises relative truth claims. The pluralism of truth claims in the present day world is the result of the history of reason and science, but it is also the consequence of social modernisation and the experience of cross-cultural relations and interaction.

4. *Religious* sentences are true in as much as an *unconditioned* reality is expressed or represented. In the end it is the certainty that things are as they are and that this suchness is finally good. This is what we can call the religious dimension of truth, as the Hebrew word *'emeth* signifies the truthfulness and reliability of God, and this is his truth which humans participate in, in so far as they dwell in God's *'emeth* (Ps 26:3; 86:11 etc.). Thus, the 'truth of God' is not a definition or expression about God, but – as a subjective genitive – a self-expression of God's being in truthfulness what he always has been in spite of all our experiences and reasons for relativity. In spite of all our relative knowledge and expressions, such or similar absolute expressions form the identity of religions. Those expressions, however, need to be experienced, they cannot be transmitted any more by authoritative communication. Therefore, the contemplative dimension of religion plays an ever growing role precisely under the conditions of religious plurality.

5. Truth, however, is not only a matter of cognition nor is it identical with understanding, but it is finally ungraspable. This is the existential or religious dimension of truth which can be enacted and realised in rites, in ethical decisions but also in the realisation of structures of thinking, such as in that which has to be assumed with necessity. But its main area of realisation is meditative experience. Each one of these realisations is dependent on culturally conditioned perceptions and interpretations, i.e. on cognition which is relativised by language. However, this does not mean that those realisations would be arbitrary, because we have to maintain the principle which is also to be acknowledged in cross-cultural discourses so as to enable rational exchange: the *principle of coherence*. Accordingly, a sentence can at least temporarily be assumed to be true if it is coherent. A sentence is coherent if it can be integrated into a system of meaning without con-

tradiction. However, the principle of coherence is only a necessary but not a sufficient condition of truth, because it cannot explain what a system of sentences finally is, i.e. the whole or the one is being pre-supposed but not explained. It remains a relative assumption. Furthermore, the principle of coherence is insufficient, for obviously immoral acts such as killing on the basis of religious and ideological reasons can be argued for quite consistently and without contradiction.

6. Hence, more criteria are required so that truth can be ascertained and distinguished from untruth. I would like to mention one important criterion, and this is the *principle of integration*. Integration means that sentences and modes of behaviour must be integrated in a rational way into the relative system of values of a specific religion or society. However, in principle a relative system is open. In Christian parlance: knowledge of truth is a matter of the eschatological future, i.e. in the present we have truth in the mode of searching for it. But now we do have the criterion of love which becomes conscious and knowable in relational patterns of cognition, feeling and action, but it can lead only to relative decisions. This is precisely the place for a productive argu-ment in interreligious controversy.

7. The basic attitude and motivation which follows from these ex-planations is esteem for the otherness of others and a tolerance which does not exclude the search for truth or the dialogical discourse which is to establish more coherence in the search for truth. However, a dia-logical discourse can no longer be built on the attempt to gain one's own identity by disgracing the other or at the expense of the other. In analogy to the field of the political notions of security in partnership, I have suggested we introduce the term 'identity in partnership' (*Identi-tätspartnerschaft*). Tolerance then is not a careless 'letting be' but the openness for the other and the own so as to work out the creativity of possibilities in the otherness of the partners in discourse and encoun-ter. Tolerance requires mutual criticism, because this is a sign of lo-ving solidarity. Otherwise religion would become irrelevant.

Let me give an example and try to formulate what this could actual-ly mean under a Christian perspective. When St Paul encourages people to critically investigate everything and retain the good (1 Thess 5:21) there is need of a criterion for the good. He mentions three of them (1 Thess 5:16-18):

(a) the *joy and happiness* which dwells in persons who are able to transcend themselves in prayer and thus live in the spirit, not in the ego;

(b) the *contemplation* or continuous prayer which is the very nature of self-transcendence, because it gives freedom from fear of losing one's identity, and thus is the precondition for dialogical openness and tolerance, for the possibility of giving up one's concepts and other ego-stabilisers is the prerequisite for growth and mutuality;

(c) finally, *thankfulness*, which allows us to accept the other or even the strange and unknown in an attitude of respect and even awe.

8. Truth is one, but under the conditions of space and time it can appear only in different and relative expressions. Christian faith depends on the claim that God has revealed himself for the whole of humankind in Jesus Christ. But as the revealed one (*revelatus*) he is at the same time and always the hidden one (*absconditus*). God becomes human, but the human is not God. This sentence implies that the human cannot fully grasp the divine. God discloses himself in loving kindness, but not in grasped knowledge. This is to say that even in his revelation God remains a secret and a mystery. He is and will always be the greater one.

9. Religions are not true by themselves, i.e. by their own claims. There are sound reasons internal to the Christian experience that truth may not be limited to one tradition but rather could or would appear everywhere: (a) because God reveals himself also in creation and in a universal history of salvation, (b) because many who do not call Christ by his name (they do not say 'Lord, lord') obviously do fulfil his will in many different ways according to the standards set forth by the gospel (see Mt 25). Whether this is the case or not can be ascertained case by case empirically on the basis of a proper historical hermeneutics.

10. The criterion for Christian theological insights is the revealed God who presents himself in Jesus Christ as unconditional love. This love sheds light on the hidden aspect of God or God as a mystery. Even if God remains greater, other and unknowable in his being he would not contradict himself – at least it is obvious that this is the Christian hope and faith. That is to say that his otherness does not and cannot contradict his love. In this way God is the *non aliud*, the non-other (Nicolas of Cusa). This is the basis for the Christian trust that

relative human knowledge can correspond at least in principle with the final truth even if this truth remains hidden and ungraspable.

11. We need to make a clear distinction between a rational and relative dimension of truth on the one hand, and a trans-rational and existential dimension of truth on the other hand. A rational truth falsifies its opposite, at least in as much as it is a contradictory contradiction. Existential truths however can refer to a deeper level where the opposite may be true as well, and yet remain true, because God as coincidence of opposites is the truth himself. Such a seeming contradiction is to be found in the two opposed sentences that God on the one hand is historically completely revealed in Christ (the relative historical truth), yet on the other hand is the one universal love which is not yet fully understood, recognised and experienced under any historical conditions (the necessary truth of reason).

12. This has consequences for the theological interpretation of the truth claims of other religions. Religions (including Christianity) are not true by themselves (or because they identify themselves as 'religions') but only in as much as God is present in them. What does that mean? It is, of course, metaphorical parlance. Whether God is present or not can be ascertained only by the consensus of a community which needs to test and give proof of respective claims. Any such claim is a claim under a specific, i.e. relative perspectival view. That is to say it is dependent on a standpoint under historical conditions which expresses the claim of certainty in uncertain language and experience. In the dialogue of such different perspectives there happens what we call the actual history of religions. Religious identification as process happens in these discourses, thus any religious identity shaped in cross-cultural contexts is informed by multiple sources coming historically from different traditions. It is a matter of conscious recognition to be aware of this fact. How this multiplicity is expressed psychologically and in terms of social organisation may differ. Some may feel they are Buddhist and Christian, some may feel they are Buddhist as Christian, some may exclude the other option and say they are 'only' this or that, but in referring to the other and representing their identity over against the other they have logically included the other already into their identity formation.

Here, we could speak of different degrees of identification. Since we said in the beginning that identity as identification depends on time, we must be careful not to neglect this factor in interpreting the psychological aspect of identity formation: I have a mother tongue, and probably also a 'mother-religion'. What is added later is learned and cognised in ways different from the primary formation. It is added, interpreting, deepening, correcting etc. something which is already given. Even if I as a born Christian would convert to Buddhism (whatever conversion might mean) I would still be primarily shaped in this specific Christian form. The same holds true the other way round, of course. Thus, identities overlap, but they are not on the same level. This is why I do not claim to be a Christian *and* a Buddhist, but a Christian who is formed, changed, hopefully deepened etc. by Buddhist identity. But even if would want to – I do not cease to be shaped by Christian identity primarily. Christianity is my religious mother-tongue, though I may want to express my experiences and beliefs much more clearly in Buddhist language and symbols.

These different levels have a direct bearing on the question of identity and emotional aspects of religious identification. It is easier to build up multiple religious identity in intellectual and even social senses, but it is much more difficult if not impossible to do so with regard to emotion. What I have experienced in childhood once and for ever has shaped me in a unique way that cannot be erased in later adult life. It is not my task here to go into details.[8]

13. The question of truth and the quest for salvation have to be distinguished. God's salvation does not depend on my religious identity or multiple construction of identities, for it cannot be conditioned by the human search for truth. In his house are many mansions, an insight which surpasses any possible religious cartography and identification processes. If in principle human beings in other religions could never be in the realm of salvation they would need to be won over into one's own camp, i.e. one would need to proselytise them for ethical reasons because otherwise one would contribute to depriving them of the highest possible goal of life. And there would be no place for dialogue, only for a conversion to one's own system of cognition and life. That is to say the whole world would need to be converted to Christianity (or Islam or Buddhism) respectively, and this would lead to intolerance and bloodshed as history shows. This, however, cannot be the will of a loving God (not to mention the problem of fulfilment of people

---

[8] See M. von Brück, 'Sharing Religious Experience in Hindu-Christian Encounter'. J. D. Gort and H. Vroom *et al.*, eds., *On Sharing Religious Experience. Possibilities of Interfaith Mutuality*. Eerdmans: Grand Rapids, 1992: 136-150.

and peoples who have lived before the alleged oneness of humankind under one religious flag).

A theology considering a multiple religious identity would have to formulate itself as a pluralistic theology of religions which takes these *aporia* into account. Like any theology it has a hermeneutic and an apologetic dimension at the same time. Hermeneutically it explains how biblical sentences take on a new dimension of meaning in the context of plurality, i.e. plurality appears to be an expression of the multidimensionality and richness of God's unconditional love. Apologetically this insight is related to the expressions, i.e. sentences, convictions and patterns of behaviour, of all present day religions. Pluralistic theologians claim that there must be many paths in which salvation can be expressed, and they can mutually correct, encourage and supplement each other. However, any possible pluralistic position itself is also a related and relative position; it does not escape the perspectival dimensionality, because humans always stand in a *specific* tradition of language, history, religions and values, which is the relative framework for any expression of truth, untruth and distinction between the two. That is why I would like to call this method an *inclusivistic* pluralism.

Josef Götz OSB
is a monk of the Archabbey of St Ottilien, Bavaria.

Thomas Timpte OSB
is a Benedictine monk in Korea.

Elizabeth J. Harris
is Executive Secretary for Inter Faith Relations for the Methodist Church in Great Britain and an Honorary Lecturer at Birmingham University.

Jørgen Skov Sørensen
is General Secretary of the Council on International Relations of the Evangelical Lutheran Church of Denmark.

Perry Schmidt-Leukel
is Professor of Systematic Theology and Religious Studies in the University of Glasgow.

José Ignacio Cabezón
is the XIVth Dalai Lama Professor of Tibetan Buddhism and Cultural Studies in the Religious Studies department of the University of California at Santa Barbara.

Paul Williams
is Professor of Indian and Buddhist Philosophy in the University of Bristol.

Kajsa Ahlstrand
is Professor of Mission and Ecumenism in the University of Uppsala.

Ruben L.F. Habito
is Professor of World Religions and Spirituality and Associate Dean for Academic Affairs in the Perkins School of Theology at Southern Methodist University, Dallas, Texas.

Michael von Brück
is Professor of Religious Studies in the Faculty of Protestant Theology and Head of the Department of Religious Studies, University of Munich.

John D'Arcy May
is Associate Professor of Interfaith Dialogue, Irish School of Ecumenics, Trinity College Dublin.

eos
Klosterverlag St. Ottilien

www.eos-verlag.de   Tel. 08193 / 71 700   Fax 08193 / 71 709

Schmidt-Leukel, Perry / Köberlin, Gerhard / Götz, Josef Thomas
Buddhist Perceptions of Jesus
Papers on the Third Conference of the European Network
of Buddhist-Christian-Studies (St. Ottilien 1999)
180 Seiten, 14,50 EUR
ISBN 3-8306-7069-9

Götz, Thomas Josef / Gerold, Thomas (Hrsg.)
Die Mystik im Buddhismus und im Christentum
und Aspekte des interreligiösen Dialogs
132 Seiten, 12,80 EUR
ISBN 3-8306-7232-2

Rötting, Martin
Berge sind Berge, Flüsse sind Flüsse
Begegnung mit dem koreanischen Zen-Buddhismus
Ein Beitrag zum christlich-buddhistischen Dialog
192 Seiten, 14,50 EUR
ISBN 3-8306-7070-2

Borsig, Margareta von
Unter dem Lächeln Buddhas
Märchen aus Indien und Japan
164 Seiten, 12,80 EUR
ISBN 3-88096-979-5